The Riddle
and
The Knight

The Riddle and The Knight

In Search of
Sir John Mandeville

Giles Milton

a&b

First published in Great Britain in 1996 by
Allison & Busby Ltd

A catalogue record for this book is available from the British Library

ISBN 0 85031 999 4

Designed and typeset by N-J Design Associates
Romsey, Hampshire

Printed and bound in Great Britain by
WBC Book Manufacturers Ltd
Bridgend, Mid Glamorgan

To Alexandra
who read countless versions of the manuscript
and gave birth to our daughter Madeleine
on the day it was finished

I, John Mandeville, saw this, and it is the truth.

The Travels, **circa 1356**

Contents

Acknowledgements

A great number of people have helped with the research and writing of this book, both in England and abroad. First and foremost my thanks are to Frank Barrett, without whom I would never have left London, and Paul Whyles, who generously spared time to read the manuscript and give me his invaluable advice.

I am also deeply grateful to Simon Denis, Simon Heptinstall and Steve Meacham, all of whom read the book at various stages of completion and suggested much needed improvements.

Special thanks are due to Alex Belopopsky and Esther Hookway for their support, encouragement and wealth of contacts throughout the Middle East; to Cyril Aslanoff, Marcus Plested and Erica Brewer for translating obscure and difficult texts; and to Jean-François Colosimo for unlocking the door to St Catherine's monastery.

Throughout my trip I met numerous people who generously dedicated hours of their time to my quest. Among them, I am particularly grateful to the Reverend Ian Sherwood, Father Isaias, Laki Vingas, and Father Tarasios in Istanbul; to the Mufti of Cyprus and Nick Cannon in Lefkoşa; to Pierre Kaspo and Father Michael in Syria; to Father Baratto and the Very Reverend John Tidy in Jerusalem; and to Fathers John, George, and Nicholas at St Catherine's monastery.

In London I am grateful to Miles Bredin, Wendy Driver, Vince Graff, Sinclair McKay, Robert Noel, Andrew Penman, James Pool, Tony Saint, Niki Tsironis; and to Dr M Bateson at the Cathedral Archives in Canterbury. And, of course, to Maggie Noach my agent and Peter Day my publisher for placing their trust in me.

Lastly, a special thank you to my mother who sadly did not live to see the finished book. It was her enthusiasm which first inspired me to write *The Riddle and the Knight*.

1 The Inscription

I remember a very old man named Jordan telling me much of Sir John Mandeville when I was a little boy . . . He didn't talk so much about his life as about the place of his grave. Alas my memory holds but a shadow of these things.

Commentarii De Scriptoribus Britannicus, **John Leland**, *circa* 1540

In the days when gods dwelt in temples, a soldier named Alban was converted to Christianity. For this crime he was hauled before Britain's Roman authorities and ordered to renounce his faith. He refused, was tortured, and executed. His body was buried where it fell.

Years passed and the Romans left. The pagan altars were overturned, churches replaced temples, and Imperial rule became little more than a distant memory. But the people of Verulamium didn't forget Alban. They canonized him, they raised a mighty building over his grave, and they renamed their town St Albans in honour of their saint. And as the Dark Ages gave way to the Middle Ages, St Alban became famous throughout the kingdom.

For a long time Alban's bones lay alone in the abbey. But there were always a few like him who led remarkable lives. Some, perhaps, were feudal lords. Others were abbots and priests who performed great and noble deeds. Whatever their achievements, these few – and they were very few – were granted the privilege of being buried inside the abbey near the sacred relics of the saint. And as the priests chanted a Latin dirge, the goodly burghers of St Albans laid their heroes to rest beneath the cold stone floor.

But with the passing of the years even these most famous of men were forgotten and people shuffled over their graves without realizing whose bones lay beneath the flagstones. Once in a while someone's curiosity would be aroused by these old tombs. Victorian genealogists would try to decipher the strange script on the stone or take rubbings from the ancient brasses. But soon that too became impossible for the limestone was worn as smooth as glass and the inscriptions faded completely. Ashes to ashes, dust to dust . . .

And so, on that cold September evening when I first visited St Albans Abbey, I found myself unable to make out a single name on the polished stone. It was almost dark by the time I turned to leave and I had long given up hope of finding the tomb I was looking for. But suddenly there was the loud clunk of a switch and the pillars lining the nave were lit by spotlights. And there before me, high up on a thick stone pillar, a row of faint Gothic letters appeared on the chalk-white surface. Much of the inscription had faded or been lost, for centuries of damp, soot and peeling paint had all but destroyed the words. But here and there a few fragments had survived:

exeu ... trus ... Mandeville ... de ... body
tr ... monument ... died ... a ... for ... by ...
a statute ...

I just had time to scribble down these words before the lights were once again extinguished and the great haunches of St Albans Abbey slunk back into the shadows.

Here, at last, was a record of Sir John Mandeville – a long-forgotten knight who was once the most famous writer in medieval Europe. He only wrote one book – an untitled volume known as *The Travels* – but within its covers Mandeville described how he had travelled further afield than any European in history – further even than Marco Polo half a century earlier.

He had set off from St Albans on St Michael's day in 1322 with the intention of making a pilgrimage to the churches and shrines of Jerusalem. But 34 years later he arrived back in England claiming to have visited not only the Holy Land, but India, China, Java and Sumatra as well. And what stories he had gathered in the years that he was away! Kings and priests studied *The Travels* to satisfy their thirst for knowledge of far-away lands. Geographers used his new-found information to redraw their maps. Monastic scribes translated his book from language to language until it had spread throughout the monasteries of Europe. By the time this mysterious knight died in the 1360s, his book was available in every European language including Dutch, Gaelic, Czech, Catalan and Walloon. The sheer number of surviving manuscripts is testament to Mandeville's popularity: more than 300 handwritten copies of *The Travels* still exist in Europe's great libraries – four times the number of Marco Polo's book.

Early readers were intrigued by Mandeville and captivated by his outrageous tales and humorous mishaps. Yet the importance of *The Travels* lay in a single yet startling passage which set the book apart from all other medieval travelogues. Mandeville claimed that his voyage proved for the first time that it was possible to set sail around the world in one direction and return home from the other. In doing so he achieved what others said was impossible: his book altered men's horizons and became the beacon that lit the way for the great expeditions of the Renaissance. Columbus planned his 1492 expedition after reading *The Travels*. Raleigh studied the book and pronounced that every word was true; while Sir Martin Frobisher was reading a copy as he ploughed his pioneering route through the North-West Passage.

Mandeville's influence on literature was also immense. Shakespeare, Milton, Keats and many others turned to *The Travels* for inspiration, and dozens of Sir John's more outlandish stories found their way into the great works of English literature. Until the Victorian era it was Mandeville, not Chaucer, who was known as the 'father of English prose'.

I discovered the book by accident during a weekend break in Paris. While searching through the shelves of Shakespeare and Co, the famous American bookshop on the banks of the Seine, I pulled down a copy of Flaubert's journal, *Letters from Egypt*. As I did so, a second volume fell from the shelf – a black-spined Penguin Classic entitled *The Travels of Sir John Mandeville*. It was a slim book and the cover was illustrated with a portrait of Sir John taken from an illuminated manuscript. He had a ruddy face, blond ringlets and a thick beard, and wore a pleated knee-length coat buttoned down to his waist. He looked a strange sort of chap: he held his right arm aloft and appeared to be hailing a ship that was already far out to sea. In the background, a castle stood with its doors open.

On this, our first meeting, Mandeville struck me as a retiring, rather serious individual. But as I flicked through his book an altogether more engaging character began to emerge. Mandeville's passion was wine and he describes the local plonk in almost every country he visits. On reaching Cyprus he is struck less by the island's glorious cathedrals as by the robustness of the local reds, while his account of Islam begins with an explanation of why Muslims don't touch alcohol. Gone was the serious explorer: Sir John revealed himself as a bluff, avuncular figure who enjoyed nothing more than regaling his friends with fantastic stories of his travels. After two or three glasses he'd be describing the maiden offered to him by the Sultan of Egypt. After four or five he'd be battling through the pepper forests of Malabar as he searched for the elusive Well of Youth.

Even in his most sober moments he can't resist repeating the local, if gruesome, gossip he has overheard on his travels. Passing a Greek island en route to Cyprus, he is told the tragic story of a knight unable to cope with the death of his lover:

> On account of the great love he had for her he went one night to her grave and opened it and went in and lay with her and then went on his way. At the end of nine months a voice came to him one night and said, 'Go to the grave of that woman and open it, and behold what you have begotten on her . . . ' And he went and opened the grave, and there flew out a very horrible head, hideous to look at, which flew all round the city; and forthwith the city sank, and all the district round about.

The book was divided into two halves with the first part beginning with a description of Constantinople. From this, the capital of the Byzantine empire, he claimed to have travelled south to Cyprus, Syria and Jerusalem as well as visiting St Catherine's monastery in the Sinai desert. Here he recorded his unique insights into life in this monastic community before ending on a dejected note: 'They drink no wine – except on days of high festival.'

It is not until the second half of his *Travels* – as Mandeville journeys across India and China towards Java and Sumatra – that his stories enter the realms of fantasy. The further east he travels the more gruesome the creatures he meets until he is mixing with women with dogs' heads, two-headed geese, giant snails and men with enormous testicles which dangle beneath their knees. He writes with relish about cannibals who eat their babies and pagans who drink from their fathers' skulls. Yet for all these vivid descriptions, Mandeville continues to give a detailed account of the cities he visits and the people he meets. What was the old rogue up to? Could he really have travelled to the Far East or was his entire book a fiction?

What kept me reading on that first afternoon in Paris was neither the pygmies of China nor the cannibals of Sumatra. I was drawn to the book's opening pages where Mandeville describes the Greek Orthodox population of Constantinople and the glittering splendour of their churches. Just two years earlier I had married my fiancée, Alexandra, in an Orthodox church in Paris and although I had not converted – as Alexandra's parents had done many years before – I was as fascinated by this eastern church as Sir John. Our marriage linked me directly to his medieval world, for the liturgy celebrated on our wedding day had been written by St John Chrysostom – one time Patriarch of Constantinople – and would once have been heard by Mandeville in the city's great church of Haghia Sophia.

The more I read of his book, the more I realized that he was a man with an extraordinary view of the world. He was born at a time when Europe was lurching from crisis to crisis: in France and Italy rival popes were engaged in an undignified tussle for power while in the east the last of the fledgeling Christian states – established by the crusaders two centuries previously – had recently been crushed by the armies of Islam. Things were little better closer to home: King Edward II was more preoccupied with flatterers and sycophants than affairs of state.

Few of Mandeville's contemporaries address this turmoil facing the west: those pilgrims who did travel in the Middle East and returned to write their itineraries advocate the wholesale massacre of the infidel, while his crusading predecessors had slaughtered the very Christians they were supposed to protect. When Muslim rulers of Syria begged the kings of England and France to protect them from the Mongol armies, the Bishop of Winchester remarked: 'Let these dogs destroy one another and be utterly exterminated and then we shall see the universal Catholic Church founded on their ruins and there will be one fold and one shepherd.'

Sir John stands a world apart from such views; he was fascinated by Islam and the eastern church because both religions demanded a genuine piety that he felt had long ago been abandoned by the Catholic church. And, like a botanist who goes in search of rare lichens, so Mandeville went looking for strange and unfamiliar customs. He collected the curious and the obscure, and each new species he found was examined and compared with the rest of his collection.

It was not only his inquiring mind that set him apart from his contemporaries. While his compatriots found themselves aspiring to a new chivalric order – the Order of the Garter – Mandeville had little interest in such high-minded pursuits and readily admits that he didn't fight in a single battle during his time away, nor did he take part in any 'honourable deeds of arms'. Instead of waltzing into battle wearing a breastcoat emblazoned with the sign of the cross – as invariably happens in medieval fables – Mandeville portrays himself as an altogether more human character. Sometimes he is frightened, sometimes ill, yet he never once loses his sense of humour. When finally he arrives home in England claiming to have travelled further than anyone in history, there is not a hint of triumphalism in his writing. Instead, he describes himself as a broken man – worn out with old age and troubled with arthritic gout. But even this doesn't stop him ending his book with a witty aside. He is laying down his quill, he says, so that future generations will still have a few new places left to discover.

Six centuries after he wrote his *Travels*, Mandeville lies discredited and forgotten. Academics, keen to demolish his reputation, wrote learned treatises on why he could never have made such a voyage and mocked the gullibility of his contemporaries. They claimed that the Holy Land was a dangerous place to visit in the 1330s, while travelling along the eastern road to China would have spelled almost certain death. Mandeville, they concluded, had copied most of his stories from the ancients while those that weren't 'borrowed' were simply invented – the products of an over-lively imagination.

It wasn't only his book that was disputed: the more I delved into old manuscripts, the more I found that Sir John's life was just as mysterious as his *Travels*. There were rumours that he was an imposter; that he was a Frenchman living in disguise. One manu-script said he had never even existed, another accused him of murder, while a few went so far as to claim he had dabbled in black magic and alchemy. The only point on which virtually every-one agreed was that Mandeville had invented the story of his birth in St Albans.

Yet the broken epitaph that I'd found on the pillar seemed to suggest that this knight really *had* lived in the town and perhaps even been buried inside the great Norman abbey. Could he also have been telling the truth about his voyage? Could he have indeed proved it possible to circumnavigate the globe? If so, his name needed to be written into the history books: after all, every schoolchild in the land has heard about the exploits of Drake and Raleigh and there are few who cannot recite the old patter, 'Columbus sailed the ocean blue in fourteen hundred and ninety two.' If Sir John was telling the truth then all this would have to change, and they would have to learn instead that, 'Mandeville sailed the ocean blue in thirteen hundred and twenty two.'

The Travels had me captivated from the very first page and I was determined to test Mandeville's amazing claims by following as much of his route as possible. I knew this wouldn't be easy for there were many practical difficulties to overcome. To turn an old adage on its head, Sir John is always more interested in the desti-nation than in the getting there and he rarely describes how he travelled from A to B. From the moment he leaves England his route is muddled and unclear, for although he lists all the possi-ble ways of reaching Constantinople – his first stop – he declines to mention which one he himself took. Nor, for that matter, does he record how long he stayed in the imperial capital: the only dates in the entire book are his departure from England in 1322 and his return in 1356.

On leaving Constantinople he almost certainly travelled by boat to Cyprus – pausing to visit the famous clifftop monasteries – before continuing by sea to Jerusalem and Egypt. From here, he seems to have backtracked to Syria before striking out eastwards across Anatolia towards Persia, India and beyond. But attempting to plot Mandeville's itinerary on a map was as futile as it was impossible and right from the outset I could see little point in ambling across the Middle East and Asia following a trail that Mandeville had only half-heartedly recorded. Instead, I headed straight to the towns and cities that caught his interest, hoping that he had scattered his book with enough clues to help me solve the mystery of his voyage.

The writers and poets of the Middle Ages loved the riddles of their Saxon forebears. They indulged in clever word plays, wrote alliterative verses, sang roundels, and wallowed in folklore. A handful of critics suggested that Mandeville's book, too, concealed a hidden message; that the entire *Travels* had been composed as an extended riddle or allegory whose meaning had long ago been lost.

Whatever the truth about this mysterious knight, I felt sure that I would only ever understand him by adjusting my own horizons and entering the world in which he himself had lived. So that when I finally arrived in Istanbul – the starting point of both our journeys – I turned my back on the modern city and went, instead, in search of Constantinople, the imperial capital of Byzantium. And as I travelled hand in hand with my medieval companion, the centuries that separated our lives began to close. Perspectives shrunk and the strange world he inhabited grew ever more distinct.

After two years in search of Sir John, I had accumulated three large dossiers of evidence about him and discovered that his life was just as extraordinary as his book. Everything about Mandeville proved to be a riddle. But he had left a surprising number of clues.

2 Constantinople

Who reads Sir John de Mandevil his Travels, and his Sights,
That wonders not? and wonder may, if all be true he wrights.
Albion's England, **William Warner, 1612**

The ferry pulled away from the quay with a deep groan
from its belly. There was the smell of diesel, followed by
a whiff of old fish, and then that too disappeared as we
hit a block of clean, chill air that smelt of fresh salt. It was October
and Istanbul was freezing.

During the summer months the *Dolmebaçe* is a pleasure boat
packed with day trippers off to enjoy a day in the sun. Out of
season it reverts to being a working ship. Its decks are laden with
provisions and the only vehicles on board are vans and lorries.
On this particular morning, the few people who sat around
drinking coffee and smoking Turkish cigarettes were returning
to their homes with crates of fruit, boxes of nails and cans of
smoked meats.

We'd scarcely left the Golden Horn before Istanbul's shoreline
vanished into the thick sea mist. First the fishermen lining the
quay were quietly swallowed up and then the Galata bridge
became a ghostly outline. Finally, the great domes and minarets
of Istanbul itself receded and were lost. A mournful blast of the
foghorn and we were away. Only the seagulls squawking around
the masthead betrayed the nearby land.

I was not going far. This rusting hulk of ferry plies its way
between Istanbul and the various islands that scatter the shores
of the Bosporus. I was getting off at its last port of call, a tiny
island some 15 miles from Istanbul. I only knew it by its Greek
name, Halki, but when I'd asked for my ticket the man had
stared at me for a moment with blank indifference then given me

a ticket for Heybeliadi. It struck me as odd that such an insignificant dot on the map should be honoured with two different names. It was only later that I realized the significance of this topographical schizophrenia.

By the time we reached Halki it was 10.30am and the morning mist had lifted. But still there was no sign of sunshine. Grey clouds loomed overhead threatening rain while the hilltop that crowned the island had yet to shake off its blurred outline. The monastery on its summit – where I was heading – kept appearing and vanishing in the cloud. It was here that I hoped to make my first rendezvous with Sir John Mandeville.

The lone barouche owner waiting at the port wouldn't let me walk to the top. I was quite possibly his only customer in months and he wasn't going to give up a couple of hundred thousand lira without a fight. We agreed to a price, I climbed into the rickety carriage and off we set up a winding hill road. Soon we were clip-clopping through an evergreen wood whose branches drooped low over the road. The sea receded into the distance and was soon far below us, and the air grew so wet it seemed to drip from the trees. Eventually, soaked through and shivering with cold, we reached a large, locked, wrought-iron gate.

The monastery of the Holy Trinity was a peaceful but lonely place. Abandoned by other monks and deserted by the faithful, one lone ascetic named Father Isaias lived a life that had remained unchanged for centuries. Though surrounded by an alien faith, though disturbed by the Muslim call to prayer that drifted up from the village, he kept alive the ancient tradition of Orthodox monasticism and carried the torch of Byzantium, flickering and fast fading, into the future.

Here atop his lonely mountain, Father Isaias lived a life of splendid isolation. Detached from the cares of the world he could sit and gaze longingly towards the imperial capital that once was Constantinople. He was truly a living fossil – a lone Greek still worshipping in Turkey – and I could scarcely contain my excitement at finding him. He was, perhaps, the last link to that ancient capital that Sir John claimed to have visited in the 1320s.

Mandeville was fascinated by the pious Greeks he met in the city and wrote in great detail about the differences between his beliefs and theirs. In his day, Constantinople boasted hundreds of monasteries housing thousands of monks, for when the city's elderly grew too frail to fend for themselves they would move to such establishments and spent their declining years in prayer. Others had less choice: a frequent punishment for troublesome ministers of state – those who fell from imperial favour – was to gouge out their eyes and confine them to a monastery. By the time Sir John says he came to the city, Holy Trinity would have been crowded with political prisoners.

Everything changed when the Turkish janissaries captured Constantinople in 1453 for many of the city's monasteries were forced to close their doors for good. Some struggled on for a few more centuries but then they, too, were abandoned and demolished. Only Holy Trinity has survived to the present day.

Father Isaias greeted me with a friendly smile and showed little surprise at my unannounced arrival. As soon as he heard why I had come he welcomed me in for coffee and a chat. 'I suppose I am indeed the last living remnant of the Byzantine empire,' he said with great pride in his voice, 'except . . . ' he paused for a moment as he sieved through his memories ' . . . except, of course, that I was born and brought up in Wimbledon.'

Wimbledon? With his faded vestments and straggly beard, Father Isaias looked the very picture of a Greek Orthodox monk. He even spoke English with a Greek accent. Yet here he was telling me he came from a genteel suburb of south London more famous for tennis and strawberries than its monastic traditions.

'I'm sorry to disappoint you,' he said. 'I thought you'd realize. You see I didn't become a monk until my early twenties. I learned Greek, lived on Mount Athos for several decades, and now I am here. But before that – well it's true – I lived with my parents in Wimbledon.'

The door creaked and an ancient ghost of a man shuffled into the room. It was Father Germanios, the abbot of the monastery, who quite possibly remembered the fall of the city in 1453. I'd been told that Father Isaias lived here alone but Germanios had apparently been holed up for years as well. He looked at me through half-blind eyes and held out his shaky hand. 'I am

London,' he said in a proud but faltering voice. Isaias looked irritated. 'He means he's been to London,' he explained. Germanios smiled again. 'London,' he said. 'Big, big . . . London.' I nodded, and his elderly face beamed with pleasure.

Together, these two monks trod the empty corridors and lonely rooms, listening as the echo of their footsteps faded into the gloom. There was a time when the monastery had been used as a summer school and the cries and whoops of students had rung out down the corridors. Now they had fallen silent for the students no longer came. Gone too were the days when the buildings housed a theological college: the last group of trainee priests had packed their bags in 1971 when the college was forcibly closed by the Turkish authorities. Walking around the Holy Trinity monastery was like entering a school in holiday time, except that the long vacation here had lasted 24 years. Being here saddened me: the life of the place was slowly ebbing away.

'This is one of the small reception rooms,' said Father Isaias as he led me into a salon the size of a tennis court. The wooden floor had a highly polished sheen and the velvet plush covering the gilded chairs was carefully dusted. There was even a fresh display of flowers that filled the ceremonial hall with scent. Someone clearly came in here every day and dusted the room. Someone polished the floor.

Next door there were classrooms which had been left, Pompeii-style, in exactly the state as when the last student waved farewell. Even the garden, with its neat pots of geraniums and carefully clipped hedges was well tended. Yet there was not a hint of behind-the-scenes activity. Who cut the grass? Who dusted the windowsills? At 11.30 am the letterbox clattered, yet I never saw the postman. A meal was cooked yet I never heard a chef. The place was run by phantoms who performed their duties then scuttled off to hide in the shadows.

I asked Father Isaias how many worked here; I asked who paid for it all. He looked at me sternly and shook his head. The few Greeks remaining in Istanbul have a hard enough time without me poking my nose into their affairs.

Despite living on a beautiful island in the Bosporus, Isaias's role as guardian of the Byzantine tradition is a precarious one and the future has never looked so bleak. Yet it wasn't always so: for more than a thousand years Constantinople was the richest city in the world – the hub of an immense empire that stretched from the shores of Spain to the coastline of the Black Sea. This empire had arisen from the ashes of the Roman world when Constantine the Great – ten centuries before Mandeville set out on his travels – was proclaimed emperor while campaigning in England. One of his first decisions was to move his imperial capital from Rome to the shores of the Bosporus and christen it New Rome. The name didn't stick and within a generation the city had become known as Constantinople after its founder. As people's horizons shifted eastwards, the lingua franca changed from Latin to Greek and the old Roman world found its successor in the Byzantine empire. The greatest turning point of all came while Constantine was doing battle in Italy. Looking into the sky, he beheld a vision of the crucifix accompanied by the words 'In this sign, conquer.' Constantine converted his empire to Christianity and, in doing so, turned a persecuted cult into a state religion.

Ever since the Turks captured Constantinople in 1453, the remnants of Christian Byzantium have been in decline and the empire that Mandeville claims to have visited has today shrunk to one tiny island in the Bosporus and a few pockets of Greeks in Istanbul. But they too are on their last legs. There are less than 2,500 heirs to the empire left alive. Thirty die every month. Many more leave the city each year, fleeing from persecution or emigrating abroad in search of a better life. Even the Ecumenical Patriarchate – home to the supreme head of the Eastern Orthodox Church and the enduring legacy of Constantine's Christian empire – is under threat. When the present patriarch dies there is unlikely to be anyone left to replace him.

But empires do not disappear completely. Customs are passed down the centuries and traditions kept alive in family homes. People also remain, and it was these descendants of the Byzantine empire that I was hoping to meet – descendants of the very families that had so intrigued my knight from St Albans.

'It won't be easy to find any Byzantines,' warned Father Isaias, 'for there are very few of us left. Most fled in the 1920s and more leave every month. I wish you the best of luck, but I don't envy your task.'

I had arrived in Istanbul knowing little more about Sir John than what he writes at the beginning of his *Travels*. He claims to have been born in St Albans and says he left England on St Michael's day in 1322 but he declines to mention his reasons for going abroad or explain why he went for so long. Instead of describing himself, he begins his book with a portrayal of imperial decline: a portrayal that could scarcely have been more accurate. For even at the time when Mandeville claimed to have visited Constantinople, the empire was teetering towards catastrophe after a long and bruising battle for power.

The fault lay squarely at the feet of the emperor's grandson, a brilliant but vainglorious youth called Andronicus. Brought up as the apple of his grandfather's eye, he was corrupted by the gifts showered upon him as a child and soon acquired a greedy obsession with money. In his youth he asked to be given a rich and fertile island to which he could retire for a life of debauchery.

But quite by accident, Andronicus found himself thrust into the political limelight. He had an instructor in the art of love – a beautiful lady described as a 'matron in rank and a prostitute in manners' – who he suspected of seducing other men in her spare time. Laying an ambush outside her bedroom one night, he butchered the man fleeing her bedchamber only to find he had killed his own brother.

Andronicus was over the moon, for this brother had deprived him of any hope of power; when his father died of grief eight days later, he realized that only his elderly grandfather stood between him and the imperial throne. Chroniclers of the time express their horror at seeing the youth unable to contain his delight at the deaths and prophesied that such an outcome could only bode ill for the empire. They were right: for the next seven years the empire was torn apart by three separate civil wars which Andronicus eventually won. His grandfather was stripped of his title, confined to a monastery, and spent his declining days locked in an uncomfortable cell.

14

By the time Sir John arrived in the city, Andronicus was busily spending the empire's revenues. His declared aim was to possess at all times a thousand hounds, a thousand hawks and a thousand huntsmen and, although he was the richest ruler in Christendom, he so depleted the empire's gilded coffers that the state could no longer equip an army strong enough to combat the threat posed by the Turks.

In his early years Andronicus had cast himself as a future Alexander the Great and cursed his grandfather with the words: 'Alexander might complain that his father would leave him nothing to conquer; alas! my grandsire will leave me nothing to lose.' But although the young emperor did wage a series of dazzlingly successful campaigns on the empire's western front – and for a short time even recovered Thessaly and Epirus – these provinces were soon lost to Serbia. In the east the situation was even bleaker: the Turks won a string of decisive victories and were virtually knocking on the doors of Constantinople by the time Andronicus died. It was a miracle, in fact, that it took them another century to capture the city.

Sir John, arriving in these troubled times, comments on the woeful position of the emperor: 'He used to be Emperor of Romany, of Greece, of Asia Minor, of Syria, of the land of Judea, in which is Jerusalem, of the land of Egypt, of Persia and Arabia; but he has lost all, except Greece.'

In this he was correct: although the Catalans still controlled central Greece and Italian familes still held the Aegean islands, Andronicus had indeed reclaimed northern Greece for the empire. It was his only lasting military success.

Few monuments remain from these final years of Byzantium and the skyline of today's city is dominated by the domes and minarets of the Ottoman centuries. The taxi driver who had met me at the airport was keen to give me a guided tour of Istanbul and although I tried to explain my interest in the city's past, he had never heard of Byzantium and kept asking if it was the name of my hotel. Keeping both eyes on the meter and none on the road, he skirted in a huge loop around the city then plunged us into the worst of the rush-hour traffic. But the detour was worth the cost for as we approached the Ataturk bridge the lights of the

Golden Horn were flickering on and the stony profile of the Ottoman city, built on the ruins of Byzantium, was spread before us. The minarets and domes lining the water's edge seemed to have heaved their bulks out of the submarine depths, dripping and cold in the chill autumn air.

My guidebook had recommended the Pera Palas: a huge, turn-of-the-century hotel built for passengers arriving on the Orient Express. It can't have changed much in the intervening years. Its dimly lit Ottoman interior is filled with huge green plants which loom like monsters from the corners of the atrium. Acres of mirrors reflect acres of carpets and, in the evenings, small parties of ex-pats gather for gin and tonics before heading into town for dinner.

The bedrooms had seen better days. The carpet in my luxury suite was threadbare and the paint peeling. And while the room faced south-west towards Halki, the island itself was permanently lost in the cloud of pollution that hangs over Istanbul like a yellowing net curtain.

A young lad was operating the hotel lift when I first arrived. As I stepped inside clutching my suitcase in one hand and passport in the other, he immediately pulled down a bench, sprinkled me with cologne, then sprayed the carriage with air freshener. As we neared the top floor he asked with great politeness: 'You wish, sir, to see Agatha Christie's room?' I declined and he shrugged his shoulders. 'Agatha is a great British writer,' he explained before opening the metal lift doors.

Half an hour later I had to pop downstairs to reception so I called the lift. Again the lad splashed me with cologne before repeating his earlier question: 'You wish, sir, to see Agatha Christie's room?' I said no for a second time but he was not easily deterred: later that afternoon he asked me for a third time, with an increasing note of desperation in his voice. He was still operating the lift the following morning so I walked downstairs to breakfast. But he caught my eye as I was on my way back to my room and called me into the lift. 'Sir,' he said with a note of determination in his voice, 'today you *will* see Agatha's room.'

'Today I am going to a monastery,' I explained. 'Tomorrow . . . I promise.'

'No, today,' he replied, and before I could say anything more the lift had stopped at the fourth floor, the metal doors were flung open, and a second lad was standing there ready to take me hostage: my tour of Agatha Christie's bedroom could begin.

Guide Two unlocked the literary bedroom and the three of us stepped inside. It was a small room that looked almost exactly identical to mine.

'Agatha-bed,' said the guide, pointing to the bed. 'Agatha-sink,' he added. 'And this . . . ' he tapped the glass firmly ' . . . Agatha-window.'

I pointed at the table. 'Agatha-desk?' I suggested.

'No sir,' he replied with a note of triumph, 'Agatha-table.'

On the way out I gave them both a tip. 'No more Agatha,' I pleaded.

'No,' promised the lad from the lift. 'Agatha-dead.'

Father Isaias suggested I spend the afternoon at Holy Trinity monastery and led me up onto the roof of the building from where there was a superb view across the island. The land fell away sharply towards the sea and far below us was the little village and port where I had arrived. I could just about make out the shadow of a tanker pushing its way through the Bosporus before it gave up its ghost to the mist.

Father Isaias pointed far into the distance. 'See that island over there?' he said. 'The Turks confiscated that from us during the war. And that one there . . . ?' He pointed towards a more definite shape. 'That monastery has been allowed to collapse. Soon it too will disappear completely. This one here is the only one left.'

A gust of wind blew rain into our faces. 'That's why I'm here,' he added. 'I have to keep this place alive. If I left, the Turks would confiscate these buildings as well, and that would be the end of everything.'

There was a moment's silence as we watched a cat chewing the geraniums: the rain began to fall harder and Father Isaias suggested we move back inside. 'Let's go to the library,' he said. 'There's just a chance we'll find something about your knight. Tell me again – what was that problem you'd found?'

I had re-read Sir John's book the night before coming to Halki and the more closely I examined his description of Constantinople the more puzzled I became. He claims to have watched a jousting tournament during his stay in the city and even describes the jousting ground as being close to the emperor's palace. Yet anyone with a concern for historical accuracy – and Sir John is normally a stickler for details – would have known that while jousting was a favourite pastime of knights in the medieval west, it was almost unheard of in the eastern empire. It was impossible that Sir John could have seen such a tournament in Constantinople and I could only presume that he had invented the story to add a little local colour to his book.

The library was deep in the bowels of the monastery, reached along winding corridors, darkened passages, and down endless flights of stairs. It hadn't been used for years. The bare concrete floor echoed the chill of the room and only a few light bulbs worked. Yet the librarian's desk was piled high with new books waiting to be catalogued. I looked at the stamps on the brown paper parcels. They had come from Greece, the United States and France and were all works of theology. Isaias told me that as chief librarian it was his job to shelve them. As the sole user of the library he was the only person who would ever read them.

He strolled through the library's central aisle, calling out the subjects as he passed them: European history, topography, theology, Byzantine studies. Here he paused for a moment and drew down a worn, leather-bound volume by Nikephoros Gregoras, chronicler of fourteenth-century Constantinople. Its title, picked out in gilt, was in Latin: *Corpus Scriptorum Historiae Byzantinae* and it had been published in Bonn in 1829. Isaias opened it with care and scanned the Greek text: 'You never know, you might just pick up some clues about Sir John's jousting anecdote in here,' he said. 'This chap knew just about everything there was to know about the city in those days.'

He flicked through the pages for a moment then stopped. 'Here . . . ' he said with a note of excitement in his voice. 'Here . . . listen to this . . . ' and he began to read from the book:

'"After the birth of his son John, he . . ." that's the Emperor Andronicus "organised two games which had been used by the

Latins for a long time in order to train the body in times of peace. They have the appearance of a duel and are called *jousting* by the Latins . . . both sides equip themselves with weapons and cover themselves with armour. Then each takes a lance which has three spikes and they rush at each other, meeting each other with great strength."'

Father Isaias gave a brief smile and looked at me. 'So your knight really could have seen jousting in Constantinople,' he said. 'Who knows, perhaps he was in the city for this very tournament?'

Jousting was indeed new to the Byzantine court for it had been introduced at the time of Andronicus's wedding to his second wife. She came from Savoy and her Italian entourage brought the martial sport to the city. Andronicus was instantly hooked and caused a great scandal amongst Constantinople's upper classes by breaking lances with the foreign knights.

'It's not so surprising that Sir John writes about jousting,' said Father Isaias. 'When people travel abroad they tend to notice things that are either extremely alien to them, or extremely familiar. Sir John must have been surprised, after travelling all that way from home, to see a sport he was more used to watching in England.'

'So you think he really did come?' I asked.

'I wouldn't like to guess whether he came or not,' he added, 'but if he didn't, he certainly knew how to do his research . . . '

We were interrupted by the chatter of voices followed by the sight of five priests emerging from the gloom. 'Hello,' said Isaias with not a hint of surprise. 'What brings you lot here?'

'The conference,' they said in unison. But already their faces had detected that something was wrong.

'The conference,' repeated Isaias with uncertainty. 'The conference . . . yes, of course, the conference. But that's tomorrow isn't it?'

Five faces fell at once. There were five sighs. Five of them muttered 'not again' under their breath. They had been told by the Patriarchate that the conference was today. Isaias thought it was tomorrow. I was surprised there was a conference at all for I was under the impression that the place had been closed down years ago, but when I asked my question it was brushed aside.

The American pastor was not at all amused. 'Well if you think I'm going to come all this way again tomorrow, you'd . . . ' he stopped when he realized he was about to be rude. The German priest was also annoyed. He looked at his watch and huffed loudly. Others were more gracious. The Italian Franciscan chuckled with good humour and the Armenian priest – a distinguished man sporting a felt trilby – allowed himself an ironic smile. The Anglican vicar, instantly spotting I was English, turned to me and murmured: 'The Orthodox are unable to organize anything. This happens every time.'

Only Isaias remained unperturbed for he knew that his monastery could take everything in its stride. I'd arrived out of the blue yet coffee had already been prepared. The bedrooms were cleaned every day, just in case. Now, five priests had turned up unannounced but it was no cause for alarm. Somewhere in the heart of the monastery, someone would already be preparing for their stay.

'Oh well,' said Isaias with a shrug, 'I'm sure lunch is being prepared as we speak. I hope you will stay for something to eat now you've come all the way here.'

The dining room was in the basement. We sat around a carefully laid table and Isaias said grace while a middle-aged Greek wheeled in lunch on a trolley. The mystery of who had cooked it increased. There were now eight of us sitting down to dine, for Germanios had also appeared, yet the kitchen staff had had less than ten minutes to prepare the endless courses. We began with clear soup, steaming hot and smelling of fresh herbs. This was followed by roast rabbit, rice cooked with pine nuts and saffron, and two different salads. When we had finished these, a second trolley piled high with cakes and fresh fruit was wheeled in.

The conversation was strained, for the American pastor was still cross at having been dragged all the way here for nothing, and at some point Father Isaias – perhaps hoping to lighten the atmosphere – decided to tell a joke. It was a strange little anecdote about Moses and Elijah and I was lost almost as soon as he began. I looked around the table at a row of blank faces, all politely facing Isaias, and realized that the others were lost too. It was quite clear that no one was going to understand the punchline.

Isaias paused for a moment and the American, thinking it was the end of the joke, had the misfortune to burst out laughing. Not only that: he clapped his hands loudly as he rocked on his chair. Father Isaias coughed, glanced at him, and continued. After several more minutes he fell silent and then began to chuckle to himself. This was our cue: from all around the table, the six of us all began to roar with laughter. Only Germanios sat there blank faced for he hadn't heard a word. But then, seeing us laughing, he laughed as well; a peal of giggles that this time had us all genuinely laughing.

'It makes a change to hear a joke,' whispered the Reverend Ian as the laughter died down. 'The Greek Orthodox are usually so serious. They're not the sort of people you can have a laugh with.'

The Orthodox in Istanbul don't have much to laugh about, for these last remaining descendants of the Byzantine empire have been brought close to extinction in recent years by the heavy-handed attitude of the Turkish government.

Yet life wasn't always so gloomy: when the Ottoman commander, Mehmet the Conqueror, captured Constantinople in 1453, he found himself ruling over such a diverse collection of nationalities that the only way he could control his empire was by giving each of them a large degree of autonomy. The city's huge Greek Orthodox community was no exception and the Patriarch – the highest Christian authority in the city – was made accountable to the Sultan for the affairs of his people.

Although these Orthodox held their church services in Greek, they still referred to themselves as *Romioi* – the direct descendants of the Roman founders of Constantinople. Even today, centuries after the Roman Empire was consigned to the history books, the Orthodox consider themselves as *Romioi* and their Patriarch is known as the *Rum* Patriarch, or Patriarch of the Romans. As one young Orthodox said to me: 'We wouldn't be doing ourselves any favours by calling ourselves Greeks. It's not very politically correct.'

But it was their overt support of Greece at the end of the First World War that spelt their downfall. When the Allied fleet entered the Bosporus in 1918, the *Romioi* were ecstatic. The Greek flag was raised in triumph from the Patriarchate, there were mass meetings in support of Greece, and virtually all the Orthodox churches in the city swore an oath of allegiance to Greece. When the supreme commander of the Allied forces arrived in Istanbul he rode into the city upon a splendid white horse – mimicking the Ottoman conqueror's entry into Constantinople four centuries earlier. The idea behind such a symbolic act came from a *Romioi*. So did the horse.

The Orthodox were over the moon. For a brief moment it seemed that the holy city of Constantinople had been wrenched back from the infidel, and the Ottoman sultan had scarcely signed the armistice before Greek troops began flooding into Turkey, determined to create a Greater Greece out of huge chunks of Turkey. Their army captured a string of coastal towns then pressed on into Anatolia, but here they met their match. A Turkish general – who later found fame as Kemal Ataturk – stopped their advance and, in 1922, routed the Greek army.

The fate of the Orthodox living in rural Turkey was decided by the Treaty of Lausanne: one and a half million were transported to Greece while half a million Muslims in Greece were moved to Turkey. But the problem remained of what to do with the half a million Orthodox Christians living in Constantinople. Although many Turks demanded they be expelled without further ado, the Orthodox protested that they had lived in the city for centuries and after much wrangling it was agreed that they must be allowed to stay. But life could never be the same for the *Romioi*. There was too much bad feeling and many soon joined the exodus and left the city for ever. By the end of 1923 the dream of Constantinople becoming once again the 'imperial' capital of a Greater Greece was over – and the city that Sir John claims to have visited entered the final stage of its decline.

One afternoon I walked across the new Galata bridge towards the Sultanahmet district of Istanbul. When I had first come to the city eleven years earlier this bridge was a floating iron hulk lined with bars and fish shops, and my schoolfriend Justin and I spent days here drinking Efes Pilsen as we prepared ourselves for the hardships of Kurdistan. It was just as well we did: when we finally arrived in eastern Turkey we discovered it was Ramadan, there was little to eat, and we returned to Istanbul two stone lighter than when we had left.

Much has changed in the intervening years: Kurdistan is no longer safe to visit and the bridge itself has gone. Dismantled some years ago and replaced by a modern concrete structure, it now lies in great rusting chunks at the farthest end of the Golden Horn. As I passed these segments I wondered which had once been home to our favourite bar of all – nameless, dirty, but serving fresh sardines with every pint.

Sadder still were the changes that had overcome the Pudding Shop. This café-restaurant – diagonally opposite the Blue Mosque and a stone's throw from Haghia Sophia – was itself a place of pilgrimage in the sixties, attracting an assortment of dropouts, wastrels and self-proclaimed philosophers all on the overland trail to India. By the time Justin and I came in 1984 these heady days were over and the Pudding Shop was already in slow decline. But even in its twilight years it was still putting on a brave face – always crowded with those, like us, who grew their hair and wore ethnic beads. There was Bernie, the groovster from New Jersey and Ragnar, a mathematician from Iceland. And who could forget Andrew, the cheery Dubliner who left a one-line message for us pinned to the wall: 'Got the runs. Gone to Kos.'

Those were still the grand old days of the Pudding Shop. Now, plates of chicken and chips are illustrated on plastic boards backed by neon lights, and Crosby, Stills, Nash and Young have been replaced by the saccharine love songs of Elton John. There is even a shiny new sign billing the restaurant as the 'World Famous Pudding Shop'. Perhaps fame has been its downfall. Ever since being featured in *Midnight Express* it has simply been too well known.

As soon as I had finished my plate of *imam bayaldi* I left the restaurant and strolled down the road to the church of Haghia Sophia. Although the coaches had left the car park and the tourists returned to their hotels, a cluster of men still stood outside the gates selling postcards and cans of drink. I was offered a Coke, a shoe shine and an ice cream before being told by a man selling guides that his brother lived in Manchester United and that his sister liked chips. His guidebooks were little better than his English: none did justice to the church that stood, for more than a millennium, at the spiritual heart of the Byzantine empire.

I had scarcely entered the cavernous interior of Haghia Sophia before two Turkish lads approached me and led me to a column at the side of the church. It was punctured by a deep hole at about head height and wrapped in a sheet of brass. Sir John had also written about this column for in his day it was famous for exuding droplets of moisture, and thousands of pilgrims flocked here to rub the miracle-working water into their wounds. But the stone's magical properties have changed in the intervening centuries, as these two Turks wished to demonstrate.

'Stick your thumb in the hole,' they said. I pushed my thumb into the column. It was clammy inside and felt damp.

'Now concentrate . . . really think hard . . . ' I concentrated and suddenly one of them jumped. 'There, did you feel it?'

'Feel what?' I said.

'The building . . . it moved. I swear the building moved.'

I told him I felt nothing and the other Turk agreed. 'Don't listen to him,' he said pointing at his friend. 'He's stupid. Dim-witted. He really believes you can move the church by twisting your finger in the hole.'

'It did move,' protested the other. 'When he turned his thumb, the whole building shuddered.'

I didn't like to disappoint him so I agreed that, yes, perhaps the building moved just a fraction. It was all nonsense of course. The church hadn't moved because he hadn't told me to twist my finger.

Sir John describes Haghia Sophia as the richest and most beautiful church in the world and he, like other early writers, was left struggling for words. 'The church presents a most glorious spectacle,' wrote Procopius in the sixth century, 'extraordinary to those who behold it and altogether incredible to those who are told of it. In height, it rises to the heavens . . . and is distinguished by indescribable beauty . . . The dome does not appear to rest upon a solid foundation, but to cover the place beneath as though it were suspended from heaven by the fabled golden chain.'

Even the Emperor Justinian who commissioned the building was taken aback by its beauty when he first saw it. Falling to his knees he uttered the words, 'O Solomon, I have surpassed thee.'

Today much of the magic has been lost and even from the outside Haghia Sophia has been swamped by the buildings that surround it. From my hotel I could see the steel grey minarets of Sultanahmet mosque and the domes of Yeni Cami clearly, but the peeling orangey-pink façade of Haghia Sophia was submerged beneath the city's Ottoman monuments. Inside it is the same. Huge plaques celebrating Allah in Arabic hang in the church as if in mockery of its glorious Byzantine past.

For days I had been struggling to picture the city in Sir John's time and imagine what sort of people the Byzantines were. Now I had the chance to find out, for the upper gallery of Haghia Sophia preserves a mosaic of the Empress Zoe and her husband Constantine. Although crafted some three centuries before Sir John arrived in the city, I hoped that by gazing into their faces and examining their expressions I might glimpse something of their thoughts as well.

Both the emperor and empress were dressed in richly decorated imperial gowns and their posture and solemn faces radiated authority. But their eyes stared back at me blankly – iconographic expressions which betrayed no hint of their personalities. What were they thinking? What made them happy? These portraits only told me what I already knew: that the Byzantines loved the solemn unchanging beauty that was expressed to such perfection in their icons. Yet to the citizens of Constantinople these finely mosaiced faces were representations of real people. Zoe had the mosaic made while still married to her first husband. When he died, his portrait was removed to make way for husband number two. When number two also died Zoe married for a third time and it is his portrait that has survived.

Despite the church's shabby condition, the monumental dome is still a breathtaking sight for it hangs above a void in apparent defiance of gravity. Here, beneath its once-gilded cupola, occurred

many of the defining events in the history of the Byzantine em-
pire. The crowning of emperors. The excommunication of the
Orthodox church by the Pope. The desperate prayers held on the
night the city fell to the Turks. And it was a service in Haghia Sophia
that converted Russia to Christianity. When Vladimir, the pagan
Prince of Kiev, wished to seek the true faith he sent emissaries to
all the world's religions. They travelled amongst Muslims but ruled
out Islam because it prohibited alcohol. They went to Rome but
found no beauty in the worship. At last they came to Constantinople
where they attended a service of the Divine Liturgy in Haghia
Sophia. And here they discovered a religion worthy to take back
to their country. 'We knew not,' they later told Vladimir, 'whether
we were in heaven or on earth, for surely there is no such splen-
dour or beauty anywhere upon earth. We cannot describe it to you;
only this we know, that God dwells there among men, and that their
service surpasses the worship of all other places.'

One part of me wanted Sir John to have been everywhere he
claimed to have travelled, if only to confound the stuffy ranks of
English professors who dismissed him as a fraud. But the idea of
Sir John inventing his entire book also appealed to me and I
could imagine him sitting in his medieval manor and chuckling
to himself as he concocted the most outrageous stories about his
supposed voyage.

While he had clearly spent a considerable amount of time
researching his *Travels* in monastic libraries, however, I found
that he hadn't always been quite so careful when he came to
record his own impressions. Take his description of the city's
famous imperial statue. He claims it stood in front of the church
of Haghia Sophia, was gilded, and portrayed the Emperor
Justinian seated on a horse. I felt sure that a remnant of such a
famous monument would have survived and indeed it has;
although the statue has long since disappeared, the column still
remains, towering over the new Sultanahmet train line. But it
could in no way be described as being in front of Haghia Sophia
– it is more than half a mile away. What's more, if Sir John really
had seen the monument he would have known that the column
was adorned with an effigy not of Justinian, but of Constantine.

There was even worse to come. I found that this gilded statue had been toppled during a devastating hurricane more than two centuries before Sir John was even born. It was never repaired or restored. It was never put back up. Sir John, I could only conclude, had not seen the statue and in all probability had not visited Constantinople.

But I had underestimated Mandeville, as I discovered on my last day in Istanbul. I was walking back to my hotel along the six-lane Kennedy Caddesi when I spotted two chunks of inscribed marble built into the wall by the edge of the road. There was something about these carefully crafted blocks that caught my eye and I went to have a closer look. They supported a small postern gate which had long ago been blocked up and was half-covered in rotting rubbish. The milky-white stone was as smooth as soap and scarred by neither blemish nor fault. It had clearly been hewn with the greatest of care and one side was decorated with a neatly chiselled row of inscriptions which were in Greek. These ran from top to bottom, suggesting that the blocks were now on their sides and had not originally been intended as gateposts. What were they doing here? Where had they come from?

When I got back to the hotel I flicked through my books on Constantinople and found a short footnote about these very posts. Every stone in Istanbul has been logged and documented by some Victorian archaeologist or German Byzantinist and these were no exception. They were not gateposts at all and their inscriptions did not belong to pagan Greece but to Christian Constantinople. They had, I read with growing excitement, once stood in the Augusteum and formed the base of the celebrated equestrian statue of Justinian.

Justinian! So Sir John was right about the statue. And if it was in the Augusteum, that would mean it was situated right in front of Haghia Sophia. It was I who had made the mistake for it had never crossed my mind that there might have been *two* imperial statues – only one of which had been blown down in the great hurricane of 1106. Further reading confirmed everything Sir John had claimed, for other writers had been equally impressed by the statue: 'Upon this horse,' wrote the historian Procopius, 'sits a colossal brass figure of the Emperor . . . he looks towards the east, directing his course, I imagine, against the Persians: in his left hand he holds a globe, by which the sculptor signifies that all lands and seas are subject to him.'

Sir John mentions this globe as well but claims that at the time he was visiting the city, it had fallen out of the emperor's hand. Could he be correct even in this tiny detail? I checked the other writers of the time and found that when William of Boldensele came to describe the glittering statue in 1332, the globe was still in the emperor's hand. Stephen of Novgorod also saw it in 1350. But the Byzantine historian Nikephoros Gregoras – whose exhaustive chronicle leaves no stone unturned – records that the globe, which was as big as a fifteen-gallon jar, was so badly damaged during a storm in 1317 that parts of it fell into the street. It took eight years to repair so that if Sir John really did visit Constantinople when he claims, he would have indeed seen the imperial statue empty-handed.

One of the most influential men in Constantinople during this period was Theodore Metochites, the Prime Minister and First Lord of the Treasury. His rise to power was as rapid and spectacular as his eventual fall from grace. Attracted to the imperial courtiers by his writing ability, he scored a diplomatic triumph when he found a wife for the emperor's son. Soon after he began to rise up the ladder of state and within a few years found himself occupying one of the highest positions in the empire. Those who hoped to gain from his promotion wrote eulogies to his warm-heartedness; those who had been overlooked described him as a pompous bore.

What was not in doubt was Theodore's immense wealth which allowed him to indulge his love of the arts. His greatest act of patronage was to pay for the restoration of the monastery church of St Saviour in Chora, close to the city walls – including a complete reworking of the mosaics – and as a finishing touch he had a portrait of himself, finely crafted from chips of coloured marble, placed over the door. And just at the time when this mosaic was being set above the entrance, Sir John Mandeville arrived in the city.

I wondered if the two men had met for they would have had

a great deal in common. Theodore loved old books and built up a huge collection of ancient manuscripts – works on geography, mathematics, astronomy and rhetoric. He was himself a great writer and many of his works survived the destruction of the city by the Turks.

When I saw this mosaiced portrait of Theodore I was at last able to imagine something of the people that Sir John himself would have met in the city. Theodore is depicted in an attitude of piety – offering a model of his church to Christ with an imploring look on his face. His beard is long but neatly clipped and his hair flows in long locks over his shoulders. He is dressed in his official robes of office – a long, dark-blue caftan gathered at the waist – while his head is covered by an astonishing hat, a vast white and gold turban known as a *skiadon*, or sunshade. But despite the pious expressions of his, and all the other faces adorning the walls of the church, these mosaics were very different to those I had seen in Haghia Sophia. There is good reason for this: at the time Mandeville was in the city there was a revival of interest in the books of classical Greece and Rome, and here in St Saviour that revival was finding expression in art. The human form, so long imprisoned by the static rules of iconography, was starting to shake off *rigor mortis*; the drapes of the robes were beginning to flow languidly over bodies; and even the trees and shrubs seemed to have been stirred into motion by the lightest of breezes. Here on the walls of this church, the first tentative movements of the Renaissance were stirring – foreshadowing the free-flowing brush-strokes of Botticelli.

Alas, this Renaissance came to an end almost as abruptly as Theodore's career for with Andronicus's victory in the civil war he was sacked from his post and driven into exile. At the height of his power he had composed a few lines of poetry to run along the edge of his portrait, and I couldn't help wondering if he had been struck by some divine foresight when he wrote: 'I have made thee, Oh most pure Lady, my hope and the *chora* [dwelling place] for the refuge of my life.'

The words came all too true, for when Theodore was recalled from exile he lived out his final days as a prisoner in his beloved church of St Saviour in Chora.

European Istanbul is cut in two by the Golden Horn – a watery inlet which curls through the heart of the city before joining the great channel of the Bosporus. On the eastern shore of this inlet stands Galata with its high-rise banks, businesses and high street stores. On the western side is Haghia Sophia and the Blue Mosque, and below them row upon row of ferry terminals. The shoreline along this western bank is derelict and noisy. A road runs along its entire length – punctured by a huge interchange for traffic crossing the Ataturk bridge – and the houses that face the water are empty and crumbling. The air of dereliction grows steadily worse as you near the Fener district which lies halfway along the shore of the Golden Horn. Even the the water seems to acquire a darker, murkier colour.

Yet as little as a century ago this was the wealthy Greek quarter of the city; home to a thriving community of businessmen who made their fortunes from trade. Its name, Fener, is derived from the two Turkish words *fena yer* meaning bad place, the home of the Greeks. Now only a few of the once grandiose wooden mansions are still standing and even these are leaning at perilous angles. The wood is rotten and the windows in danger of falling out. Baggy Turkish bloomers hang from makeshift washing lines, witnesses to the vanished riches and cosmopolitan lifestyle that this area once boasted.

These days, the narrow streets are filled with women wearing veils and bearded men in Islamic dress. Many are clutching the Koran – the only book that the shops here seem to sell – and most are on their way to or from the local mosque. You won't hear the sound of Turkish in these streets: people chat to each other in Arabic and the shop signs are decorated with beautiful Arabic calligraphy. The families living here are newcomers, peasants from Anatolia, who have come to the city in search of employment. Lacking money and jobs they find themselves inexorably drawn into religious fanaticism.

High above the streets of Fener and looming over everything like a huge russet cliff-face is one of the city's few remaining Greek schools. Its walls are blackened by pollution and surrounded by barbed wire and not a sound comes from the playground. The surrounding streets are derelict and I soon found myself among alleys filled with rubbish. Passing a church and finding the door open, I stepped inside to ask the way to the Patriarchate. The woman at the door gave me directions and, when she had finished, I asked her if she was a *Romioi*. 'No,' she said. 'I'm Italian. From Bologna.'

She didn't look Italian and I asked when she had moved to Istanbul. She paused for a moment then said: 'I think we moved here four centuries ago.'

The Ecumenical Patriarch has lived in the city since the time when Constantine converted his empire to Christianity. In Mandeville's day the offices were housed in the massive Church of the Holy Apostles: today they are in a building so heavily fortified that you could be forgiven for thinking you are about to enter the Bank of England's bullion vaults. There is a round-the-clock security guard outside the building. Close-circuit television cameras monitor every inch of perimeter wall. There is chain-link fencing. And everyone entering the site is questioned before being asked to pass through an airport-style metal detector to check for weapons and explosives.

I had arranged a meeting with Father Tarasios, a youthful deacon who lives here and, after finally gaining entry to the building, I suggested to him that they were, perhaps, going a little over the top.

'Even this isn't adequate,' moaned Tarasios. 'Last year, on the eve of the anniversary celebrating the Turkish capture of the city, three huge explosive devices were discovered along the perimeter wall of the main building. The gardener noticed the trip wire at 2.25 am. The bombs were timed to go off at 2.45 am, 3 am, and 3.15 am. Bang, bang, bang. We would have been blown sky high.'

Every week, there is some new altercation outside the Patriarchate. Rocks are hurled at the building, petrol bombs are tossed over the gates and vandals cover the walls with radical Islamic graffiti. The new Islamic mayor of Istanbul recently said that there was no place for the Patriarch in an Islamic society, and the fundamentalists are continually threatening to break down the main gate to the complex of buildings, which was sealed in 1821 as a sign of respect to Patriarch Gregory V who was hanged from it by a bloodthirsty mob.

'We are forever hearing how the fundamentalists will smash down the gate and destroy the Patriarchate,' said Tarasios. 'They claim we will not open that gate until the Patriarch has personally hanged the Chief Mufti from it in revenge. It is ridiculous. These things are reported in the press as fact. Everything we do is distorted and misquoted.

'We are not allowed to wear our vestments in public,' he added. 'We accept that. It is Turkish law. But no one would ever dare tell the fundamentalists not to wear their dress which is also forbidden. It is highly ironic that our community had far more freedom under the Ottoman Sultans than in a modern democracy. We feel like prisoners in our own homes.'

Things could soon get even worse, for a member of the Turkish Parliament recently proposed opening Haghia Sophia once again to Muslim worship. The suggestion caused deep anxiety in Parliament for controversial legislation is not allowed to be discussed in public lest it damage Turkey's image in the eyes of the west. To raise such a matter openly was a deliberate provocation and a clear breach of this policy. But to those who work within the Orthodox community such provocation confirmed all their worst fears.

'It would be the last straw if that happened,' said Tarasios. 'It would be almost impossible to bear. But I suppose we would have to bear it.'

Although Sir John doesn't write about the Patriarchate, he does record a letter sent by the Patriarch to Pope John XXII. It was a reply to a missive from the Pope and can have done little to heal the rift between the Orthodox and Catholic churches for its tone was as curt as it was critical: 'We well believe your power is great over your subjects; we cannot support your great pride; we do not purpose to slake your great avarice. God be with you, for God is with us. Farewell.'

Most medieval writers would have been scandalized by such a letter and used it as a pretext for launching an attack on the Orthodox church. But Mandeville shows a curious restraint, commenting on neither the author nor the contents. It is almost as if he agrees with the sentiments expressed.

The Patriarch who wrote it – a man named Esaias – had been reinstated in his job as soon as Andronicus won the civil war. The chronicler Nikephoros Gregoras records that the event was a cause for joyous celebration and Esaias was led back to the patriarchal palace with a bizarre procession accompanying him. There were not only bishops and priests by his side, but also a band of musicians and a troupe of dancing girls. Esaias was said to be so delighted by the bawdy antics of one of these girls that he was helpless with mirth as he made his way through the streets of the city. Such happiness was short-lived, for relations with Rome were going from bad to worse and the reunion of the two churches was as far away as ever.

Before I arrived at the Patriarchate I had imagined a rundown building gathering the dust of centuries and pictured antique priests shuffling along corridors while muttering to each other in Greek. Such a picture was the outcome of a letter I had received from the Patriarch some months earlier. I'd been hoping to travel to the monastic community on Mount Athos in Greece to write an article for the *Telegraph Magazine* and had been told that when dealing with the Orthodox Church it pays to have numerous letters of support from a hierarchy of priests and bishops. On this occasion I went straight to the top and wrote to the Patriarch, the spiritual head of Mount Athos, asking for his help.

What I received in reply was a letter so impressive I immediately had it framed. Written on thick paper and composed in the language of classical Byzantium, it had been penned in this very building and was signed personally by His All-Holiness the Ecumenical Patriarch Bartholomeus I, Archbishop of Constantinople and New Rome. His signature, decorated with a flourish of calligraphy, stretched from one side of the paper to the other and underneath he had added, 'At Constantinople; with the prayers of God.' But if the language of the Patriarchate harked back to Mandeville's medieval world, the buildings themselves could not have been more high-tech. As I chatted with Father Tarasios, an international communications network was whirring away around us. Cable TV picked up the Patriarch being interviewed on Greek television. Every second, a fax would arrive from somewhere in

Most venerable custodians and representatives
of the community of the Holy Mountain,
beloved children in the Lord of our
Mediocrity, may the grace and peace of God
be with you.
The bearer of this letter, the most honourable
Mr Giles Milton, of London, comes to this
holy place with the sanction of the Church, to
visit and make pilgrimage to the sacred
dwelling-places therein.
We commend him to your beloved
venerability and we exhort you that he might,
through your earnest care, be granted all that
will facilitate the fulfilment of the purpose for
which he has come.

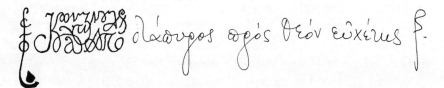

the world. The telephone rang continuously. We could have been
part of a Bond film were it not for the conspicuous absence of
Bond girls.

'We are continuously being accused of trying to set up a
second Vatican,' said Tarasios as he put down the phone. 'Of
acting like a state within a state. But this shows a profound
misunderstanding of the Patriarchate. The Patriarch is not a
political leader and nor is he just the head of the Greek Church,
he is the *spiritual* head of all Orthodox churches.'

A second phone rang. He picked it up, shouted something in
Greek, and hung up. 'I'm sorry,' he said. 'We're busy today.'

'Wouldn't it be easier to move the Patriarchate elsewhere?' I suggested. 'Somewhere less controversial.'

'This is impossible,' replied Father Tarasios. 'Constantinople is the historical and spiritual centre of Orthodoxy. This is where St Andrew came. This is where so many martyrs have died for their faith. We could set up in Geneva, or wherever, but then it would be merely an administrative centre. It would be missing the point entirely.'

He stopped talking for a moment in order to bang the television set, for the reception had broken out into a rash of fuzzy dots. Worse still the video had packed up. Tarasios cursed the machines and, as he did so, the television burst into life once more and Cagney and Lacey appeared on the screen. There was a shooting followed by a car chase, before the picture once again disappeared into a fuzz of dots.

'The Patriarchate has to be, and will always be, in Constantinople,' said Tarasios. 'It was here when your chap came and it will be here in the future . . . '

He offered me a tour of the buildings, recently rebuilt after a disastrous fire in 1951. For years the Patriarchate was not allowed to touch the charred remains and it was only after the personal intervention of Jimmy Carter that the government relented.

The exterior had to be an exact replica of the old building but inside the designers were allowed greater freedom and unleashed a riot of gilt and regal purple. In the throne room where His All-Holiness meets his most distinguished guests a long red carpet leads the eye towards a raised platform atop which stands a carved and gilded chair. The room is lit with chandeliers dripping with plum-sized lumps of crystal and I suddenly felt as if I had left the centuries-old traditions of the church behind and stepped through the doors of Hollywood. At any moment Joan Collins could have wafted into the throne room.

This room changed my perception of the Patriarch. Before, I had imagined him as a remote and dignified person radiating gravitas and imperial authority. Now he had become a walk-on part in an American soap.

'Who paid for all this?' I asked Father Tarasios.

He pointed upwards suggesting, I thought, that the money had descended like the Holy Spirit from on high. But when I looked above my head I saw an oil painting of a Greek shipping billionaire who had generously donated huge sums to restore these buildings.

But billions of dollars will not keep the dwindling population here alive and the Patriarch is well aware of that. He takes an interest in every single *Romioi* in the city, helping them gain university places abroad (they are not allowed to study at Turkish universities) and offering them career advice.

'Every single one of us counts in the city,' said Tarasios, 'and it is absolutely devastating if a family leaves. People often move abroad temporarily to enable their children to study, and once they have seen a different life they choose to stay. Sometimes we have thirty funerals in a month. On the rare occasions there is a wedding or baptism it's a huge celebration.'

The Patriarchate also tries to keep the few surviving Greek schools open, even though some have only one or two pupils. Children are bussed from all over the city to attend these schools for once they close – even if only for a year – they are never allowed to reopen.

'The other night we were tipped off that one of our churches was going to be knocked down in the middle of the night. We sent the local bishop and his parishioners to defend the building. When they got there a bulldozer was about to knock it down. They got there just in time.'

The attitude of the Turkish government towards the Patriarchate mirrors the state of diplomatic relations with Greece. When relations are running smoothly the Patriarchate is left in peace. When relations break down – as they constantly do – there is certain to be trouble. One night, above all others, is for ever etched on the memories of the *Romioi* community here. On a September evening in 1955 a mob of thousands systematically ransacked *Romioi* property in the city and attacked the Orthodox community. A ninety-year-old priest from the monastery of Balikli was burnt alive. Women were raped. And the destruction to property was immense. The police watched on passively as thousands of shops, houses and churches were looted and people attacked. Some even fraternized with the rioters. There was eventually some semblance of justice, but not until many years later. After the military coup in 1960 the Prime Minister, Adnan Menderes, was ousted and accused of complicity in the anti-Greek riots. Fifteen members of his government were found guilty and the disgraced Menderes was hanged. He instantly became a martyr.

The present Patriarch, Bartholomeus, is a shrewd man who walks the diplomatic tightrope with skill and is enough of a realist to have accepted that his community is in an endgame situation. Every year there are fewer and fewer Orthodox left in Istanbul and it has been calculated that by 2020 there will be no more *Romioi* left in the city. Yet under Turkish law the Patriarch has to be a Turkish citizen. What happens when there are no Orthodox 'Turks' left?

The Patriarch has taken the high risk strategy of raising his profile on the international scene and his aim is to publicize the problems faced by the Orthodox in Istanbul. To this end, he has recently invited a number of important visitors to the patriarchal buildings. Chauffeur-driven limousines have been spotted drawing up in the steep alleyways carrying foreign ministers and diplomats from all over the world. Recently he welcomed Prince Philip here. Soon he will visit the Pope, a meeting of great symbolic significance which suggests that after more than six centuries of cold shouldering one another, the Catholic and Orthodox churches might at last begin working towards *rapprochement*. Even the Anglican church maintains close contacts with the Orthodox church, and the Archbishop of Canterbury has his own ambassador to the Patriarch permanently living in the city.

When Tarasios had finished his grim tale he folded his arms and asked if I had any questions. I told him about Mandeville's interest in the Orthodox church and explained my quest to discover whether there were any true Byzantines left in the city. 'Perhaps,' I said hopefully, 'I have already reached my goal. Perhaps your family have lived here for generations.'

He chuckled for a moment. 'I'm afraid not,' he said. 'You see I'm from Texas. But there is a person you ought to see . . . '

Dr Yagcioglu peered at me over the frame of his glasses in a way that only doctors can. 'You're looking for a real Byzantine,' he said in a slow, considered voice. As he did so he let out a long, low whistle followed by a series of tut-tutting noises.

'That won't be easy,' he said. 'You see most of our community only arrived at the turn of the century. My family came from Anatolia. Others come from the islands or from Greece. But a Byzantine . . .' again he tutted. 'I think this calls for a cup of tea.'

I was in the psychiatric ward of what had once been Istanbul's largest Greek hospital. But the Greek patients have long since been supplanted by Turks and Dr Yagcioglu – who was in his late seventies – was one of only five Greek doctors remaining. When built, the hospital had been surrounded by pleasant suburbs but times have changed. Nowadays it is overshadowed by the squalid Topkapi bus station and the nearby streets are littered with rubbish and smashed-up cars. Even the great Byzantine walls of the city, which I could see from the window of Dr Y's room, have seen better days. Home to beggars, tramps and gypsy families who build ramshackle shelters amongst the rubble, they have acquired a dangerous reputation in recent years. A group of tourists trampling across people's homes recently found themselves at the receiving end of a hail of bullets.

Sir John would almost certainly have entered the city through one of the stone gateways that puncture these walls. If he had arrived from Europe by land – as seems likely – he would probably have walked through the Yedikule gate as I had done just half an hour before. Perhaps he, too, had looked up and noticed the stone carving of a Byzantine eagle; blackened by pollution these days but still as proud a symbol as ever. It seemed a telling comment on the ancient empire of Byzantium that I was now scrabbling around for the descendants of that empire in the psychiatric ward of a decaying hospital.

Outside Dr Y's room, a queue of Turkish women were waiting to see him. Some were moaning. Some were silent, staring at the walls with blank eyes. Others had wild, dishevelled expressions that gave their faces a frightened and frightening look. At first Dr Y had been reluctant to see me for he was a busy man. But he was intrigued to see a foreigner in his hospital and as soon as he learned of my quest he jumped me to the front of the queue, invited me in for tea, and visibly relaxed as he chatted about his life.

He had worked here since the fifties. In those days, he said with a tone of regret, it was a splendid hospital but now – he threw up his hands – he was weary. His children had left Istanbul: his son had emigrated to the United States, his daughter to Greece. But he would remain in the city; yes, he would remain . . .

His ageing face contained the last vestiges of middle age. His hair was Ronald Reagan black though a touch of silver grey was visible at the roots. His saggy jowls hung from his face like heavy curtains and he sipped the tea with prolonged and noisy slurps.

'And you say you are following Robin Hood?' he asked. I corrected him for the second time, but he didn't seem to hear. Instead he repeated in a puzzled voice: 'Tut, tut, tut . . . a Byzantine family . . . ?'

Suddenly his face lit up. 'Of course. There is a lady in the old people's home here. I'm sure her origins are in the city.'

Mrs E – her name was unpronounceable – was eating a bowl of mashed potato when I knocked on her door. She didn't ask who I was or what I wanted when she invited me in to her tiny room. Instead, she told me to sit down and said she'd be ready as soon as she'd finished her dinner. She shared her room with a blind lady who must have been in her nineties, but although I'd been told they were friends, they scarcely spoke to each other for the whole time I was there.

I sat quietly while Mrs E ate her bowl of potato and as soon as she finished she turned to me and thanked me for coming to see her. 'My dear, it is very sweet of you to come and visit me. You see I get so few visitors these days. My family have all gone abroad. It *is* good of you to pop in.'

I was just about to tell her of my quest when she stopped me. 'Now my dear, I expect you want to hear all about my life. But you mustn't interrupt me with questions or I shall forget everything I've told you.'

She had, in fact, led a fascinating life. Her rouge face and black mascara hinted at a lifetime in the arts and I soon discovered that she had been a concert pianist and spent many months in Paris and Vienna. She had also worked in her parents' fashion business and, although her tales of the cosmopolitan lifestyle of Istanbul in the twenties were fascinating, they were not entirely relevant to my quest. But Mrs E was in her element and not going to stop for anything. Whenever I tried to interrupt she would raise her hand and say, 'Hush, my dear, hush.'

Finally she finished and I got to ask my question. 'It sounds like your family have lived here for generations,' I said. 'You must be one of the last people who can truly claim descent from the ancient empire of Byzantium?'

'I don't know where you got that idea from, my dear,' she said. 'I'm not Greek and neither are my family. Didn't I tell you? I'm from Bulgaria.'

It was Sunday and the feast of St Dimitrios. The Patriarch was back in town after his visit to Greece and would, I was told, be celebrating the Divine Liturgy at the little church of St Dimitrios.

Whenever Patriarch Bartholomeus goes abroad he is feted in the streets and tens of thousands of people turn up to receive his blessing. In Istanbul it is not quite the same. Because of his precarious position he keeps a low profile in public and besides, there are few people left to greet him. Despite this, the church of St Dimitrios in the Kurtalus suburb of Istanbul was packed on that last Sunday in October. More than two hundred people – young and old – had turned up for the liturgy and more arrived every minute. As I stood in the doorway the worshippers – unused to a foreigner in their midst – turned around and stared at me.

I peered back at them through the gloom and could make out 12 men singing in the choir. Priests and deacons appeared and disappeared in billows of incense and women prostrated themselves on the floor. But where was Patriarch Bartholomeus? He didn't seem to be here after all. Slowly my eye was drawn towards a lavish golden throne on the right side of the iconostasis. It was surmounted by a gilded canopy which glittered in the candlelight and there on the throne, swathed in imperial purple (an effect only slightly marred by his thick spectacles) sat His All-Holiness the Ecumenical Patriarch Bartholomeus,

Archbishop of Constantinople and New Rome. In his left hand he held a golden staff topped by a ruby-red cross.

At certain moments he would rise from his throne and bless the crowd. Once he took a few steps towards the altar and two monks leaped up to carry his train. But more often he sat in dignified silence, stirring occasionally to cross himself. There were readings from the Epistles and the Gospels. The faithful received communion. And, as the long service in St Dimitrios drew to a close, the assembled throng queued up to receive the Patriarch's blessing. I was last in the queue and wondered what to say to him. Should I thank him for his letter? Tell him I'd met Tarasios?

Suddenly I found myself staring into his spectacles. He looked at me inquisitively as if to ask what I was doing here. Then he held out his hand for me to kiss, gave me a piece of blessed bread, and murmured a few words in Greek.

It was all over in seconds and I forgot to say anything. But I was more than content for here in this little church of St Dimitrios I had at last caught a glimpse of the city that Mandeville himself claims to have visited. For the legacy of the medieval empire of Byzantium still lives on in the Orthodox Church. The vestments worn by the priests are modelled on the costumes of the imperial court and the robes that the Patriarch was wearing that Sunday were the same as those the emperor himself would once have worn. His crown, too, represents the imperial authority invested in him by the first Ottoman sultan – a symbolic replacement for the crown lost by the last emperor in 1453. Bartholomeus, in fact, looked as if he had just stepped out of the mosaic on the wall of the little church of St Saviour in Chora.

3 The Manuscript

Mandeville, Sir John, was the ostensible author of the book of travels bearing his name . . . there are strong grounds for the belief that his name is as fictitious as his travels.

Dictionary of National Biography, **1893**

When I returned to London I went to see one of the earliest copies of Sir John's *Travels*, kept behind lock and key in the great manuscript vaults of the British Museum. This was a copy of the greatest rarity and before I was allowed to look at it I had to produce letters of reference and photographs of myself, as well as fill in numerous forms promising not to eat, smoke or destroy the manuscript. Forty minutes later, the handwritten edition of Sir John Mandeville's *Travels* was brought to my desk. It had been rebound in red Morocco leather in 1757 and was embossed with the emblem of King George II. But open the covers and Georgian England gave way to a medieval fantasy world of dwarfs and monsters.

The Gothic script, in gold, was difficult to read and the scribe had added at the beginning in spidery red letters: 'Here bygynneth the book of John maundeile, knyght of Ingelong that was born in the town of seynt Albons . . . '

As I turned the vellum pages they crackled with age. Each sheet was decorated with pictures illustrating Mandeville's pilgrimage to Jerusalem. On one page there were depictions of St James and St John; on another, a Crown of Thorns dripping with blood. But as soon as Mandeville embarked on the second half of his travels these illustrations became increasingly outlandish. There were dwarves with holes for mouths and men with gigantic upper lips, while the borders were decorated with giant snails, men with ears trailing along the ground and trees giving birth to lambs.

The monk chosen to illuminate the book must have read its stories with wide-eyed astonishment. True, the first half of the book was a religious text, but had the abbot read beyond the chapters about Jerusalem? Did anyone realize that the last part of the book, which purported to be the pilgrimage of a religious knight, described every sort of wickedness and abomination? Most likely he decided to keep quiet, for *The Travels* was far more interesting than the Bibles and Prayer Books he was normally given to illuminate, and while his fellow monks in the *scriptorium* were producing devotional pictures, he had been given free reign to draw the most ghastly creatures imaginable. It was only on the last page that he returned to the devotional theme with a pious portrayal of the crucifixion. Perhaps he felt that at the end of this strange story the reader needed a visual reminder that all creation is due to the benificence of God.

By the time of Sir John's death there were dozens of such editions circulating around Europe for *The Travels* had achieved a quite extraordinary success and medieval cartographers scanned its pages for new information about the world. With the passing of the centuries, however, Mandeville's reputation was steadily undermined and his work discredited. As the world was charted by geographers, his stories of magical valleys were shown to be nothing but figments of his imagination until, by the seventeenth century, he was being mocked in stage satires as the archetypal lying traveller.

The following century brought a brief reprieve. The chattering classes of Georgian London found that Mandeville's monstrous tales appealed to their bawdy sense of humour and *The Travels* was republished as a tuppence-ha'penny chapbook. Stripped of its devotional material, the book focused on the pygmies, monsters and cripples that Mandeville met in the east. Sir John himself underwent a character change: in the rough woodcuts that illustrate these cheap editions he is portrayed in eighteenth-century costume, a parrot in one hand and a stick in the other, shooting at a blackamore with his blunderbuss. Any anachronism was easily circumvented by the publisher who simply changed the date of the travels from 1372 to 1732 and altered the title to produce a maximum impact on his potential readers. *The Travels of Sir John Mandeville* became, 'The Foreign Travels and Dangerous Voyages of the Renowned English Knight Sir John Mandeville, wherein he gives an Account of Remote Kingdoms, Counties, Rivers, Castles, Giants of a prodigious height and strength, the people called Pigmies, very small and of a low stature. To which is added an Account of People of odd deformities; some without heads. Also enchanted wildernesses, where are fiery Dragons, Griffins and many wonderful beasts in the country of Prester John. All very delightful to the reader.'

While the eighteenth-century public may not have believed Sir John they cheerfully lapped up his tall stories. But such popularity was short-lived. Victorian England found itself unamused by his book and dismissed Mandeville as a charlatan and a liar who never even left England. In 1820 the critic Hugh Murray summed up the prevailing opinion when he denounced Sir John's book as 'a pure and entire fabrication' which had been copied and pillaged from other books. 'What he added of his own,' he concluded, 'consists quite exclusively of monstrous lies.'

The Victorian critics who did so much to bury Sir John's reputation started from the premise that he hadn't travelled at all and cited the tall tales as proof that his entire voyage was a fiction. But in doing so they overlooked the fact that even men who definitely *did* travel in the Middle Ages recounted marvels they had clearly invented. They also ignored the fact that to sustain the fiction of having travelled – if indeed it was fiction – would have been no mean feat. Other writers who have attempted similar deceits have almost always come unstuck because of a simple error or foolish slip.

Their attempt to blacken Mandeville's name by accusing him of copying from other travel books was similarly unfair. Medieval writers had a very liberal attitude to plagiarism and it was deemed perfectly acceptable to lift interesting passages from other books and incorporate them into your own. Chaucer himself had few scruples when it came to borrowing stories from his contemporaries. Mandeville had copied vast chunks of William of Boldensele's *Itinerarius*, lifted wholesale from Vincent of Beauvais's *Speculum Historiale*, and transcribed verbatim from William of Tripoli's *Tractatus de Statu Saracenorum*. He had even

Egypt: 'The sultan has four wives, of whom
one shall be a Christian and three Saracens.'

Egypt: '[The sultan's] men stand round with
drawn swords in their hands.'

St Catherine's monastery, Sinai: 'Rooks and
crows come in a great flock [and] each one
brings in its beak . . . a branch of olive.'

Land of Amazon: 'These women are noble and
wise warriors [and] kings of neighbouring
realms hire them to help in their wars.'

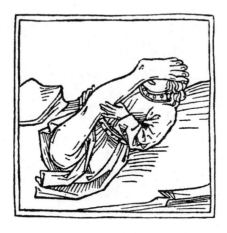

Ethiopia: 'There are some who have only one foot . . . it is so big it will cover and shade all the body.'

India: 'They say that the ox is the holiest animal . . . and therefore they represent their God as half man and half ox.'

Quilon, India: 'In that land pepper grows in a forest [which] is 23 days' journey in length.'

St Thomas' shrine, India: 'His hand lies in a reliquary [and] men of that country judge who is right by that hand.'

skilfully interwoven passages from Albert of Aix's *History of the First Crusade*, despite the fact that it had been written two centuries earlier.

My trip to Istanbul set me thinking that Sir John could have been telling the truth after all, for the more I examined his book the more clues I found scattered throughout its pages. It was entirely possible, indeed plausible, that Mandeville really did undertake a lengthy pilgrimage to Constantinople and Jerusalem for the route through the Holy Land was a popular one in the Middle Ages and thousands visited the holiest shrines in Christendom. Even his claim to have travelled to the Far East held an inkling of truth for trade had opened up the route to India and China and Marco Polo was not long returned from his historic voyage. A trickle of papal emissaries had also reached the Mongol court and survived to tell the tale. And although Mandeville claims to have gone even further afield – to Tibet, Borneo, Java and Sumatra – it would be surprising if a man so fascinated by foreign travel had not even attempted a trip. Though it would not have been easy, it was by no means impossible.

But would it ever be possible to discover whether he had gone or not? Although a few scraps of evidence had emerged in Istanbul, it seemed unlikely that any concrete record of his travels would have survived the centuries. After all, it was proving difficult enough to find out anything about him in this country.

Despite his early fame Mandeville left behind little trace of his life. History picks and chooses its heroes and can discard of even the most famous of men within a generation. Time has not been kind to Sir John; no statue, carving, or stained glass window has been left as a memorial to the knight who, six centuries previously, was being celebrated right across Europe.

Only the inscription in St Albans Abbey has survived and, although it is almost illegible today, its words had been clearly visible in the seventeenth century for, in 1657, the famous Elias Ashmole, whose notes are housed in the Bodleian Library, scribbled them into the margin of a book. They were, as I had thought, half in Latin and half in English and this is what they said:

Siste gradum properans; requiescit Mandevil urna
Hic humili; norunt et monumenta mori.
Lo, in this Inn of Travellers doth lye
One rich in nothing but a Memory.
His name was Sir John Mandevil content
Having seen much, with a small continent.
Toward which he travelled ever since his birth,
And at last paun'd his body for that Earth
Which by a Statute must in mortgage be
Till our Redeemer come to set him free.

This transcript was an exciting find for I could recognize several of the words that I myself had noted down from the St Albans pillar. The lines in Latin were especially interesting for although the first phrase is a formulaic reflection on mortality, the second sentence records that 'here rests Mandeville in an humble urn'.

This had me confused: since cremation was not the practice of the Middle Ages, did this mean that Mandeville's entire body had been placed in an urn and buried at the base of the pillar? If so, what had happened to this massive object? Is it even today resting under the flagstones?

It is impossible to know for certain (I felt sure that the dean would not allow me to dig up his floor) but the most plausible explanation is that Mandeville's heart was removed from his body after death and carried to the abbey. This would be entirely in keeping with burial practices in the Middle Ages, for many distinguished people had their hearts cut out and buried separately from their bodies. But it also opened up the possibility that Sir John died abroad . . .

The more I read about Sir John the deeper the mystery became for it soon became apparent that not everyone has been as attracted by his charms as me. Disturbing rumours have followed him down the centuries; his contemporaries said he had written books on the magic properties of herbs; that he dabbled in the black arts; that he indulged in necromancy. I found several manuscripts on alchemy that purported to be written by him, while other manuscripts claimed he was the author of a subversive treatise on pagan philosophy. And while a small group of supporters said he had undertaken secret negotiations on behalf of King Edward II, a different group suggested he had been involved in a political assassination. Strangest of all was a curious little tale concerning the foreign alphabets scattered throughout his book.

These unrecognizable squiggles, it was suggested, were not alphabets at all. They were a secret code containing instructions on how to overthrow the Pope.

For all its tales of monsters and giants *The Travels* must have made depressing reading to Sir John's contemporaries for it systematically charts the loss to Islam of the great Christian cities of the Middle East. Two centuries before Mandeville's voyage tens of thousands of crusaders had marched across Europe towards Jerusalem, brutally wresting the Holy City from the infidel in 1099. For almost one hundred years the Holy Land was ruled by an uneasy alliance of Christian kings and princes but it proved impossible to defend these precarious kingdoms. Jerusalem fell back into infidel hands in 1244. Acre was lost in 1291. And within a century of Sir John arriving in Constantinople, the imperial capital itself would fall into the hands of the Turks.

Ever since a shocked Europe learned of the loss of Acre, the reconquest of the Holy Land had been the objective of all in positions of authority and throughout Sir John's childhood the idea of a new crusade was continually being mooted. In his old age Edward I had expressed the wish to lead such a crusade and the English Parliament enthusiastically backed his calls for an armed expedition. The king of France, too, was said to be keen on an anti-Turkish alliance with the Tartars, although plans never got beyond the drawing board.

It was in this climate that Mandeville wrote his *Travels*, and it would have been extraordinary if he hadn't mentioned the subject. But even in the prologue, where he discusses the possibilities of such a campaign, his call to arms remains muted: 'Each good Christian man who is able, and has the means, should set himself to conquer our inheritance, this land, and chase out from there those who are misbelievers [for] if we be true children of Christ, we ought to lay claim to the heritage that our Father left to us, and win it, out of strange men's hands.'

He stops short of calling for a rally to arms, perhaps because he knew that at the time of writing the Hundred Years' War between England and France had all but destroyed any hope of an alliance against the Turks. There had been other setbacks as well: the great crusading Order of the Templars had been suppressed not many years earlier and, when the Knights of St John of Jerusalem set up their new headquarters in Rhodes, the different nationalities spent most of their time bickering among themselves. Yet this passage – right at the beginning of *The Travels* – is just one in a series of anti-climaxes scattered throughout the book and it left me wondering what on earth had been in Sir John's mind when he set pen to paper.

It was a similar story in the second part of *The Travels*. By the time Mandeville came to write about Persia, India and China, the great explorations to the Far East were almost over. The Turkish domination of the Middle East had all but closed the trade routes to India and the last papal emissaries were on their way back from China. But unlike most medieval writers who pleaded for missionaries to go back to the east and demanded the forcible conversion of the Mongols, Sir John's only object seems to be to fire people's imaginations with fabulous tales from the Orient.

Even the short chapter in which he 'proves' that it is possible to circumnavigate the world had me scratching my head. For although he presents details of his theory and backs it up with scientific observations and astronomical calculations, the passage is seemingly plonked into the book at random and, once discussed, is never mentioned again. If Sir John had really made such a momentous discovery then surely he would have returned to it again and again, especially since he was challenging many of the accepted theories of his day. Most of his contemporaries had a view of the world that today seems deliciously naïve and their maps were more like romances than today's atlases. Jerusalem was always placed right at the centre of the world and enclosed by a giant circle. The upper half of this circle represented Asia while the lower half contained Europe and Africa. The British Isles, if they made it on to the map at all, were squeezed into the bottom left-hand corner – not only on the fringes of Europe but right on the edge of the world. Yet even the most accurate of medieval charts showed only the top half of the world for it was widely believed to be impossible to cross the Equator into the southern hemisphere. As late as the 1580s – more than two centuries after Sir John wrote his *Travels* – church fathers were arguing that the heavens did not extend around the earth but were only above.

Had Sir John *really* written the controversial passage about circumnavigation or had it been added at a later date by an unscrupulous scribe? I was beginning to doubt Mandeville's word when I stumbled across two medieval documents in Paris that seemed to vindicate him entirely. One of these recorded that in the very year that geographers were converging on Paris to debate the issue of circumnavigation, a young man named John de Mandeville was living in the city. The second fragment was an even more exciting find: it was part of a Comptus Roll of students attending the University of Paris and it recorded that a Johannes de Sancto Albano was studying there in 1329. If this Johannes was the author of *The Travels*, his tutor, perhaps, was the controversial John Buridan, rector of the university, whose lectures questioned whether the extreme fringes of the globe were inhabitable. And if Sir John was attending such lectures, a thought might one day have come into his head. Instead of listening to endless debates on whether it was possible to circumnavigate the world, why not set out on a journey – a journey around the world – that would prove it once and for all.

4 Cyprus

Mandeville wrote an Itinerary, or Account of his Travels, in English, French, and Latin; which were falsified by the monks, who destroyed much of their credit, by mingling them with legendary tales and stories out of Pliny.

History and Antiquities of Hertfordshire, **Robert Clutterbuck, 1815**

orthern Cyprus was on holiday when I arrived. It was the festival of *Kurban Bayrami* and the seaside town of Kyrenia was crowded with Turks. This is one of the great religious feasts of the year, when the Muslim faithful gather to celebrate the thwarted sacrifice of Ishmael by Abraham. It used to be a time for family celebrations. In the mountain villages that overlook the town sheep would be slaughtered and roasted on spits, while in Kyrenia there would be merriment and three long days of festivities. But times have changed. I was sitting in a bar beside the harbour when the Muslim call to prayer – the wail of *allah akbar*, God is great – rang out across the harbour to announce the start of *Kurban*. No one stirred. No one moved from the bar. No one even seemed to hear it.

I finished my drink and wandered up to the mosque which was set in a narrow street just up from the harbour. Inside there were just five men standing in a row behind the imam who led the prayers facing in the direction of Mecca. Five men stood, kneeled, then prostrated themselves in the empty mosque while the rest of the town sat enjoying their beers.

'We are not a religious people,' an elderly Cypriot told me later. 'We are not like the Arab countries. A few of the older people might occasionally go to the mosques but the rest of us . . . well, we go maybe once or twice a year.'

He chuckled as two young Turkish girls in bikinis walked passed. 'Even the immigrants from Anatolia seem to give up going to the mosques when they get here. The first thing the women do is get rid of their veils. If your knight was worried about Cyprus being overrun by Islam, he needn't have been. You won't find the mosques overcrowded here.'

Cyprus was never over-enthusiastic about embracing Islam. Even after the Ottoman conquest of the island in 1571, which saw the principal churches converted into mosques, only a minority of the population were Muslim. The vast majority on the island were Greek Orthodox who, like their compatriots in Constantinople, were left to practise their religion in relative peace.

Everthing changed with the Turkish invasion of 1974, and a brief glance at a map illustrates the full tragedy of Cyprus. A line of red dots weave their way across the mountainous backbone of the island and down into the dusty central plain. They run from Famagusta in the east to Lefke in the west and even plough through the heart of Nicosia, one-time capital of the island. South of the red line is the Republic of Cyprus, the Greek half and the rump of the once united island. In the north is the smaller, self-styled Republic of Northern Cyprus recognized by no country in the world except Turkey. Anyone not familiar with the political situation will learn about it long before arriving in the north of the island: the worldwide boycott of Ercan airport requires that all international flights touch down in Turkey before continuing on to Cyprus.

Though the division of the island occurred more than two decades ago it is still the main topic of conversation. The Greek Cypriots have a well-oiled publicity machine that blitzes newspapers with angry letters as soon as there is any possible hint – real or perceived – of support for the position of the Turkish Cypriots. The travel article I wrote on my return prompted hundreds of letters from Greeks outraged that I had even set foot in the north. Most provided me with an outline of the 1974 invasion, followed by horrific details about mass rapes, tortures and destruction of property. While they varied in tone, virtually all ended with a similar sentiment: 'Do not allow such articles to appear without an accurate account of the island's unfortunate history . . . '

It is not just the Greeks who are keen to promote their point of view. I had scarcely entered a bar on my first night before an elderly Turk, a retired teacher, approached me and asked what I thought about Cyprus's problems. When I explained that I had only just arrived, he welcomed me to the island and said he would like to tell me briefly what *he* thought.

'I have no quarrel with the Greeks,' he said with a sigh. 'I speak fluent Greek. I used to have Greek friends. I even played football in the streets with my Greek schoolmates. The problem with today's Greeks is their wealth. They are millionaires, multi-millionaires, and they build luxury hotels and huge houses.'

He stretched out his arms to show me just how rich they were. 'Do you know a song called "Money, Money, Money"? Well that, my friend, is the Greeks. And us? We have nothing. If the Greeks were allowed to buy property in Northern Cyprus they would buy us up. They would cover the island in hotels and we wouldn't stand a chance. We Turks would be ruined.'

He ordered two more beers and thanked me again for coming to the north half of the island. 'It is good that you wish to understand the history,' he said, 'for the only way of discussing the future is to look into the past.

'Cyprus's problems go back many many centuries. Ottomans . . . Byzantines . . . Muslims . . . Christians . . . who can say when it all began. Perhaps the last time the island was truly united was when your knight Mand . . . '

' . . . deville.'

' . . . yes, when your knight Mandeville was here. For in his day Cyprus was one island under one ruler. My dream is to see this happen again, but I fear it will not be possible before I die. It is very simple problem: in Greek Cyprus they have too much history. And in Turkish Cyprus, we have too little money.'

It was very different in Mandeville's day. At the time when he says he visited the island, Cyprus was one of the richest kingdoms on earth and the monuments that lie scattered around the northern half of the island all date from that period. The country found itself in such an extraordinary position only after the Muslim armies recaptured the Holy Land from the crusaders. For while the Pope forbade direct trade with the infidel, he decreed that goods from Islamic countries could be bought and sold if they first passed through the hands of a middleman. These middlemen were based in Cyprus and the wealth they accrued left them richer than many of Europe's monarchs.

It was an extraordinary state of affairs presided over by an extraordinary succession of kings. The Lusignan family had bought Cyprus from Richard the Lionheart and as they grew rich they built cathedrals, sumptuous castles and monasteries – Gothic edifices that still crown the mountaintops of Northern Cyprus.

Not all their money went on cathedrals and monasteries. The lavish banquets they held, and their debauched parties and riotous living became renowned throughout Europe. Monarchs, princes and dukes flocked to the court of King Hugh IV and the Lusignans gradually married their eligible offspring into all the royal houses of Europe: even Queen Elizabeth II has Lusignan blood coursing through her veins.

The chroniclers of the time – many of them prudish monks – filled their writings with tales of over-indulgence. They were horrified and fascinated in equal measure, watching the debauchery as a child watches a horror movie – hands clapped over their eyes but fingers open to allow them the occasional peek. A few joined in the fun; after all, they could always atone for their sins when they reached Jerusalem.

One straightlaced pilgrim, a German rector named Ludolph von Suchem, recounts many anecdotes about the wealth of the nobility. There was the tradesman's daughter who wore more jewels on her head than were owned by the King of France. There was the merchant who sold a golden orb to the Sultan for 60,000 florins but, regretting his decision, offered to buy it back a few days later for double the amount. Others sound more like Imelda Marcos than medieval knights: the Count of Jaffa owned 500 hounds and employed 250 servants to bathe, guard and anoint them. And in one celebrated incident, a wealthy merchant hosted a banquet for his friends and served powdered diamonds instead of salt and pepper.

Despite his love of the good things in life, Sir John was filled with foreboding by such wanton extravagance and – following the loss to Islam of Jerusalem and Acre – he predicts the downfall of Cyprus as well. He even records an extraordinary conversation he had with the Egyptian sultan, setting out why Christian countries are doomed:

'The Sultan asked me how Christians governed themselves in our countries. And I said, "Lord, well enough – thanks be to God." And he answered and said, "Truly, no. It is not so. For your priests do not serve God properly by righteous living as they should do. For they ought to give less learned men an example of how to live well, and they do the very opposite . . . [and] when people should go to church to serve God, they go to the tavern and spend all the day – and perhaps all the night – in drinking and gluttony . . . "'

The attack lists dozens of reasons why Europe is on the decline and is an impressive piece of rhetoric: so impressive, in fact, that another medieval writer called Caesar of Heisterbach copied the story word for word. Or so I thought. But I had hardly finished reading Heisterbach's manuscript when I spotted a problem. He wrote his book in 1235. Mandeville didn't write his *Travels* until the 1350s. It was Mandeville who had copied the speech from Heisterbach, and not the other way around.

What on earth was he up to? Did he *really* know the situation in Cyprus or had he gleaned it all from other books?

I was fascinated by the tales of the Lusignan kings and had vain hopes that the Lusignan name might have lingered on until the present day in some remote mountain village, especially as the legacy of the Latin occupation of the island is still apparent in the many people with blue eyes and mousey hair. But if Lusignans did remain on the island they must have kept a low profile for their name disappears altogether from the history books and I could find nothing more about them. Until, that is, I went to Lefkoşa, the northern half of Nicosia, where I stumbled across an intriguing footnote to the Lusignan story.

I had hired an interpreter named Mustafa and, as he drove me through the dilapidated streets of the city, we passed his clubhouse and he suggested we stop for a beer. Housed in a nineteenth-century villa and with a tidy patio at the front, the Brotherhood Club was a retirement home for gentlemen; a place where elderly Turks could while away their final years in peace.

As we sat swilling bottles of Efes Pilsen we were joined by a few of Mustafa's friends, and within a few minutes we were chatting about the Lusignans of Cyprus. I asked if there were any descendants of these fabulously wealthy monarchs left on the island but they all shook their heads.

'No,' said one. 'They disappeared centuries ago.'

'If there were any left . . . ' added another, 'they would have disappeared in 1974.'

'There weren't any even then,' said a third. 'They were sent packing by the Ottomans.'

But then there was a croaking noise which came from a table in the corner. A very old man, whose stunted chest, thick neck, and ancient suit gave him the look of a respectable frog, sat up and wagged his finger in the air.

'There was a Lusignan,' he said. 'Sherki Lusignan. Don't you remember him?'

A few men began to nod, scratching their heads as they tried to remember this Sherki and encouraging the man to continue.

'Sherki came from Famagusta,' he said. 'He was a wild one – a real adventurer. No one really knew where he came from or who he was, for he never spoke of his past or about his family. In the war he volunteered to go to Crete at the time of the German invasion. Volunteered! He said he was a doctor and wanted to go to nurse the troops, but it later turned out he wasn't a doctor and didn't know the first thing about medicine . . . '

The others in the bar had fallen silent and the old man continued with his story. He knew he had a captive audience and he chose his words with careful deliberation, pausing occasionally for dramatic effect.

'He had a quick hand did Sherki. People said he was for ever stealing things – slipping papers and bills into his pocket when people weren't looking. All sorts of rumours went around. Some sounded plausible; others were clearly ridiculous. Well one day he suddenly produced a series of documents claiming he was a direct descendant of the Lusignans. No one ever knew if these documents were stolen, or forged, or where they had come from. Everyone assumed they had been thieved from the archives. But what he said was true – he really did have the papers and they really did seem to prove everything he claimed. They gave Sherki the right to be king of Cyprus and from that day onwards he liked to be known in all seriousness as king of the island.

'We were young children at that time and, well, we all knew him as Sherki the Foolish. We teased him in the streets, followed him into the shops, and gave him a terrible time until one day Sherki vanished and was never seen again. I later heard that he had gone to Paris to pursue his case through the French courts. But that failed as well and he was said to have gone to live in England. When he finally died he was over ninety. He left no children and no heirs for he was never married. With Sherki's death, that was the end of the last king of Cyprus.'

Everyone in the bar was silent for a moment as they waited to hear if there was more. Then one man began to speak. 'You know, I think I do remember Sherki,' he said. 'I remember him from when I was young.'

'I think I do too,' added another. 'He was a *very* odd man.'

Suddenly there was a chorus of similar recollections: I felt like adding that I remembered him as well.

The Lusignan line, then, ended in a dubious claim from an untrustworthy eccentric and memories of the kings who ruled Cyprus in Mandeville's day had drifted into legend. But many months later – when I was back in England – I read about a second claimant to the throne whose case seemed much stronger than Sherki's. She was an eccentric old lady named Miss Eliza de Lusignan and she lived in Lower Edmonton near London at the end of the last century. According to records she was quite content with her life as a governess and although she enjoyed telling people she was descended from the Lusignans, she never pressed her claim to the throne.

I also discovered that a handful of Lusignan descendants do still remain on Cyprus although they no longer bear the distinguished name for they are merely scions of lesser lines. A female offspring of the family married the commander of the Ottoman army in the sixteenth century and her descendants now live in Greek Cyprus, distinguishable by their blue eyes and fair skin.

When I had arrived in Northern Cyprus I had gone straight to the seaside town of Kyrenia, the only place in the north half of the island that could possibly be called a resort. Even so, it is only half-heartedly waking up to the potential of tourism and, at the time I was there, only a handful of guests were staying at the hotel. Three of these were matronly Italian women who would nod politely to me at breakfast each morning before sitting themselves down at one of the seventy empty tables. Each was huge – three fortresses of flesh squeezed tightly into cotton dresses – and one by one they would help themselves to vast quantities of food from the buffet. Cold meats, cheeses, slabs of butter, sausages, boiled eggs and toast would all be heaped on to their plates before they waddled back to their tables. And then the feast would begin: forks were lifted, mouths opened, and in a flash the piles of food were transferred from plate to mouth. Occasionally the women would groan slightly. Sometimes they would dab the beads of sweat from their foreheads. But only when the last morsels had been sucked up from their plates would the Italian chatter begin: '*Salsiccia . . . delizioso . . . cetriolino . . . buono . . .* '

One morning, one of the women winked at me. I was horrified and immediately began reading my book. But when I looked up she winked again, smiled, and stuffed a giant gherkin into her mouth. When the three had finally finished their breakfast she led them out of the dining room, passing my table and rubbing my chair with a deliberate swing of her hips. And then she pointed at the empty seat opposite: '*Perche?*' she said. 'Why?'

I gave a wan smile and she winked again. 'Kyrenia,' she said pointing at her bulging purse. They were off to the shops.

Kyrenia was a fishing port long before Mandeville visited Cyprus and its mellow stone buildings all face the sea, turning their backs on the grand chain of mountains that begin their ascent just outside the town. The town must look even more beautiful from the water for a picturebook Venetian castle – rough-built from golden limestone – stands guard over the entrance to the harbour. I clambered up to the top of its castellated tower, from where there is a fine view of the mountains behind the town. Their lower flanks are covered in thick green vegetation but as the rock turns towards the vertical the trees and shrubs disappear leaving exposed bluffs and crags. In the early evenings I would sit in one of the bars that surround the harbour and turn my chair towards these mountains. Towards six o'clock the bank of thin cloud that had rested on their shoulders for much of the day would slowly lift and the limestone would be lit by the dying sun.

For centuries it was these mountains that kept the Lusignans in power. Anyone who controlled their cloud-covered peaks also controlled the passes that led to the fertile plains at the island's heart. Little has changed in the intervening six centuries: when the Turkish army invaded in 1974 one of their first goals was the peak of Mount Didymos where the ruined summer palace of the Lusignan kings still stands guard over the island.

I asked a taxi driver to take me up to the summit and he jumped at the chance for he hadn't had a client all morning. If he polished his Mercedes any more, he joked, the paint would start to wear thin.

The road swung uphill as soon as we left the town. At first it curved around a series of sharp bends but soon we joined the main Kyrenia–Lefkoşa highway which sliced its way effortlessly through the mountain range. As we reached the highest point on the main road – though still far below the summit – we turned right on to a single track lane and continued upwards, climbing steeply towards the castle of St Hilarion which Sir John himself claims to have visited. In his days the approach to the castle would have been guarded by soldiers loyal to the Lusignans. Today the roadsides are cluttered with red skull-and-crossbones signs – a reminder to drivers that the mountain range is overrun by the military. At one point we passed an army camp surrounded by reams of barbed wire. A young Turkish conscript, machine gun in hand, stood next to a sign warning ASKERI BOLGE – GIRILMEZ: Military Area – No Entry. A few minutes later we passed a family having a picnic under a similar sign. It seemed an odd place to stop for lunch.

Another camp, more picnickers, and we swung around a huge bend in the road. And there before us – clinging for dear life to the uppermost reaches of Mount Didymos – stood the ruins of St Hilarion castle.

Sir John mentions both the castle and the relics of Saint Hilarion that were kept here, but he refers to the place as the Castle of Amours. This puzzled me until I found that other writers called it Dieu d'Amour, which was itself a corruption of the Greek name for the mountain. Perhaps Sir John had picked up the abbreviated name from the locals?

Little is known about Saint Hilarion: the few surviving records of him agree that he was a seventh-century hermit who had a neurotic passion for solitude. He fled the Holy Land for the deserts of Libya, but finding even the sandy wastes too noisy took ship to Cyprus and lived out the rest of his long life on a diet of 15 figs a day.

When the castle was first built his tomb was enclosed within its walls and Sir John says it was looked after with great honour. But the walls of the shrine, as well as those of the castle, have suffered over the last six centuries. Rain and wind have buffeted the ramparts. The towers have crumbled and the chapels slowly broken apart. It is only near the mountain's summit – a steep climb from the roadway – that a few traces of carved stone remain to hint at the palace's former luxury.

The queen's chamber has lost its roof and three of its walls, leaving a pair of Gothic windows which stare westwards across the plunging countryside below. I sat on the narrow window ledge where Queen Eleanor must once have sat; the warm sandstone curved upwards to form a window frame, carefully chiselled into arches and decorated with fine tracery. It was hard to imagine that this shell was once the most comfortable room in the royal palace, yet in Sir John's day it would have been adorned with tapestries and silken cushions, glassware from the east and manuscripts from France.

My vision was rudely shattered by the babble of voices. 'That's Margaret's house down there . . . and that is George's over there.'

A group of English ex-pats had appeared and were showing their friends where they had set up home.

'Isn't Margaret's garden a mess?' said one. 'She really ought to get someone in to help her.'

'George's isn't much better,' said another. 'Of course, you know his daughter's getting divorced . . . '

I scrambled up the broken walls above the royal bedchamber and on to a narrow ledge which dropped away sharply on either side. At one point my foot slipped, dislodging a stone, and I watched it bounce off a rockface and fall hundreds of feet to the road below. Finally I reached the highest point, a square-walled tower from which the paranoid Prince John of Antioch massacred his Bulgarian bodyguards. He had been warned by Queen Eleanor that they were planning to assassinate him and, fuming with rage, made them jump the 2,500 feet to their deaths. The Queen, it was later revealed, had invented the story but by the time John discovered their innocence it was too late. Their last view, at least, must have turned their thoughts heavenwards for the tower commands a fantastic panorama. On a clear day you can even see the Turkish mainland.

Sir John also visited the abbey of Bellapais which sits upon a bluff of rock thousands of feet below. He was not alone in describing the famous abbey for many medieval pilgrims travelled to Bellapais, on their way to Jerusalem, in order to venerate a piece of the crucifix. The abbey grew wealthy from the royal patronage it enjoyed, and with the steady increase in the number of pilgrims it found an even more lucrative source of income. Successive kings granted the abbots the rare privilege of wearing golden spurs – a custom normally reserved for the knights of court – as well as the right to keep a large town house in Nicosia.

Few records survive from the peacable times when Mandeville was visiting but as soon as things began to go wrong at Bellapais, the chroniclers reached for their pens and the whole sordid tale galloped into the history books. First the prior was jailed for disobeying his archbishop and then the Genoese sacked the place and carted off its treasures. But this was only the beginning: by the sixteenth century, life here was more akin to a brothel than a monastery for the monks had abandoned their vows of chastity and the cloisters of Bellapais – which for centuries had heard only the solemn chanting of prayers – now echoed with the laughter of debauchery. Most of the monks married: some, not content with monogamy, took two or three wives. It all added to the fun.

With the Ottoman conquest, however, the good life came to an abrupt end. The monks fled and the abbey fell into ruins and by the turn of this century the British were using its carved stone blocks for road building.

The monks of Bellapais were never to return although their Premonstratensian order still exists. Unmarried and back to their vows of poverty and chastity, their base has moved to the sober area of Tongerloo in Belgium.

The more I read Sir John's tales from Cyprus the more I found myself scratching my head, for although some sounded both plausible and accurate, others appeared to be figments of his imagination. He only alludes to the Lusignan wealth – a surprise, since most travellers left the island wide-eyed – but occasionally records details that no other writer mentions. Take the bizarre eating habits of the locals: 'It is the custom that all men, both lords and others, eat their food in the earth. For they make pits in the earth around the hall, knee-deep, and have them well paved; and when they want to eat, they go into these pits and sit down. And this is in order to be cooler, for that land is hotter than it is here.'

Could this be true? No earlier traveller describes such a custom, but when a sixteenth-century Englishman came to recount his *Voyage of Master Laurence Aldersy to Jerusalem*, he too was struck by these habits. 'The people there are very rude,' he wrote. 'They eat their meat sitting upon the ground with their legs a crosse like tailors.'

This is only one in a string of curious details. As a knight of the realm, Sir John would have been accustomed to hunting in the Hertfordshire countryside and it is not surprising that he writes about the hunting on Cyprus. But what strikes him is not the number of hounds or the quality of the falcons. Instead, he is fascinated by a strange animal that the nobles use during their hunts. 'Men hunt with *papions*,' he says, 'which are like leopards; and they catch wild beasts as well – better and more swiftly than hounds. And they are somewhat bigger than lions.'

These *papions*, or hunting cheetahs, were indeed used in Cyprus in the fourteenth century for they had been imported from India more than a century before. But Mandeville's *Travels* is the first recorded account of them being used on the island, and as such is an important piece of evidence in his favour. His final detail, however, casts a cloud of suspicion over his story; to assert that cheetahs are bigger than lions is an astonishing error for anyone who has actually seen a cheetah.

But he is not the only writer to get the size of the animal wrong: the French pilgrim Seigneur d'Anglure – who definitely did visit Cyprus in 1395 – also describes these hunting cheetahs yet assures his readers they are smaller than a fox.

Where Sir John does agree with all travellers is in his description of the wine. Virtually every account of the country mentions it and several pilgrims remonstrate that their less pious compatriots drink disgraceful quantities on reaching Cyprus. The local plonk was renowned for its potency and was so strong that it was usually mixed with water. But not everyone took this precaution: one English traveller was shown a row of tombs of English knights who had dropped dead after a long evening's binge.

Mandeville's description of the wine bears a remarkable similarity to a passage in a book by William of Boldensele. But there is one important difference: unlike Boldensele, Mandeville names the wine, singling out *de marrea* as having the finest and most delicate bouquet of all. 'In Cyprus [there] are many vines, of which a very strong and noble wine is made; the first year it is red, and after a year it turns to a white, and, the older it gets, the whiter it becomes and the clearer and stronger, and the better the bouquet it has.' Mandeville is the first in a series of writers to praise *de marrea* as the best of all. Seigneur d'Anglure is the next to enthuse about this wine but Sir John could hardly have copied it from the Frenchman for by the time Anglure wrote his book Mandeville had been dead almost 30 years.

I had arranged to meet a family friend as soon as I arrived in Lefkoşa. Nick Cannon worked for the British High Commission in Greek Cyprus but he also spent part of his time overseeing

British relations with Northern Cyprus. This dual job has led to an absurd anomaly. Since the British government doesn't recognize the self-styled 'Republic of Northern Cyprus', it cannot be seen to have any formal diplomatic relations. As soon as Nick crosses the green line from the south to the north – in official terms at least – he no longer exists.

The Turkish army's advance in 1974 was finally halted in Nicosia and a boundary hastily scribbled across the city map. This divided the former capital in two and for ever separated Greek from Turk, Christian from Muslim. But it also produced some ludicrous situations: the British High Commission fell into Greek Nicosia, the British Residence fell into the Turkish side, and there is a minefield running between the two. Even less fortunate was the Ledra Palace Hotel which found itself trapped in the middle of no-man's land. Once the finest hotel in the Middle East it now rises forlornly from behind its fence of barbed wire – home to United Nations' squaddies and the scene of futile diplomatic meetings.

But the barriers, barbed wire and machine guns have in no way marred the splendour of the British Residence, for although surrounded by ruined tenement blocks pockmarked with gunshots, Her Britannic Majesty's servants strive to keep up the standards. A chandelier brightens the Residence's grandiose hallway while a resplendent portrait of the Queen hangs above the stairwell.

Only diplomats are allowed to pass freely over the green line. Nick had crossed the military checkpoints earlier in the morning and before lunch he showed me around the northern half of the city. Lefkoşa is a shabby place and Northern Cyprus's lack of cash is visible in the crumbling buildings and peeling paintwork. The streets are crowded not with shoppers but with thousands of Turkish conscripts who are based in nearby barracks and who patrol the town as if it were an army compound.

We walked through the covered market but were soon stopped in our tracks by a 20-foot high wall topped with barbed wire. Other roads and alleys were similarly uninviting: most became cul-de-sacs overnight in 1974 and now boast red warning signs bearing the skull and crossbones. But the landmines buried in this bleak strip of no-man's land haven't stopped nature from colonizing: rusting oil drums, set up to block streets more than 20 years ago, now sprout trees and flowering plants.

Suddenly I heard the sound of Italian voices and dived into a shop with Nick in tow. But it was too late – the women had caught a glimpse of me and they entered the shop just behind us, beaming with smiles and throwing their hands into the air. Walking had overheated them and their faces were glistening with sweat. The woman who had winked at me at breakfast now gave me a sickening smile then pointed in the direction of Kyrenia. Did I want a lift back in their taxi? I declined and they waddled off in the direction of the Saray Hotel.

Over a huge lunch of *mezze*, *brochettes* and *kofte* Nick told me the latest green-line gossip. 'Recently a Turkish pizza delivery boy accidently strayed into the no-go area,' he said. 'He was immediately arrested and detained by Greek soldiers. Of course, as soon as the Turks heard about this there was a huge campaign to free him. Eventually he was released but his moped was held for three months while the Greeks negotiated the return of a Greek car which had strayed through a Turkish checkpoint. When the moped was finally exchanged for the car there was much rejoicing. The pizza, it was said, was still on the bike.'

Other incidents don't have such happy endings. An English tourist who fell desperately sick in Northern Cyprus was allowed to cross the green line so she could be flown home from one of the British military bases in the south. But before she reached the airport she died. Her husband, meanwhile, was stuck on the Turkish side of the island . . .

Nick had to return to the south that afternoon and left me outside the medieval cathedral which dominates the city. It looks as if it has dropped out of provincial France – hardly surprising since it was designed by French architects and built by French craftsmen – and in Mandeville's day its golden sandstone must have provided the city with a glittering skyline. Today it is in a sorry state; the west front once boasted a huge stained glass window but the glass has long since disappeared and the delicate Gothic tracery replaced with pre-fabricated concrete mouldings. The surround to the huge double doors used to be decorated with finely chiselled statues of the Virgin but all were smashed when the Ottomans seized the city. Only two carvings remain: miniature figurines of angels whose pious expressions are captured for ever in stone.

One glance at the west front is enough to warn you that there is something not quite right about the building. Rising up from either side are two towers, and on top of these towers are minarets pointing their slender fingers into the blue sky. This, then, was the fate of the building: in 1570, the cathedral of St Sophia was converted into the Selimiye Mosque.

I took off my shoes and entered through the west door. It was cool inside and completely silent. A few Turkish conscripts stood peering in, and those with cameras took snapshots of this strange mosque. But they soon lost interest and left and, as their chatter died away, I wandered down the aisle in the presence of medieval ghosts.

Converting the building into a mosque has created a strange effect. On entering, the eye is drawn down the long nave towards the apse. But Islam has re-aligned the church's interior in the direction of Mecca and the focal point of today's worship – the *mihrab* and *mimber* or prayer niche and pulpit – is set at a diagnonal to the south wall. It looks as if a giant hand has given the church's innards a sudden twist whilst leaving the outside walls in the same position.

If Sir John came here he didn't mention it: a pity, for the cathedral was consecrated in a splendid ceremony in 1326 when he was already four years into his travels. It was here in St Sophia that the Lusignans were once crowned kings of Cyprus before travelling to Famagusta to be anointed as kings of Jerusalem. Long after Jerusalem had fallen to Islam they continued receiving this hollow honour. The nobles, too, liked to keep the titles and pretensions of their lost kingdoms and for decades they continued to style themselves as princes and counts of Antioch, Galilee and Tripoli, even though they had never set foot in their realms.

I lifted up the carpets to see if I could find any remaining tombstones. There were a few fragments but none was complete. The feet of a knight in armour poked out from the bottom of one rug but when I removed the heavy cloth I found that the body and head had disappeared. Here and there I discovered traces of inscriptions in Latin, but they too were worn or broken. Only the faintest outline of a cross remained on one of the walls as testimony to the building's former usage.

As I stood on the spot where the altar must once have been, I re-read the local bishop's sermon to his people just hours before the Turkish attack. He urged them to remain steadfast in faith and pleaded that they defend their city to the death: 'You do not only defend religion,' he said, 'but also your wives, children and estates; so as all things, both human and divine, invite you to shew invincible valour; and that the more readily and boldly, as that you being free men, and generous, are to fight against slaves, base and unarmed people, wont to overcome more by their numbers than their valour.'

It was not the greatest of speeches and it was all to no avail. A few days after this sermon, in September 1570, the city was captured, the population enslaved, and St Sophia turned into a mosque. Of all the major towns and cities in Cyprus, only Famagusta still remained in Christian hands. If that, too, fell to the Muslims, the island would be lost for ever and Sir John's great fear – that the defeat of Christendom in the region was inevitable – would have been proved all too true.

The following day I took the bus to Famagusta, the main port in Northern Cyprus, and was sitting in a café in the old town when a young student entered, looked around for a table and, finding none free, asked if he could sit at mine. Before I could answer he had sat down, ordered a coffee and swallowed a sugar lump.

'You are English . . . ?' he asked, before proceeding to bombard me with questions about where I lived. When I told him that my wife was a teacher in Haringey – home to a huge Turkish-Cypriot community – his face lit up. 'I have an uncle in Haringey,' he said. 'Where does your wife teach? What age are the children? Perhaps my nephews go to her school?'

Mehmet had studied history at Ankara University and when I explained why I had come to Famagusta he jumped at the chance of telling me a few stories.

'You know, of course, about the battle of Famagusta?' he said.

I did know a little about the battle, for the siege of Famagusta had been a defining moment in Cyprus's tragic history. But before I could say anything, Mehmet was in full flow. 'You need to know more,' he said without a moment's hesitation. 'It was the most wonderful battle . . . a glorious, extravagant battle.'

I told him I'd never heard of a battle described as extravagant before but he brushed my comment aside. 'That is because battles are not normally extravagant,' he said. 'But the battle of Famagusta was, I assure you, an extravagant battle.'

Meeting Mehmet was a gift: in Istanbul, Syria, Jerusalem and Egypt I had tried to arrange meetings with people who could help me explain the world in which Mandeville had lived. In Northern Cyprus this had been much more difficult for I'd been unable to establish contact with anyone before leaving England. But now Mehmet had walked in off the street and started to explain the history of his home town, grabbing the salt and pepper to help him demonstrate the battle.

'This,' he said as he pointed to the pepper, 'is Mustafa Pasa, the fantastic general of the Ottoman army. Try to imagine him; he has waged many successful campaigns and won many battles, but like all great men he has a weakness . . .' He paused for a moment to let me guess, but when I shook my head he continued. 'His weakness,' he said, 'was his uncontrollable temper.'

He then reached for the salt and brought it nearer to the centre of the table. 'This,' he said, 'is Marcantonio Bragandino, commander of the combined Venetian and Greek forces and the defender of Famagusta. The town's defence is dependent upon him and he is as brilliant as Mustafa.'

Mehmet put down the salt and reached for the pepper once more. This time he poured a large pile onto the table as he gulped down the last of his coffee. 'But here is the problem. The Turks have huge cannon – hundreds of them – which rain down cannonballs on the town. The defenders only possess a few light arms but they have the huge city walls to protect them.'

This much I knew was true. Before coming to the café I had climbed on to the battlements and seen for myself the dozens of cannonballs still scattered around the defensive walls. These walls had been mined and rebuilt during the lengthy siege. The Ottoman troops had caught the plague and the defenders had starved yet still the battle went on. But by August, with less than 2,000 soldiers left alive, the Venetian commander knew that all was lost. Deciding to spare the lives of the rest of his troops, he sued for peace.

'When Bragandino walked out to surrender,' explained Mehmet, 'he carried his commander's umbrella and walked with great pride. Mustafa treated him kindly at first for he was a good man, but suddenly, bang . . . ' Mehmet banged his fist on to the table at this point, rattling his coffee cup ' . . . he flew into one of his rages.'

There was now a small pool of coffee on the table, as well as a pile of salt and pepper, and Mehmet mixed them together with his spoon.

'Bragandino accused Mustafa of dishonour – not a clever idea – and without warning Mustafa screamed at him, grabbed his head and sliced off one of his ears before ordering another soldier to cut off his other ear and his nose. The other generals were all executed but Bragandino was thrown into prison for 12 days.'

I pulled a face but Mehmet had not finished. He told me how, on the following Friday, the Venetian was released from prison and forced to carry heavy sacks of boulders around the city walls and ordered to kiss the ground each time he passed Mustafa. He was then hauled into a chair and hoisted on to a yard arm while the victors jeered at him to scan the horizon for the fleet that would save him. And that, said Mehmet, was the end of the Venetian. He was killed and the town had been won by Mustafa.

But whether by design or through ignorance, he had not told the end of the story as it really was. For what actually happened to Bragandino was far more terrible, even in an age noted for its barbarism and cruelty. He was stripped, tied to a column, and flayed alive while Mustafa watched with glee as the executioner's knife slowly sliced off Bragandino's skin. Mustafa screamed at the Venetian to convert to Islam but Bragandino remained silent. Not until the knife had cut down to his waist did Bragandino finally expire, muttering a quiet prayer.

Once he was dead, Mustafa had Bragandino's skin stuffed with straw and tied to a cow with the red umbrella mounted over his head. This gruesome spectacle was then led through the city. Medieval chroniclers agree that even the Turks were shocked by such a display of barbarism.

Mustafa eventually took the skin back to Constantinople where it was kept as a memento until a member of the Bragandino family managed to acquire it for a vast sum of money. It was transferred to an urn in the church of Saint Giovanni e Paolo in Venice where it is kept to this day.

It was a brutal end to a brilliant commander. Mustafa had secured his victory and Islam had come to Cyprus. But the glorious medieval towns of Cyprus lay in ruins and the population had fled or been massacred. It was worse than anything Sir John had predicted.

The Ottomans never took advantage of their victory. The country, which had prospered under the Lusignans and Venetians now became a backwater – run virtually as a private estate by rapacious Ottoman governors (often Greeks from Constantinople) who shamelessly extorted taxes from the local population. Little was repaired or restored after the conquest and Famagusta, like Lefkoşa, has remained a town in ruins for the last four centuries. Vast areas lie buried under piles of rubble for there has been neither the money nor the inclination to repair them. There are scattered remnants of churches everywhere. Sometimes these are nothing more than shells, their roofs long since staved in. In other places, skeletal arches rise skywards like the ribcages of giant dinosaurs. Windows gape at the sky and buttresses lean against nothing but the wind. Soon the walls themselves will collapse into powder for everything here is constructed from sandstone and the salty corrosion of the sea air scratches away at its surface. The name Famagusta means 'Sunken in Sand' and it could scarcely be more appropriate: the sandstone walls will one day make a lovely beach. Even the huge port – the pride of Northern Cyprus – is overcome with neglect. There was only one ship in the harbour on the day I arrived and its rusting hulk looked less than seaworthy. I checked the name: it was called the *Tirana* and was heading for Albania.

There are few places in the world where history has so dramatically repeated itself. Turn towards the old town and it is still in ruins from the 1571 invasion. Turn towards the new town, Varosha, where the large Greek population used to live, and it is still in ruins from the 1974 invasion. Today the whole area is strictly out of bounds, fenced off with barbed wire and patrolled by the UN, but it is possible to get an overview from the top of Palm Beach Hotel. Several miles of seafront hotels lie abandoned, along with thousands of shops and homes: the buildings are said to have been kept in exactly the state in which they were left all those years ago and thousands of Greeks hope one day to return to their homes. But after more than 20 years of abandonment and neglect most are in a sorry state. Many are visibly crumbling and the damage they sustained during the fighting gets worse by the year. A single light burns at night from one of the 40 disused hotels: it is the UN observation post which overlooks the wreckage of war.

The day after my visit to Famagusta I had an appointment with the Mufti of Cyprus, leader of Northern Cyprus's faithful, whom I hoped would be able to verify Mandeville's account of Muslim beliefs. I had expected him to be dressed in a long cloak with a flowing white turban wrapped around his head and imagined I would find him in a mosque, seated in front of an open Koran. As it happened, I couldn't have been more mistaken.

The Mufti is a pleasant-looking chap called Ahmed Djemal. On the day I met him he was wearing the bottom half of what looked like an old pinstripe suit, an open-necked shirt, and was chain-smoking Royals cigarettes. 'Fifty a day,' he said with a sigh, 'except during Ramadan.'

I had brought with me Mustafa, my interpreter, for the Mufti didn't speak English. When I asked Mustafa if he'd ever met his spiritual leader, he shook his head. 'I didn't even realize he lived in Lefkoşa,' he said.

We climbed up to the first floor where the receptionist – a pretty girl with bright lipstick and colourful clothes – smiled and pointed to the Mufti's room. 'Just walk in,' she said. 'You'll find the Mufti in there.'

I opened the door and was greeted by an immense poster of Kemal Ataturk, founder of the Turkish secular nation. It was the first clue to the message that the Mufti was keen to express; that Islam does not have to dance hand in hand down the road of political extremism.

His room could have come straight from an MFI catalogue. The black leather sofa perfectly matched the formica coffee table; a lava lamp and some seventies chrome would have completed the decor. As the Mufti called his secretary and asked for coffee, the sun broke the cloud in two and poured through the window, momentarily brightening Ataturk's frown.

Mustafa chatted with the Mufti in Turkish then turned to me with a smile. 'The Mufti is most interested in your knight,' he explained, 'and is glad you wish to present the good things about Islam.'

I asked if there were bad things. The Mufti lit a cigarette and nodded. 'In some parts of the world, yes. But remember; we're not like the Islamic regime in Iran nor do we practise the Islam of the Arab countries.' He paused before adding with a note of pride: 'Here in Cyprus we are open-minded and strive for the truth in Islam. We are a secular country which is more modern even than Turkey. We are very forward looking.'

He was beginning to sound like a spokesman for the former Soviet Union and I suggested, with a hint of mischief, that what he really meant was that no one cared about religion any more.

'It's very true that the attendance rates in our mosques is extremely low,' he said. 'Our big problem is that the education of the imams is lower than the education of the local people. How can they attract new people into the mosques when they are so poorly educated? Most are over sixty and it is too late to re-train them.'

I asked if foreign tourists had a bad effect on Islam; if people were attracted by more alluring lifestyles. 'It is the foreigners who always stir up trouble,' he said. 'There are always a few who want to start up fights . . . '

Fights! This surprised me. I knew that the Greek part of the island had a reputation for attracting English lager louts but I'd never heard of any problems on the Turkish side.

'No, no, no', he said. 'Not the English. I'm talking about Saudi Arabians and Iranians. It is the extremist Arab students who come here and start fights with the modern students who don't like their Islamic views. It is these foreign tourists and students who cause all the problems. They pray in the streets and the schoolyards. They are very negative minded and this is not what Islam is about. We don't need that sort of thing here.'

The Mufti was outspoken in his criticism of Islamic extremists and he proudly told me that the Turkish Cypriots were even keener followers of Ataturk's secular policies than the Turks. They got rid of the Arabic language before Turkey. They abandoned their national dress. They threw away their fezes. And to cap it all, the Mufti of the time agreed to become a civil servant appointed by the Prime Minister. When Ahmed reaches 60 he has to retire. But all this, he assured me, has enabled Cypriots to come to a closer understanding of Islam: 'There are those who argue that imams shouldn't be paid because they weren't paid in Mohammed's time. Next they'll be saying that mosques have to be built with palm leaves as they were in the earliest days. But Islam has to be open to the modern world. Extremism is a deviation from the faith.'

He stopped talking and I asked Mustafa to read the Mufti a few extracts from Sir John's book. Although Mandeville was fearful of Islam he writes from an extremely informed point of view. Unlike many of his contemporaries – to whom the killing of Muslims was a moral obligation – Sir John was both curious and tolerant, and instead of stressing the differences between Islam and Christianity he was interested in the similarities.

'I will tell you,' he writes, 'something of their laws and their creed, as is contained in the book of their law, the Koran . . . The Saracens accept the Incarnation, and they will willingly speak of the Virgin Mary . . . and that the angel Gabriel told her that she had been chosen by God before the world's beginning to conceive Jesus Christ and bear Him; they say she bore Him and yet was a virgin afterwards as she was before . . . Each year they fast for a whole month, eating only in the evening . . .'

The Mufti listened carefully to Mustafa and nodded at the end of every sentence. 'He was an intelligent man,' he said at last.

'He's right in nearly everything he writes.'

But once again, the story was not as straightforward as it seemed. For although Mandeville was indeed one of the first Europeans ever to write about Islam, I had unearthed a little-known book by a Dominican friar named William of Tripoli. His *Tractatus De Statu Saracenorum* – written some 20 years before Sir John was born – also gave details about Muslim customs and seemed to have provided Mandeville with a large number of his details. But *The Travels* differed in two significant respects: its tone was far more tolerant than William of Tripoli's book and, more importantly, it was far more widely read.

The Mufti let out a long sigh and muttered something in Turkish. 'The Mufti has something important to say,' said Mustafa.

'What your man said is true,' began the Mufti. 'Christians and Muslims are very similar. They both believe in God and they both have the same goal.' He paused to light a cigarette. 'But there is a difference, and it is this. God gave his book *directly* to Mohammed who wrote down God's word in the Koran. The Bible is merely an interpretation, written through the pens of your saints. Where the Koran *records* the word of God, the Bible merely *interprets* the word of God.'

He drank his coffee in one gulp and drew heavily on his cigarette. 'There is only one edition of the Koran and that is in Arabic. There are 18 editions of the Bible worldwide: translated and rewritten. When we pray from the Koran, we always do so in Arabic for God's word is in Arabic. When we interpret the Koran, we are permitted to do so in the language of our country. Interpretation differs from country to country, from people to people. But the text – the core of the book – always remains the same.'

The ash on his cigarette had grown perilously long and as he moved his hand it dropped off, sending a fine spray of ash on to his trousers and shoes. 'So when you enter a mosque you will always hear people praying in Arabic. That is because you can *only* pray in Arabic. And as the Koran says, when you are called to prayer, you should run as fast as you can.'

'People don't,' I said.

'No,' said the Mufti. 'I'm afraid they don't.'

He chatted away in Turkish for a moment then fell silent as Mustafa translated what he had said. The Mufti, he told me, would like to inquire as to the health of the British royal family.

I said that, as far as I was aware they were very well, thank you. His voice dropped to a whisper and he moved his chair closer. 'Did you know,' he said as he pushed the door shut with his foot, 'that Prince Charles has converted to Islam. Yes, yes. He is a Muslim.'

When? How? Where? I bombarded him with questions.

'Ssshh,' he said. 'I can't say any more. But it happened in Turkey. Oh yes, he converted all right. When you get home check up on how often he travels to Turkey. You'll find that your future king is a Muslim.'

I asked him more but he wouldn't tell me. Instead he told me that many Christians become Muslims and that what had happened wasn't at all unusual. I then asked if Muslims ever became Christians but he shook his head. 'You cannot convert from Islam,' he said.

This I knew, but I had heard rumours of Muslims praying at Christian shrines. I was told that local Turkish Cypriots would leave flowers on the tomb of St Barnabas near Famagusta and that they would light candles in the few remaining churches in Northern Cyprus.

The Mufti nodded slowly. 'This, I'm afraid, is true,' he said. 'I haven't heard of it happening at the tomb of St Barnabas but I do know that people go to Apostolos Andhreas monastery and light candles there in the chapel. It is very bad. In Islam you cannot ask for help from anyone but God. There are no saints in Islam.'

Some days after meeting the Mufti I drove up the coast road from Famagusta to Bogaz, turning away from the sea shortly after the ruins of Salamis. The land here is almost completely flat, yet the road twisted around imaginary bends as if climbing the mountains that stood in the distance. I had promised to deliver a letter to the grandmother of a woman who worked at my wife's school but had been given the wrong directions to her village. Once I was off the main road there were no more signposts to

Sinirustu and I asked a couple of farmers for the quickest route. They all pointed across the fields towards the mountains. A few minutes later I asked some other farmers and they pointed me back across the fields towards the sea.

When I arrived finally in the village, which stood in the heart of the dry and airless plain that covers the middle of the island, I noticed a large crowd gathered in a field. Women in homespun clothes and men in jackets were standing in a circle. It was a funeral, and as I drove past the body, wrapped in a white linen sheet, was slowly lowered into the ground. The women of the village were weeping while overhead a falcon wheeled on the warm currents of air. It seemed to present a complete picture of death.

I suddenly had a panic. What if this was the old woman I was meant to be visiting? Perhaps she had died since I'd left England. It would be awful to have to take that news back to London. I drove into the village and – heart pounding – asked two women sitting by the roadside where I would find Aysa Husseyni.

'Up there,' they said with a smile. 'You'll find her at home. But she's upset . . . her neighbour died only yesterday.'

Muslim funerals happen very quickly after the person's death. Aysa's neighbour had indeed died only the day before yet her body had already been interred. Preparation of the corpse is full of ritual. The body is washed and its nose and mouth cleaned three times. Then it is wrapped in a white cloth and taken to the cemetery where five or six men pray for the deceased. It is lowered into the ground facing Mecca and covered with earth. Within a day of dying, the person has been buried.

But the grieving is not over and, among the Turks in Cyprus, there are many traditional customs to honour the dead, some of which are still practised in the remoter rural communities. On the third and the fortieth day a long and beautiful sixth-century poem, known as the 'Mevlid' after its author, is traditionally recited. Then the guests are given sweets and rosewater, followed by a feast of the deceased's favourite food.

In ancient times the Turks used to dance after a burial and weep when a child was born. The deceased, they said, no longer had to suffer the trials of living; the child, sadly, had the misfortune of being brought into the world.

Sinirustu was thoroughly rural and most of the inhabitants were farmers. Apart from a couple of tractors parked in a field the village could have belonged in another century. Despite the massive population exchanges between Turks and Greeks after the 1974 war, the landscape of rural Cyprus can't have changed a great deal since Sir John's time. The feudal system lingered on until the Ottoman conquest and even today many peasants live on smallholdings and work small plots of land.

I walked slowly up to Aysa's house. The garden had gone to seed and the tumbledown cottage was in a sorry state of disrepair. Aysa Husseyni, ancient and wizened, sat in an armchair in the shade.

'Who are you?' she asked as she emerged from a snooze. But before I had a chance to answer her mind had trailed off on to other things. She was not well, she told me. She was old and her neighbour had just died. It was sad because she was too old to go to the funeral and it was a shame because she was such a kind woman. She pointed to her two little grandchildren who were playing in the yard. 'Birth . . . and death,' she said. 'Birth and death.'

I slowly nodded my head for there was little I could add. Two grandchildren had been born and a woman had died, and for a small village in Cyprus this had been the pattern for thousands of years. There were no headstones in the cemetery to record the passing of lives. No inscription had been placed in the mosque to honour the famous. A name could live on for a generation or two, but then it was forgotten. Ashes to ashes. Dust to dust . . .

5 A Second Sir John

I would censure all *Pliny's, Solinus', Strabo's, Sir John Mandeville's, Olaus Magnus', Marco Polu's* lies, correct those errors in navigation, reform Cosmographical Charts, and rectify longitudes, if it were possible . . .

The Anatomy of Melancholy, **Robert Burton, 1621**

For all his descriptions of the places he visits and the people he meets, Sir John is almost completely silent about himself. He says nothing about his family, his home, or when or why he was knighted. Was he married? Did he have children? If so, he thinks it of little interest to the reader and for much of *The Travels* only his thoughts and opinions provide clues as to what sort of a person he might have been.

Not until the end of the book does he describe exactly how he feels after 34 years of travelling:

> I have been on many honorable journeys . . . [and] I am now come to rest, a man worn out by age and travel and the feebleness of my body, and certain other causes which force me to rest. I have compiled this book and written it, as it came into my mind, in the year of Our Lord Jesus Christ 1356 . . . On my way home I made my way to Rome to show my book to our Holy Father the Pope. And I told him of the marvels I had seen in different countries, asking that he with his wise council would examine it . . . And a little while afterwards, when he had examined it all the way through, he said to me that certainly everything was true that was in it.

This claim to have visited Rome and got papal approval for his work immediately aroused my suspicions for I felt sure that no book so openly critical of the Catholic church would have received a blessing from the pontiff. More damaging for Sir

John's credibility was a glaring inaccuracy that convinced me he had invented the whole tale. For the popes of the time were living in exile in Avignon and they didn't return to Rome until 1377. If Mandeville really had taken his book to the Pope, he would have travelled not to Rome but to Provence.

It was most unlike Mandeville to make such an obvious mistake and the more I investigated this anecdote about Rome, the more I felt sure that this passage was not the work of Sir John. For it only occurs in a few of the surviving manuscripts, suggesting that it was added at a later date by a scribe who was either too young, or too ignorant, to know that the popes were living in Avignon at the time when Sir John was on his travels.

His reason for adding such a passage was easier to explain: the anti-papal criticisms in *The Travels* are rarely far from the surface and it would provide a convenient explanation to anyone questioning why a monastic library owned such a subversive book.

The story reminded me that I couldn't believe everything I read by Sir John – or about him . . .

I uncovered a few other scraps of evidence about Mandeville, but the more I delved into them, the deeper the mystery became. It soon became apparent that someone, for some unknown but possibly sinister reason, had at one time had a vested interest in concealing Sir John's true identity. For while I myself had seen Sir John's epitaph in St Albans Abbey, I was surprised to discover that he had also had an epitaph in a church in Liège, Belgium, and that Liège claimed him as a citizen of their town. Unfortunately, this Belgian church was demolished at the time of the French Revolution, but not before the epitaph had been seen by many English travellers who reported what it said. Its words are of great importance, for virtually everyone has believed the following version of events over the last five centuries:

Here lies Master John de Montevilla knight alias
ad Barbam, Master of Compredi, born in England,
professor of medicine and most devout in prayer
and most liberal giver of his goods to the poor, who
traveled over the whole world. He ended the last day

of his life in a house in Liège, in the year of our Lord 1372, the seventeenth day of the month of November.

This inscription clearly indicates that Sir John Mandeville died and was buried in Liège, not St Albans, and it was supported by other evidence. English travellers who visited the tomb were also shown Mandeville's saddle, spurs and bridle-bit, as well as the two knives he supposedly used on his travels. But the story has a twist in the tale. In the words of a local Liège chronicler and contemporary of Sir John:

In 1372 died at Liège on the twelth of November a man who was greatly distinguished for his birth. He was content to be known by the name of John of Burgundy, called With the Beard. He, however, opened his heart on his death-bed to Jean d'Outremeuse, his gossip, whom he appointed his executor. In truth, he entitled himself, in the deed of his last will, *Sir John Mandeville, knight, Earl of Montfort in England and lord of the isle of Campdi and of the castle Perouse*. When dead at last, he was buried with the brethen Wilhelmites, in the suburb of Avroy.

This chronicle brings a dramatic new element to the story. For while it agrees that Sir John died at Liège, it records that he had been living in secret and under the assumed name of John of Burgundy. Not only that – it gives him a string of new and distinguished titles which raises him from small-time provincial knight to the rank of a highly influential nobleman.

This extraordinary story has been the basis for virtually every portrait of Sir John Mandeville from the sixteenth century to the present day. But there is one major problem with it. The only man who was party to the deathbed confession was, as this passage reveals, Jean d'Outremeuse. And the man who wrote the story? None other than Jean d'Outremeuse. This means that Outremeuse was the sole witness to the confession and therefore the only person who could make it public. It only took him to be lying for the whole Liège story to come crashing down.

I sat back and considered the evidence. I was now dealing with not just one Sir John, but two, whose lives were similar but whose deaths were very different. The first Sir John had been born into a provincial St Albans family, had travelled, and been buried in his home town. The second Mandeville was a distinguished nobleman from the powerful Montfort clan who had lived under the assumed name John of Burgundy, had concealed his identity up to his dying breath, and had been interred in Liège.

Further clues only confused matters more. The Liège Mandeville was apparently the author of a host of other books, including a manual about gemstones and a treatise on the magical properties of herbs. The more I sieved through the evidence the more I suspected the hand of Jean d'Outremeuse in all this. He seemed to have a secret motive in pretending to have known Sir John Mandeville. What I couldn't figure out was why.

Jean d'Outremeuse was a romancer who wrote fanciful tales using imaginary sources. His greatest work was *Ly Myreur des Histors*, an encyclopedic world history which mixed legend with fable. On the rare occasions he had reliable sources he used them. When he didn't he made them up.

Outremeuse's story certainly sounds likely for there was indeed a distinguished doctor called John of Burgundy who had settled in Liège late on in his life. He was an eminent scholar and an authority on the plague and his 1365 treatise *De Pestilentia* was translated into several languages and circulated throughout the Mediterranean lands. But there is no evidence that this doctor ever travelled, nor do any of his writings show any knowledge of the dozens of books that the author of *The Travels* had read. To use the jargon of modern detectives, he simply does not match the psychological profile of the author of *The Travels*. But he was a particularly convenient person for Outremeuse to claim to have been Mandeville, for by the time people might want to question the doctor it was too late: he was already dead.

In making his Sir John the 'Earl of Montfort in England' Outremeuse betrays his weakness in genealogy, for of all the dozens of English Mandevilles, not a single one ever held that title. The arms displayed on the Liège tomb, too, are suspect: according to early travellers they depicted a silver lion with a crescent on its breast. No English Mandeville ever bore these arms.

But none of this would have bothered Jean d'Outremeuse for his object and obsession was to glorify the Montfort family. His *Ly Myreur des Histors* never stops talking about how wonderful they are. If his was the only book left about medieval history, you could be forgiven for thinking the Montfort family the most illustrious in Europe.

When Outremeuse wasn't inventing stories about the Montforts, he invented stories about himself. He frequently takes famous people and links them by invented genealogy to himself or, at the very least, to his home town of Liège. He had already done it many times before in his *Geste de Liège* in which a succession of historical and mythical characters find themselves visiting the town. And since there is not a shred of evidence, apart from Outremeuse, to suggest Sir John died in Liège but plenty – as I was later to discover – to show he returned to St Albans, it seems certain that on this occasion he went one step further. He connected the writer of *The Travels* (a man he was obsessed with) to the Montforts (a family he was devoted to) and placed all of them in Liège (his home town). It was a pack of lies, but it is testimony to his imaginative ability that he has been believed for more than 550 years.

So much time has passed since his great voyage that it will probably never be possible to do more than guess about Sir John's life. Records have perished or been destroyed. The great monastery of St Albans was sacked during the Reformation and its priceless treasures lost or carted off and never seen again.

Despite this lack of evidence – or because of it – both the *Encyclopedia Britannica* and the *Dictionary of National Biography* have remained sceptical about Mandeville. The *Britannica* records that his life is as mysterious as his travels, while the *Dictionary of National Biography* takes a less generous line: 'Mandeville, Sir John, was the ostensible author of the book of travels bearing his name . . . there are strong grounds for the belief that his name is as fictitious as his travels [for] no trace of him can be found in England [and] the legend of his burial at St Albans was of late growth.'

While records of the Mandeville family are scant, none of us dies without leaving behind cuttings and papers, bills and letters.

A few manuscripts have survived the centuries and from these fading scraps and snippets I hoped to build up a picture of this spirited knight who forsook his home, his family, and his friends for more than three decades.

According to the *Rolls of Medieval England*, there were a great many Mandevilles living in the St Albans region in the fourteenth century, all of whom were ultimately descended from Geoffrey de Mandeville, a liegeman of William the Conqueror. Geoffrey must have been a loyal kinsman for William granted him vast estates amounting to 118 lordships scattered right across England, many of them in the wealthy St Albans area.

Yet by 1227, the Mandevilles had reached a point of crisis: the eldest line of the family had died out and the title passed by way of marriage to Humphrey de Bohun, the Earl of Hereford and Essex. From this point onwards all remaining Mandevilles looked towards the de Bohuns as the holders of the Honour of Mandeville and – disastrously as it turned out – their fortunes were inextricably linked to those of the de Bohuns.

My problem was in finding the Sir John who wrote *The Travels*, for I had soon unearthed dozens of records of a John Mandeville, Maundeville or Mandevil. By the early 1300s there were John Mandevilles living in Dorset, Ulster, Devon and Lincolnshire, and most could be dismissed immediately. The one in Dorset sounded promising for he had gone on a pilgrimage to Jerusalem and ended his days as a monk with the Hospitallers of St John, but further investigation showed he had left England several decades before *The Travels* was written. The Sir John from North Antrim also sounded like a candidate for he had murdered his overlord, the Earl of Ulster, and then hastily fled overseas. But once again the dates didn't match and besides, there was no other evidence to link the Mandeville of *The Travels* with Ireland. It was a similar story with all the remaining Sir John Mandevilles. One by one I was able to strike them off my list.

One scion of the Mandeville clan lived at the village of Black Notley in Essex – a headstrong family with a reputation for taking the law into their own hands. The head of this family was a certain Sir Thomas Mandeville who had inherited Black Notley, along with other lands, in 1303. His eldest son was named Walter, and Sir Thomas transferred property into Walter's name some four years later. But there is a second name that keeps cropping up in these land records – a John Mandeville, who would appear to be Sir Thomas's younger son. If so, there is a strong possibility that he is the author of *The Travels*. As a younger son he would be free from many of the obligations incumbent on his elder brother and therefore more able to travel. He would also have been the right age to have written the book; he appears to have left England for a long period of time; and could quite feasibly have been educated at the abbey of St Albans.

By the 1320s this John Mandeville was managing substantial amounts of property and land in the area around Black Notley – lands owned by Sir Thomas. Records show he held land in Borham, as well as the neighbouring villages of Little and Great Waltham. Yet in 1321 – just months before the author of *The Travels* claimed to have left England – he sold everything he owned and disappears from all records for the next 37 years. According to one of the few surviving land registries from that year, a 'John de Mandeville and Agnes his wife' sold ten acres of land to Richard and Emma Filliol. Furthermore, 'John atte Tye of Terlying and Alice his wife had a settlement with John Mandeville of Borham and Agnes his wife by which the former secured for twenty marks of silver one messuage, sixteen acres of land, and one and a half acres of wood in Borham.'

Men didn't dispose of land in the Middle Ages unless they had an extremely good reason. But it is entirely possible that Sir John did have a good reason. He was going abroad for a very long time, and needed a huge amount of cash to fund his voyage.

After 1321 the records fall silent and John Mandeville disappears without trace. The next mention of him is in 1358, when he pops up once again as the witness to a large amount of property.

Slowly it was all beginning to fall into place: the inscription, the documents, the family, the sale of land. But even if this was the man I was after, one nagging question remained. Travel on the scale of Mandeville's voyage – while not unheard of – was far from common in the Middle Ages. What on earth would drive a well-educated and prosperous landowner to sell everything he owned in order to risk his life in unknown countries? Maybe he was simply hungry for fame, although there was every possibility he fled England because he had to.

His own account of why he went abroad is straightforward: people, he says, always enjoy reading yarns from foreign lands. But the terrible events of 1322 present a far more compelling reason to explain his departure.

Humphrey de Bohun – the Mandevilles' overlord – had turned against the King. Furious with Edward II's favouritism and incompetence, he, along with a handful of other headstrong barons, challenged the King to do battle and within months the two armies were marching northwards towards Boroughbridge. But scarcely had the fighting begun before the rebels were overtaken by catastrophe. Humphrey de Bohun was killed in a surprise ambush, the rebel army lost its nerve, and the troops surrendered to the King.

It was a *fait accompli* and King Edward was in no mood for clemency. Hundreds of rebel soldiers were massacred as they fled from the battlefield while those lucky enough to escape with their lives were thrown into prison. Things had never looked so bleak for the Mandeville family for – as liegemen of the de Bohuns – they shared in the treason of their overlord. Worse still, King Edward was determined to have his bloody revenge. All leading members of the de Bohun family were jailed and their tenants heavily fined. Those who had money fled overseas, for rumours abounded of royalist soldiers lusting after the rebels' blood. If ever there was a time for a Mandeville to flee St Albans, it was in 1322.

6 Syria

It is very certain that many things in his book which were looked
upon as fabulous for a long time, have been since verified beyond
all doubt. We give up his men of fifty feet high, but his hens that
bore wool are at this day very well known, under the name of
Japan and silky fowls, &c. Upon the whole, there does not appear
to be any very good reason why Sir John Mandevile should not
be believed in any thing that he relates on his own observation.

The General Biographical Dictionary, **Alexander Chalmers, 1815**

There was confusion when I landed at Damascus airport.
As I walked into the arrivals hall I was greeted by the
sight of two men each holding a placard bearing the
words 'Mr Milton.'

I walked up to one and he smiled as he shook my hand. 'Mr
Milton?' he said. 'I'm from the Meridien. Welcome to Damascus.'
I saw the other man approaching, but before I could say
anything he said with a note of surprise: 'Mr Milton, I'm from the
Sheraton. Welcome to Damascus.' The two men looked at each
other and then looked at me. I was surprised to have been met
by anyone at all, for I'd been expecting to take a bus to my hotel.
Both men pointed towards their black Mercedes outside. They
both told me they had driven all the way from the centre of town.
And then the one from the Sheraton, who was beginning to grow
suspicious of an unshaven 28-year-old being accorded the
privilege of not just one Mercedes, but two, asked what I was
doing here.

'I work in tourism,' I said casually. I had to be careful what I
told him, for I had lied in order to get a visa – a dangerous thing
to admit in Syria.

He looked at me suspiciously. 'Tourism, eh?' he said with a
mischievous glint in his eyes. 'And what *exactly* do you do in this
tourism business?'

'Well . . . ' I said, 'I sort of write up reports on places.' At this he nonchalantly tossed back his head and made an expression that told me he knew exactly why I was here.

'Aha . . . ' he said slowly. 'I think what you're trying to tell me is that you're a journalist, Mr Milton. That's what you are. A journalist.' And with that he took me by the hand and led me away from the crowd of people standing nearby. 'And do you have a journalist's visa?' he whispered. 'Or did you, er, how shall we put this . . . did you perhaps pretend that you were something other than a journalist?'

I confessed to the latter and he let out a long, low whistle through his teeth. '*Veeeery* dangerous,' he said. 'Very, very dangerous. But, Mr Milton,' he said. 'I assure you my lips are sealed. It can be our little secret. You know, just between the two of us.'

I smiled nervously and he smiled back. He said he would allow me to stay at the Meridien and forgive my travel agent for booking two hotels. But he warned me to be careful. 'Don't tell anyone else,' he said. 'Keep it a secret.'

I thanked him and left with the other driver. It was an inauspicious start to my stay in Syria.

Perhaps I had been foolish to lie about my visa but I'd been warned by a specialist travel agent in England that it was extremely difficult for writers and journalists to get permission to enter Syria. My visa would have to be processed in Damascus and be personally approved by the Minister of Information. It could take nine months and there was every chance that my application would be refused. If that happened I would never be granted a visa and all my Syrian plans would be brought to an untimely end. So, when I headed off to the Syrian Embassy in Belgrave Square I told them I was a student of English Literature and arrived with all the necessary documents and letters.

I was surprised to discover that Sir John had faced similar difficulties. At the time when he was travelling, Syria was a difficult country to visit, especially if you were Christian. The crusaders had lost their last stronghold in the Middle East just two decades earlier and the great stream of pilgrims who once flocked here from Europe had all but dried up. There was great suspicion of any western traveller who suddenly turned up unannounced in a land that still had vivid and bloody memories of crusader rule.

The wily Sir John – always able to keep his critics on their toes – neatly sidesteps these problems. Because he was a close personal friend of the Sultan, he says, he was able to acquire a special permit which allowed him to travel unhindered wherever and whenever he wished.

'I had letters,' he writes; 'under the great seal of the Sultan, in which he strictly commanded his subjects to let me see all the places I wanted, and show me the relics and the holy places as I wished; and they were to conduct me from city to city if there were need . . . and obey my requests in all reasonable matters unless they were against the royal dignity of the Sultan or against their law.'

I was instantly suspicious of these 'letters' for they were too convenient for words. They would allow Sir John to write about everywhere in Syria – even the remotest of places – without any of his readers being able to challenge him on how he was able to travel there.

I turned to the other books written by medieval pilgrims. None of them mentioned these permits and none of them had felt it necessary to get letters from the Sultan. But then most had been travelling in less troubled times when the crusaders had opened up the pilgrim trail and the road to Jerusalem was less dangerous. No sooner had I dismissed Mandeville's story as fiction, however, than I unearthed a little-known account that seemed to vindicate it entirely. An Anglo-Irish friar travelling in the same year as him had also found it necessary to ask the Sultan for a permit and he, like Mandeville, was so struck by the usefulness of this 'visa' that he wrote about it at length: 'He, [the Sultan's interpreter] gave us a patent letter bearing the Sultan's seal . . . drawn with a reed and ink, which the Sultan himself draws with his own hand and never commits to another to draw. And hence it is that all the admirals and all the rest bow themselves partly out of respect for him . . . while all the time uttering glorious praises, honours, and reverences on the Sultan.'

My chauffeur-driven Mercedes sloshed through the drab suburbs of Damascus. It had been raining for hours and the streets were awash with filthy water. In places it had grown so deep that it slopped against shop doors.

My arrival in Damascus had not gone according to plan, for even before my brief encounter with the two chauffeurs I'd found myself with a problem. As I stood in the arrivals lounge waiting patiently for my luggage to appear, I watched the carousel churn out every conceivable rucksack and suitcase except my own. When I asked at Baggage Inquiries what had happened to my luggage the man threw up his hands: 'It could be in London,' he said. 'It could be in Bombay. It could be in Oman. Who knows, it might even have gone to Riyadh.'

'Well let's just hope it has good weather,' I said with weary irony.

'Oh yes, Riyadh is always . . . ' He stopped in mid-sentence and looked at me as if I was mad. When I asked him to fax London he wearily shook his head. 'We have no fax machines in Syria,' he said. 'But just be patient. You worry too much. Your baggage will arrive . . . if God in His merciful wisdom wills it.'

I hoped that God would will it. If not, I was in for a cold and miserable time in Syria.

The outskirts of Damascus are shoulder to shoulder with garages and bicycle repair shops yet despite the cold weather, groups of mechanics in greasy overalls stood in doorways drinking tea. Hanging from every lamppost was a picture of President Assad – pale-faced, moustached, and looking like an early-evening chat show host. But his was not the only face on display: the capital was adorned with banner-sized portraits of someone whose good looks, dark glasses and unshaven face bore a striking resemblance to George Michael.

'Who is this George Michael?' asked my irritable driver. 'This is not your George Michael . . . this is Basil, the son of the President of Syria. Or rather, it was.'

'Was?'

'Yes, he is dead. Basil was killed in a car crash. But we still like to remember him.' He paused for a second then asked: 'Who *is* George Michael?'

We had soon left the outskirts behind and were passing through the city's medieval centre. There was the flash of a crenellated battlement, a blur of neon, and the fading smell of kebab before we were whisked on to a flyover that carried us high above the city, leaving the puddles and lakes far below us. We passed the Army Museum with its gardens adorned with tanks and wreckage from the 1973 war, and a few minutes later we had arrived at our goal – the Damascus Meridien.

I didn't normally stay in such luxury but I was writing a travel article for *The Mail on Sunday* and had been offered two complimentary nights by a PR agency in London. Unfortunately, I didn't have quite the right clothes. All my luggage had been lost – right down to my toothbrush – and I was dressed in filthy travelling clothes. Heads turned for all the wrong reasons as I walked into the glittering hotel lobby.

'You are welcome in Damascus,' said a voice behind me. I spun around to be greeted by a man dressed in a slick dinner jacket, dress shirt and bow tie. 'Mr Ali,' he added as he held out his hand. 'Sales director of the Meridien.'

He led me up to a private lounge for a drink and soon we were joined by the managing director and the financial director who arrived on a breeze of cologne. All were in their fifties and dressed in dinner suits. In the Arab world, where sharp dressing is *de rigeur* for businessmen, they seemed bemused to behold an unsightly and unshaven British journalist.

'So you write about Syria?' said the managing director.

'Syria,' said the financial director, 'is a beautiful country. She is one of the most beautiful countries in the world.'

The sales director agreed. 'She is more beautiful than a woman,' he said. 'I think you will adore her.'

All three men nodded in agreement and stroked their moustaches. 'And what, sir, do you wish to see in Syria?' asked the MD.

'Palmyra?' suggested the FD.

'Crac de Chevalier?' said SD.

I explained that I was following the route of a medieval knight and they glanced at each other then smiled at me politely.

'How interesting,' said MD.

'Very interesting,' said FD.

'I'm sure he too found Syria a beautiful country,' added SD.

The financial director handed me a complimentary fruit cocktail adorned with an umbrella. 'Whatever you want, Mr

Milton, you only have to ask.' The others smiled as they stared at my steel-capped boots. I wished they would sit down, but instead they remained standing in a semi-circle in front of me. When I moved to pick up my drink the umbrella collided with my nose and the marischino cherry plopped on to the floor. Everyone saw the disaster happen and all eyes looked down at the carpet. Was it under the desk? Had it rolled under my chair?

'There it is,' said FD at length. It was squashed between the heavy tread of my boots.

By the time Mandeville set off on his travels, Damascus had long been eclipsed by its more powerful neighbours. To the north lay Constantinople and the Byzantine empire while to the south was Cairo, capital of the powerful Mameluke dynasty. These Mamelukes had achieved huge successes on the battlefield, expelling the last crusaders from Syria.

Yet Damascus had a history that more than matched its neighbouring cities: six centuries before Sir John wrote his book it had been the centre of a formidable Islamic empire that stretched from the Bay of Biscay to the banks of the Indus, from the Aral Sea to the cataracts of the Nile – a greater area of land, even, than the Roman Empire.

Ruled by the brilliant and cultivated Umayyad dynasty, it had controlled the great caravan routes from the east, and the wealth that poured into Damascus allowed its rulers to lavish money on palaces, mosques and religious schools. It was a city of such legendary beauty that the prophet Mohammed hesitated to visit it because, he said, he wished to enter paradise but once.

Although this empire had long since crumbled by Sir John's day, Damascus in the 1330s was undergoing something of a renaissance. Governed by a capable bureaucrat sent from Egypt – a man whose love of building was matched only by his wealth – Tengiz set about beautifying his provincial capital. By the time Sir John claims to have visited the city, its streets must have been alive with the clatter and banging of building work. These were the buildings I wanted to find and I turned to Sir John to see what he had written about them. Unfortunately he scarcely mentions either builders or buildings, preferring instead to write about the local fruit: 'In Damascus there are many wells,' he writes. 'There are also many fair gardens, giving great plenty of fruit. Nowhere else is a city like it for gardens of fruit. There is a very large population in that city, and it is well walled, with a double rampart.'

And that was it. A walled city filled with gardens, and populated by prodigious eaters of fruit. I flicked back through his book to see how he had travelled to Damascus but that was equally vague. He offers a number of routes, most of which started from Constantinople. The first was to take a boat to Cyprus, to Syria and from there travel overland to Damascus. Another possibility was to go overland across Cappadocia and reach Damascus by way of Antioch. Finally – and rather vaguely – he suggests passing through Syria and into Palestine by travelling along the banks of the River Jordan.

But what route did he himself take? And in what year did he arrive? As ever, he didn't say.

A freezing wind swept through Damascus and my linen jacket provided inadequate protection against the winter chill. On my first morning I headed to the souk to buy some new clothes since God, in His merciful wisdom, had not willed my luggage to arrive. Underpants seemed in great supply – voluminous Y-fronts that would have fitted an elephant – but pullovers were not to be found so I wandered deeper and deeper into the souks in search of them.

Like all the great medieval cities of the Arab world, Damascus's old quarter is surrounded by a high defensive rampart. Until the beginning of this century the city was still contained within these fortifications but now they mark only a tiny island in the midst of an ever-growing metropolis. Damascus's historic heart has been turned into a giant roundabout surrounded by a never-ending circuit of tarmac and the city's Los Angeles-style road network ensures that it is almost impossible to go anywhere on foot. Those wishing to visit the historic old town must cross at least two dual carriageways and a main artery road before landing up safely inside the city walls. Woe betide anyone caught in the middle of the road, for drivers delight in using pedestrians as target practice while simultaneously playing the *Dallas* theme tune on their horns. I survived three roads, two green lights and a roundabout before finding myself washed up safe and sound inside one of the city's ten gates.

The western end of the famous Souk al Tawil – known to all as Straight Street – is narrow and lined with stalls selling spices, cloth and decorative copper plates. But as I walked along this street I noticed a gradual change in the atmosphere. The noises began to change and the spice stalls were replaced by shops with window displays and fancy lighting. Once you have passed the ruined Roman archway this change becomes even more apparent: not only do the alleys widen and buildings become smarter, but the people are better dressed too. There is a very good reason for this: the Roman arch marks the end of the Muslim part of the city and the gateway to the wealthier Christian quarter. Ever since the city was conquered by Islam, this area of little more than one square kilometre has been home to thousands of Christians – all belonging to different churches with a bewildering array of beliefs.

But it was neither patriarchs nor churches that I was after. Having given up on finding a pullover, I was looking for Damascus's greatest building, the Umayyad Mosque, for there was something of a confusion in Sir John's book that needed clearing up. According to several sources, this was the final resting place of one of the most important relics in Christendom – the head of St John the Baptist. The earliest tales recount how Herod sent the head to Damascus so that the Romans would believe that the execution had taken place. But the popular tradition records that on the day Damascus fell to the Muslim armies, John the Baptist's blood bubbled up from beneath the old Byzantine church. Horrified onlookers tore up the floor and unearthed the head still covered in skin and hair, prompting the caliph of the time to mark the spot with a column. Because of this, the mosque became an important shrine and was frequently praised for its beauty, as the medieval Muslim traveller Ibn Battuta testifies: 'The Umayyad Mosque is the most magnificent mosque in the world, the finest in construction and noblest in beauty, grace and perfection; it is matchless and unequalled.' He adds, 'Damascus

Mailapur, India: '[The worshipper] stands in front of the idol with a sharp drawn knife in his hand, and with that knife he cuts off a piece of his flesh.'

Sumatra: ' . . . the men and women go completely naked and they are not ashamed to go show themselves as God made them.'

Sumatra: 'Merchants sell their children . . .
those that are plump they eat; those that are
not plump they feed up and fatten.'

Indo-China: 'The king . . . has castles made
and tied on the elephants.'

Indo-China: ' . . . when their friends are seriously ill, they hang them on trees, so they can be chewed and eaten by birds.'

Nicobar Islands: 'Men and women of that isle have heads like dogs, and they are called Cynocephales.'

Sri Lanka: 'There are also wild geese with two heads . . .'

Andaman Islands: ' . . . there is a race of great stature, like giants. . . they have one eye only, in the middle of their foreheads.'

surpasses all other cities in beauty, and no description, however full, can do justice to its charms . . . the variety and expenditure of the religious endowments are beyond computation . . . and the people vie with each other in building mosques, religious houses, colleges and mausoleums.'

Despite the Arab historians' fascination with the building, Sir John doesn't even mention it in his *Travels*. This was strange, for if the Umayyad Mosque really was the site of St John the Baptist's burial it would be unthinkable that he should pass through the city without visiting the shrine of one of Christianity's most revered saints.

From the outside, the building looks like a fortress, and is constructed from giant and roughly chiselled blocks of stone. But this rugged exterior shields a fragile and delicately adorned inner courtyard which was converted from a church into a mosque by the great Caliph al-Walid in AD715. The decoration of the mosque was so costly that it was said to have deprived the state of seven years' revenue and its greatest wonder was its mosaics, an unrivalled masterpiece created by the finest Byzantine craftsmen loaned by the Emperor of Constantinople. Even under a drab grey sky, their vibrant colours and patterns still hint at their former splendour. Here the eye could lose itself among a fantastical world of towers and columns, palaces and pavilions, all surrounded by luxuriant palm fronds, orchards and groves. The plants seem Oriental while the buildings, depicted iconographically, belong to the Byzantine tradition. These mosaics were the last flourishing of Byzantine art in Syria. After this, the imperial craftsmen packed up their tools and left.

The shrine of St John the Baptist is inside the mosque, covered by an iron and glass protective screen which stops the devout from touching the reliquary. The tomb looks neglected: a single plastic rose gathers dust, and even the pile of money that visiting pilgrims have pushed through cracks in the glass lies untouched. The skull itself – if it exists – is contained within the reliquary which is draped in green cloth decorated with Arabic calligraphy. As I stood there, a constant stream of pilgrims approached the tomb hoping for intercession from the miracle-working relics.

Two Muslims suddenly came up to me and made cutting motions to their throats. 'Yahia,' said one as he slashed his throat again. 'For you it is John the Baptist but we call him Yahia.'

He stuck his hand deep into his pocket and handed me a fistful of warm, squashed and sticky marshmallows. They came complete with a generous coating of fluff from the inner lining of his jacket pocket. 'There are other heads too,' he said. 'The head of Hussein is over there,' he pointed to the far side of the courtyard, 'except that some say his head is really in Medina. Then, of course, there's his sister's head. She was called Zeinab and her head is in the suburbs of Damascus. And as well as all those heads . . . '

I stopped him. 'I'm interested in this particular head,' I said, pointing at the reliquary. He nodded gravely. 'This is a very interesting head. You see we worship it and you worship it. To us, Yahia – John the Baptist – is a forerunner of Jesus Christ. He is a prophet in our religion as well as yours.' He paused and then added thoughtfully: 'This, I think, is good.'

What the Mufti of Cyprus had told me about the shared heritage of Christianity and Islam was true, and the Umayyad Mosque was the tangible expression of these common roots. Here, Muslim and Christian alike would fall on their knees before the funerary cask of Yahia or John the Baptist.

I still didn't understand why Sir John hadn't visited these relics for he always discusses miracle-working bones and icons with enthusiasm. When I turned to the accounts of other medieval pilgrims I noticed they, too, had a similar lack of interest in the shrine of St John the Baptist. Ludolph von Suchem only mentions the building in passing while Burchard of Mount Sion ignores it completely. Why had so many pilgrims overlooked one of Christendom's greatest shrines?

The Travels, perhaps, holds the key to this mystery. The tradition in which a caliph found John the Baptist's head in Damascus is not as straightforward as it first appears, for the more I read about the shrine the more heads of St John the Baptist there seemed to be. And it wasn't just heads – I soon had legs, arms, and every part of his anatomy popping up in the most unexpected of places.

Mandeville was desperate to clear up the confusion over the relics before venerating them but the more he investigates the history of the bones the more puzzled he becomes. First he is told that John the Baptist was buried in the city of Sebastiyeh between the prophets Helizeus and Obadiah, but others disagree and assure Mandeville that he was beheaded beside the Dead Sea: 'There Julian the Apostate, when he was emperor, had his bones exhumed and burnt and the ashes were scattered in the wind.'

While this second story satisfactorily explains the decapitated body, it doesn't account for John the Baptist's head. Where had that been buried? 'The head,' Mandeville is told, 'was enclosed in a wall in Sebastiyeh but the Emperor Theodosius had it taken out, and found it wrapped in a bloody cloth.'

Even this is not the end of the story. Mandeville records that half the head was sent to Constantinople while the other half found its way to Rome where it was stored in the church of Saint Silvester.

Such confusion explains, perhaps, why Mandeville didn't visit the relics stored in the Umayyad Mosque. He didn't believe that this was the head of St John the Baptist and was in no mood to venerate a skull that he had already seen in Constantinople.

Sir John stumbles across a host of different Christian religions in Syria. He writes about the Syrian Church (which still exists) and the Greek Orthodox Church (which also exists). He also mentions the Franciscans (who still have a church in Damascus), the Arians (who died out centuries ago) and the Nestorians.

The *who*? I had never heard of this last lot and wondered whether they still existed. If so, where did they live? What did they believe?

It is not just in Syria that Sir John writes about the Nestorians; the further east he travels the more he meets these peculiar people. In India he claims that the emperor himself is a Nestorian priest, while in China huge communities of Nestorians are said to be scattered throughout the land. Had Mandeville invented such stories or simply repeated some garbled tale he had heard from another traveller? The further I delved into the history of the Nestorians the more remarkable was the story that

I uncovered. The Nestorians had indeed existed in Sir John's day and were, as he says, Christians – but they were Christians whose beliefs were dramatically different from those of the Catholic or Orthodox churches.

They had come into existence in the fifth century when a Patriarch of Constantinople named Nestorius – renowned for his melodious voice and mastery of rhetoric – repudiated several of the Orthodox church's central tenets. He separated the God and Man in Christ and thereby threatened the Virgin Mary's position as the Mother of God.

For a patriarch to be saying such things caused such appalling furore in the imperial capital that the emperor immediately summoned a great church council at Ephesus in AD429 to decide if his teachings were correct. Nestorius was confident of winning his case; he already appeared to have gained the Emperor's ear and had gathered around him 16 like-minded bishops as well as several hundred soldiers just in case things went wrong.

But right from the outset the council did not go according to plan. His chief supporters failed to arrive in time for the meeting and Nestorius, protesting at the decision to begin without his allies, refused to appear. In the council's first session Nestorius was condemned *in absentia*, deposed, and banished to a remote monastery in the Libyan desert. This should have spelled the end for his supporters but it only succeeded in strengthening their convictions. A group of them founded their own theological school and their teachings spread like wildfire through the Byzantine empire, especially amongst those communities disaffected by the Emperor's policies. Within a few decades much of Persia had converted to Nestorianism and missions began springing up right across Asia. By the time Sir John was claiming to have travelled, the Nestorian church was so mighty that their Patriarch, ruling from his palace on the banks of the Tigris, had half the world under his sway.

I wondered what had happened to these people for they seemed to have vanished from the pages of history. And then I learned, to my great excitement, that it was just possible that a tiny community of Nestorians were still living in the remote north-eastern corner of Syria . . .

The town of Hassake stands guard over a slender finger of land that pokes insolently into the great desert of Iraq. The traveller coming from Damascus has little choice in how to reach Hassake. There is no airport, there is no train. The only way to arrive in this remote town is by bus – a wearisome seven-hour journey across the desert.

As soon as the bus leaves Damascus the landscape changes: the city is on the cusp of a fertile crescent and the desert is for ever knocking on its door. Within minutes of leaving the suburbs we had entered a flat and inhospitable terrain, and for the next three hours there was nothing to break the monotony except shards of stone and the occasional scrap of litter caught by the wind. This was wasteland without grandeur; there were no sand dunes marching triumphantly into the wind; no green-fringed oases to brighten the horizon.

We stopped at Palmyra, the greatest ruined city of antiquity in the Middle East, and I stepped off the bus to be greeted by a blast of freezing air. It came from the north; chilled amongst the rocky peaks of Kurdistan before being sent shooting across the flat Syrian desert. I had no reason to visit Palmyra for Sir John doesn't even mention the town. But the bus was going no further so I had no choice. I would have to stay overnight and wait for the next bus to Hassake.

It came as no surprise that Mandeville had not visited Palmyra, for by the fourteenth century the city was already in ruins and only the newly garrisoned fort atop the sugarloaf mountain marked the strategic significance of this outpost. Yet in the days of the Roman Empire, Palmyra had been an immensely rich caravan centre which lived off the taxes it gathered from merchants passing through its gates on their way to Damascus. Even in its ruined state the city appears huge, spread over a vast pan of desert. At the eastern end of the great colonnade stands the Temple of Bel, a massive honey-coloured stone structure built to protect the central shrine within. The inner sanctum of this shrine, where bloody sacrifices to the gods were once made, is in a remarkable state of preservation; the cupola still displays a proud bust of Jupiter surrounded by the signs of the Zodiac.

From here it is possible to get an overview of the colonnade which cuts through the town and leads the eye towards the Camp of Diocletian, reduced over the centuries to a pile of rubble. On the left there is a theatre. On the right stands the temple of Bel-Shamin. And in every direction temples and homes poke out of the desert – tombstones on a truly epic scale.

I felt a twinge of excitement as I stumbled over these ruined temples and colonnades. Brushing my hands along the carved stone blocks I sensed, like Sir John, that I was about to leave behind a familiar world and enter one entirely different: Asia Minor, the Unknown. For while these classical façades belonged firmly within the Graeco-Roman tradition, the sculptures and statues told a different story. The more I gazed at these faces and looked into their eyes, the more I saw that these people were not of Roman stock. They have long eyelids and shallow faces, ringlet beards and weird hats. These were Persians, Assyrians, Mesopotamians, whose statues and deities fill an entire room of the British Museum.

For the Romans, Palymra was *ultima thule* – the last outpost of the known world beyond which lay the formidable Persian army. As I stood at this one-time border between civilization and barbarism, the elements suddenly unleashed themselves on the desert. It began to rain – furious sheets of water driven horizontal in the gale. It lashed the temples and columns, transforming static statues into weeping faces and threatening at any moment to turn to snow.

I turned my back on the colonnaded main street of old Palmyra and, stumbling over a half-buried column, walked back into the new town. The red, green and blue fairy lights that decorated the outside of the Palmyra Restaurant provided a welcoming sight. Palmyra may no longer mark the end of the known world but it still felt like a frontier town.

My spirits lifted when I entered the small museum for the man selling tickets was a cheery chap, though surprised that I wanted to see the artefacts dug up from the site. 'There's nothing to see here,' he said. 'It's only old stones. Come and watch the football instead.'

His small office was crowded with seven young lads, all smoking and drinking tea. Aleppo were playing Damascus and in the few brief moments when the television wasn't a haze of fuzz, it appeared that Damascus was winning. Three of the lads were happy about this and each time there was a near goal they went through a hand-slapping give-me-five routine. The other four sat silently throughout the match, smoking endless cigarettes and slurping tea.

At half time I asked my new friend if I could pop out and see the museum. 'If you're not enjoying the football,' he murmured with a shrug.

I promised I'd come back afterwards and was about to walk away when he motioned me to come nearer.

'Perhaps you would like . . . ' his voice dropped to a whisper ' . . . to *buy* some of the exhibits?'

I laughed but saw that he wasn't joking. 'Jewellery . . . coins . . . you must only ask.'

When I returned half an hour later having seen everything in the museum, I told him I'd like to buy a couple of mummies.

His face fell for a moment before he realized I was joking. 'The pots are very nice,' he said. 'What's wrong with the pots?'

It was bitterly cold at night and I sat in bed with the blankets around my ears. My hotel was in the new part of town and was a newer building than most. It had three windows missing, the back wall had yet to be built, and the corridor to my room was ankle-deep in gravel and sand.

In the flickering electric light I began reading a fascinating book I had brought with me. It was called *The Monks of Kublai Khan* which I'd mistakenly thought was a history of the Nestorian church. But when I looked closer I saw that it was a translation of a Syriac document which told the extraordinary story of two Nestorian monks who had travelled along exactly the same route as Sir John – except in reverse. It had been written in the last decade of the thirteenth century, just a few years before Sir John's journey and threw a flood of light on both the Nestorian communities in the Middle East and on Mandeville's claims to have visited these communities.

The story began in China where an interesting rumour had just reached the ears of the great Mongol Emperor Kublai Khan (of Xanadu fame). He had heard that two Nestorian monks from his lands were planning to undertake a pilgrimage to Jerusalem, and he immediately summoned them to his palace in Peking. Their names were Sawma and Markos and the reasons for their journey – if their own account can be believed – was to seek absolution for their sins in Jerusalem. But right from the outset, their voyage was shrouded in mystery for as soon as Kublai Khan heard of their intentions he decided to put these two monks to good use: he had long dreamed of capturing Jerusalem but had always lacked intelligence information. There could be no better people to send on a clandestine spying mission than two simple monks whose object was to pray at the holy places and whose travels would arouse no suspicion. To this end he provided them with special permits which would allow them to travel unmolested through all the lands under his suzerainty.

Although Sawma and Markos found themselves welcomed by all the local rulers as they crossed China on their journey westwards, the journey stretched their endurance and it was only after great hardship that they reached Kashgar, Khorasan and finally Baghdad.

At this point they were within striking distance of Jerusalem but their mission was suddenly stopped in its tracks. The Nestorian Patriarch in Baghdad died and an assembly of bishops met to decide on his replacement. The fame of these monks from China had preceded them and Markos's holiness drew the attentions of many in the Church. The assembly argued that his spirituality outshone all others and that he should be confirmed as supreme head of the Nestorian Church. It was a political decision; Markos was well acquainted with the manners and customs of the Mongols and would prove extremely useful as an adviser to the Persian king – a fellow Nestorian.

He turned the job down but was immediately overruled and given the honorary name Yahbh-Allaha, or 'God given'. Sawma too was honoured. He was awarded the title of Visitor General which gave him the right to travel anywhere in the world in the name of the king.

He was soon ordered to do so. The King of Persia also harboured dreams of capturing Jerusalem and felt that he was now in a position to do so. He sent Sawma to the Emperor of Byzantium, as well as the kings of Italy, France and England, and the Pope in Rome, in order to enlist their support.

Sawma was treated nobly in Constantinople and then headed to Rome where he was showered with vast quantites of gold, jewels and relics. In France he was taken by the king to see the Crown of Thorns and in Gascony he was granted an audience with King Edward I of England. Edward was delighted by the idea of retaking Jerusalem and told Sawma: 'We the kings of these cities bear upon our bodies the sign of the Cross, and we have no subject or thought except this matter. And my mind is relieved on the subject about which I have been thinking, when I hear that King Arghon thinketh as I think.'

But tragedy was about to beset the two monks. First Sawma died, exhausted from his travels. Then the Persian king dropped dead and his country was plunged into civil war. The fanatical Muslims rose up and massacred thousands of Nestorians and local warlords carved out private fiefdoms. Most notorious of all was a warrior-leader called Nawruz who made the annihilation of the Nestorian Church the centrepoint of his policies. 'The churches shall be uprooted,' he decreed, 'and the altars overturned, and the celebrations of the Eucharist shall cease, and the hymns of praise, and the sounds of calls to prayer shall be abolished; and the chiefs of the Christians, and the great men among them, shall be killed.' The very night of this decree a band of brigands broke into the Patriarch's cell and tortured him. Markos was lucky to escape with his life.

When the civil war finally came to an end, things had never looked bleaker for the Nestorians. The new king favoured Islam over Christianity and by the time Markos died in 1317 – just five years before Sir John left England – the Nestorian Church was in a critical position.

It wasn't long before its death knell was ringing right across Asia. In 1392 the Mongol Emperor Tamberlaine the Great swept westwards and captured Baghdad, massacring all the Christians in the city. Only a handful escaped, fleeing for their lives into the desolate mountains of Kurdistan.

The Nestorian Church had been broken. Within less than a

century this vast Christian community – which had stretched from the Yangste river in China to the shores of the Black Sea, from Siberia in the north to the present Sri Lanka in the south – had shrunk to a pathetic and persecuted community of a few thousand living in terror in the snow-covered wilderness of Kurdistan. Never before in history had a faith and a people been so totally annihilated in such a short space of time. Sir John, it seemed, had been one of the last westerners to meet them.

And that, it was assumed, was the end of the Nestorian Church. But in 1820 a certain Claudius James Rich, a Resident of the British East India Company in Baghdad, decided to visit the ancient site of Nineveh. While on this trip he made a most astonishing discovery. He stumbled upon a remote and backward people who still spoke the language of Christ and who – he was convinced – were the last remants of the ancient Nestorian Church.

The discovery was an accident. He had sent his Tartar servant to Constantinople to deliver a letter and on the return journey, this Tartar took a short cut across the mountains and stumbled across a ruthlessly hostile Christian population. 'These Christians were a ferocious, vindictive, and capricious set,' Rich later wrote, 'extremely irritable withal, and that the slightest offence might be his destruction . . . his march was one scene of difficulties; they plundered him of his money and arms and told him they refrained from further violence for the sake of Zebeer Pasha's letter of recommendation.'

Any further investigation was going to be dangerous in the extreme for these Nestorians were renowned for their ruthlessness. They shared their territory with the devil-worshipping Yezids and were surrounded by tribes of Kurds who murdered for sport. But Rich had thrown down the gauntlet and within a few years an American missionary called Dr Asahel Grant took up the challenge, despite being warned by the Pasha of Mosul that he would never return alive from these desolate mountains: 'To the borders of their country I will be responsible for your safety. You may put gold upon your head, and you will have nothing to fear; but I warn you that I can protect you no further. These mountain infidels acknowledge neither pashas nor kings, but from time immemorial every man has been his own king.'

Grant was not to be deterred: he climbed high into the mountains and found, to his amazement, that these few villages were indeed inhabited by Nestorian Christians who worshipped God in the way they had done for centuries. Grant couldn't believe what he found:

Here, in the munition of rocks, has God preserved, as if for some great end in the economy of his Grace, a chosen remnant of his ancient church, secure from the beast and the false prophet, safe from the flames of persecution and the clamour of war. My thoughts went back to the days when the Nestorian missionaries were spread abroad throughout the East, and for more than one thousand years continued to plant and sustain the standard of the cross throughout the remote and barbarous countries of Central Asia, Tartary, Mongolia and China . . . I looked at them in their present state, sunk down into the ignorance of semi-barbarism, and the light of vital piety almost extinguished upon their altars, and my heart bled for their condition.

A flurry of missionary activity followed in Grant's wake. English Bibles were translated into Syriac and money sent to restore their churches. But lavishing such gifts on them led these pitiful people astray. They began to harbour vain and impossible dreams of being granted statehood and, to this end, they descended from their mountain strongholds during the First World War and joined the Allied forces in Iraq in their fight against Turkey. After the war the Nestorians discovered just how fruitless their dreams were to be for they were abandoned – despised and persecuted – on the hot plains of Iraq. There was even worse in store: offered the choice of abiding by Iraqi law or leaving Iraq, they chose to leave. But as they crossed the frontier into Syria, an Iraqi regiment – supported by local Kurds and Bedouin – attacked them. Thousands of Nestorians were massacred in cold blood. Of the already depleted population who had descended from the heights of Kurdistan, only a few families managed to cross the Euphrates into Syria.

And there, in a remote corner of desert, I was told they had remained to this day.

The bus to Hassake pulled up in Palmyra's town square the following afternoon. It was a rattle-bag of rusty metal and most of the passengers on board were not Arabs but Kurds.

'Why do you go to Hassake?' asked the man behind me. 'Hassake is horrible. There is nothing to see. There is nothing to do. Palmyra is good, Hassake is not good.'

I told him it sounded like an interesting place. 'You are crazy,' he said bluntly before adding in his strangely formal English, 'there is so much for the tourist person to see in Syria. We are pleased to offer you ruins. We are pleased to offer you crusader castles. We are pleased to offer you souks. And yet you choose to come to Hassake where we are not pleased to offer you any of these. Excuse me, good sir, but I consider you a crazy man.'

I explained that there was a church I wanted to see in Hassake. I was interested in the Nestorians; did he know anything about these people?

He shook his head and asked if they were friends of mine. When I said no, he had one more thing to say.

'You will arrive in Hassake tonight and you will be gone in the morning,' he predicted, and passengers in the nearby seats nodded in agreement. 'But we are pleased to welcome you in Syria,' he added, as if by way of apology.

It grew dark as we neared Hassake and the flat landscape melted into the night. Occasionally the darkness would be broken by the firelight of a Bedouin encampment or the bright flare of an oil well, for the Syrians have recently discovered oil in this remote land. But more often, for hour after hour, we rattled along in silence and in darkness. At some point I must have drifted off. The continuous hum of the engine made me drowsy and when I closed my eyes I found a succession of images dancing before me: medieval ramparts, monks wandering through the streets, and a string of brightly coloured fairy lights decorating the cathedral. We are pleased to offer you palaces . . . we are pleased to offer you castles . . . you are welcome in Syria . . .

I awoke from my dream. The bright lights of Hassake lit the

horizon, the road opened into dual carriageway, and the bus swung into the bus park. I stepped off the vehicle into an oily puddle and my left foot was sodden.

My friend from the bus offered to take me to a hotel and I readily accepted. My guidebook took just two lines to dismiss Hassake, warning that there was nothing to see here and nothing to do. This became all-too apparent as we walked from the bus park into town: a 20-minute hike through one of the most depressing urban landscapes I have ever seen. There were half-finished concrete buildings littering the roadside and half-finished concrete walls. There were roundabouts which had been abandoned long before they had been connected to the chaotic road system. Acres of wasteland filled with heaps of broken rubble. I had travelled seven arduous hours across a windswept desert only to arrive in Slough.

Worst of all was the mud, for Hassake was bogged down in the stuff. Cars sloshed through it with a satisfying squelch and people walked along the pavements with giant moon steps, as large clumps stuck to the undersides of their shoes. But the mud was not my only problem: my presence in the town seemed to be attracting considerable attention and as I walked down the main street people gathered in little groups to discuss what I was doing here. Who was I? Why had I come? It was not just the locals who seemed curious. The police, too, were watching me from the corner of their eyes: I hoped they would leave me alone.

When I got to my hotel the owner – a shifty fellow with one eye the size of a gobstopper – demanded to know who I was and why I had come to Hassake.

'I'm a student,' I told him.

He looked me up and down and muttered something in Arabic to his friend who stirred from the television set and came to have a look at me.

'Why Hassake?' he demanded.

'I'm following a medieval . . . ' I stopped and began again. 'The churches,' I said. 'I've come to see the churches.'

He let out a sarcastic laugh and examined my passport. He wanted to know why my profession wasn't written in, and when I told him I'd forgotten to do so he stared at me through his wobbly eyeball. 'You are not a student,' he told me. 'I don't know who you are or why you are here . . . ' he coughed for dramatic effect 'but I have one room for 40 dollars.'

I refused and he laughed again. 'In that case,' he said, 'you will sleep on the pavement tonight.' His friend chuckled as I handed over four ten-dollar bills. It was a rip-off but there was nothing I could do.

I took my bag to my room, stood over the toilet and was sick. The room was disgusting. The floor was awash with stagnant water, there were four cockroaches in the cupboard, and I could only guess at what had taken place on the mattress. It looked as if it had been the site of a massacre. Worse still, I was ill. As I did battle against the cockroaches, my stomach was waging war with the kebab I had eaten.

Because I had expected Hassake to be tiny I'd thought that finding the Nestorian church – if there really was one in the town – would be simple. As it happened, the place was immense and sprawled over many miles. It could take me days to track down the Nestorians, and even then I would have no way of communicating with them.

I was never going to find them without help, but Hassake had little in the way of information for the foreign visitor. There was no tourist office and no large hotel. There didn't even seem to be a town hall. But a shop on the main street had caught my eye: it was smarter than the rest and was called Kaspo's, a patisserie with windows piled high with cakes. It was decorated with a string of lights and its French sign looked so out of place in this ghastly town centre that I wondered for a moment whether I had stepped into Paris's seventh arrondissement. I felt sure that someone here must speak French or English, for whoever ran the shop had clearly been abroad.

As I opened the door a bell tinkled and a plump and prosperous man – clearly the owner – looked up and smiled. His name was Pierre Kaspo and he welcomed me in French. Would I like a cake, perhaps, or a glass of fresh juice? As I drank the juice he asked what I was doing in Hassake. I told him about Sir John and the church I was looking for – careful to call it the Assyrian, and not the Nestorian church for I'd read that the word Nestorian had long ago become pejorative and had been replaced by the term Assyrian.

Kaspo smiled as I told him of my quest for this church. His prosperity revealed itself in excess fat: the bags under his eyes drooped slightly, his cheeks sagged under the weight of gravity, and his double chin hung from his jaw like a bag filled with water. But Pierre Kaspo turned out to be a charming and generous man. He was also extremely helpful. Of course there was an Assyrian church in Hassake, he said. *Oui*, there would be a service tomorrow. *Certainment*, he would drive me there himself.

'*Revenez ici vers neuf heure*,' he said as he shook my hand. 'I will take you to this church. It will be my pleasure.'

I couldn't believe my luck. Tomorrow I would finally meet these Nestorians that Sir John had described all those centuries before.

I woke with a start: was that the sound of bells I could hear? I jumped out of bed, ran across to the window and threw open the curtain for a view across the town. I'd forgotten that my bedroom looked on to an unfinished concrete wall.

But I could hear bells – perhaps even now summoning the Nestorians to church. Were these the same bells that had once rang out over Tartary? The same that Sir John had once heard pealing throughout Persia and China? I threw on my clothes and ran to Kaspo's shop, but on arriving I found that he was in no hurry to move. 'First we must take tea,' he said, '*et puis* we must wait for my brother. Perhaps we shall even eat a few cakes? My cakes are the best in Hassake.'

While we waited for his brother, Kaspo told me of his life. He was not Syrian at all, but Armenian – a Christian refugee who had lived in Syria for many decades. He had been to Paris in his youth and had hoped to go to London but – he threw up his hands – he now had a wife and two children. How could he possibly go abroad? Anyway, business was good. He couldn't leave the shop.

I asked him more about the Assyrian church. Did anyone still call it the Nestorian church? He gave me a confused look. '*Nestorian* church?' he said. 'You're interested in the *Nestorian* church? I thought you wanted to see a Syrian Orthodox church.'

My heart sank. We had spent the whole of yesterday afternoon talking at cross purposes and my excitement over the Nestorians had all been for nothing. Kaspo must have noticed my disappointment for he grabbed my arm and chuckled. 'Don't worry, don't worry,' he said. 'If you want to meet a Nestorian, then you need go no further than my shop. 'Mustafa,' he called. 'There's someone to see you.'

Mustafa, a small, thin man with a bald head, appeared from the basement. He was dressed in jeans and a black polo-neck jumper and certainly didn't look like a descendant of one of the wildest tribes on earth. He shook my hand and I asked him, with Kaspo's help, if he was indeed a Nestorian. He gave me a quizzical look then nodded. 'Yes,' he said. 'I am a Nestorian . . . why?'

Mustafa was of Iraqi origin but had no idea from where his family originated. It was possible, he said, that he came from Kurdistan but it was all a long time ago and he was Syrian now and happy living in Hassake. He was a taciturn man who answered every question with either a yes or a no (usually it was no) and seemed bemused to learn that I had travelled thousands of miles to meet him.

Perhaps his reluctance to talk was the last vestige of that rebellious nature that had once been the hallmark of his tribe. For there was every likelihood that Mustafa was indeed descended from one of the families that – only a few generations ago – had left their mountain strongholds. In fact it was possible that it was his very forefathers that Sir John had met six centuries previously.

Kaspo interrupted our conversation. 'My brother's obviously not coming. Let's go and see Mustafa's Nestorian church. But I warn you now – don't get excited. The church is not at all interesting. There is no colour and no icons. You will find it very . . . very bland.'

The church was 15 minutes' drive from Kaspo's shop and stood right on the edge of town. To get there we drove through a building site, past unfinished houses and shops and eventually drew up outside a building with no roof and gaping holes where windows ought to have been.

'*Voila*,' said Kaspo. 'The Nestorian church.'

'But it's a building site,' I said.

'We use the underground crpyt,' explained Mustafa. 'A few years ago we decided to build a new church but we haven't got very far. No money.'

That much was apparent. It would be many years before this church, half-built from breeze blocks, would be ready for services. Mustafa opened the door to the crypt and we entered a long room filled with neat rows of chairs stretching from the front to the rear wall. The front row was taken up by four comfortable armchairs; the rest were made of moulded plastic. Three enormous chandeliers hung so low from the ceiling that they almost reached the ground, while the paint had become so loosened by damp that the floor was scattered with flakes. The altar was concealed from view not by an iconostasis but by a theatrical pair of red velvet curtains and when Kaspo pulled them open I half expected him to reveal a cinema screen. But there was only a plain altar and an unadorned crucifix. Nothing else cluttered the sanctuary and it was a far cry from the lavish descriptions Sir John gives of the Nestorian church. He speaks of gold crucifixes and grand buildings containing untold riches. This place looked like a committee room.

I asked Mustafa about the services; how, for example, would they be celebrating Christmas in a few weeks' time? He looked puzzled and muttered something in Arabic to Kaspo before turning back to me.

'We've had Christmas already,' he said. 'Christmas is 7 November.'

Now it was my turn to be puzzled. Even taking into account the change from the Gregorian to the Julian calendar, I couldn't understand how the Nestorians arrived at 7 November for Christmas day.

'What's wrong with 7 November?' said Mustafa defensively. 'It's an excellent day for Christmas. Who can accurately say when Christ was born? – 7 November is as good as any other.'

I asked him if there were many Nestorians left in Hassake. 'We are not so many,' he said. 'There are only about 2,000 of us left. We have one church and one priest. It is sad.'

We had arrived too late for the liturgy and the congregation had returned to their homes. I was annoyed but couldn't complain. Without Kaspo I would never have found this last fragment of a once great and ancient church. Here, in the remote north-eastern corner of Syria, the bells of the Nestorian church still ring out across the desert, as they did in the days when Sir John claimed to have travelled through the Holy Land.

I returned directly to Damascus from Hassake and was walking along the congested trunk road that winds around Damascus's medieval walls when two men stopped me in the street. It was always happening in Syria. People stopped me and tried to sell me things, or invited me into their shop, or to meet their uncle for tea. But these two had an altogether different approach.

'Excuse me,' they said. 'How can we help?'

I looked at them. Was this a trick? Were they going to open their bags and produce a carpet for me to buy?

'Forgive us,' they continued. 'You look like a gentlemen who needs help.'

As it happened I did. I was looking for the chapel from which St Paul had fled the Jews of Damascus. I had been told it was inside the city walls but couldn't find it anywhere. They pointed me in the right direction then one of the men said: 'You are Protestant. I, too, am Christian. I am Syrian Orthodox.'

I had been told that there were a few communities of Syrian Orthodox who still spoke Aramaic, the language of Christ, and asked him if this was true. He paused for a moment's thought. Until recently, he said, Aramaic was still in use. But now it had all but died out. A few elderly people might remember the language but the young didn't care about their traditions. No, he concluded, it was doubtful that I would find people who still spoke Aramaic.

His colleague muttered something in Arabic. 'Ah yes,' he said. 'It's true. There are a couple of villages in the hills above Damascus where it is said they still speak Aramaic. If you're interested, that is where you should go.'

I had been intending to visit these villages for they had aroused Sir John's curiosity as well. While his description of Damascus had been vague, his account of the hilltop village of Saidenaya – or Sardenake, as it was then called – was extremely detailed:

From Damascus men come past a place called Nostre Dame de Sardenake. It is on a rock. It is a beautiful and delightful place, somewhat resembling a castle – there was one there once. There is a fine church where live Christian monks and nuns. They have excellent wine there. In this church, behind the High Altar on the wall, is a wooden panel on which a portrait of Our Lady was once painted, which often became flesh; but that picture is now seen but little; nevertheless that panel constantly oozes oil, like olive oil; there is a marble vessel under the panel to catch it. They give some to pilgrims, for it heals many of their illnesses; and it is said that if it is kept well for seven years, it afterwards turns into flesh and blood.

I wondered if this icon would still be there. I doubted it for such a relic was unlikely to have survived six centuries of Muslim rule.

The road to Saidenaya weaves slowly upwards towards the Lebanese mountains, curving around gentle pink hills. There were seven of us in the Mercedes taxi and everyone stared out of the window in silence as the car struggled across moulded valleys and dry riverbeds. Soon the ground was dusted with light snow; collected by the wind, it lay across the stony ground in lace-thin folds. The driver gripped the wheel as he turned the last sharp corner in the road and a magnificent sight suddenly swung into view. Saidenaya – a fort-like monastery sat stacked high upon a chunk of rock, and behind it was the massive bulk of Jebel ech Sheikh, its rounded shoulders dolloped with snow.

The entrance to the monastery looked every year of its vast age. The massive stone lintel had slumped like molten cheese to little more than four feet above the ground and the shallow steps scooped out of the rock were worn down with the footsteps of nearly 20 centuries. The courtyard was reached through a dark passage that once served to keep out hostile Bedouin but inside the monastery all was bright and tidy with lovingly tended pots of geraniums betraying a feminine touch. Saidenaya is a nunnery, cared for by a handful of Greek Orthodox nuns.

The oldest chapel in the monastery stands in a corner of the

main courtyard. Inside it was almost completely dark, the only
light coming from three candles which sent a soft light dancing
over the silver censers. Gradually my eyes grew accustomed to
the gloom and a startling sight emerged. An ancient and
blackened iconostasis cut the tiny room in two, and from it hung
hundreds of templates of hands – all beaten from fine silver.

A young nun was tending the shrine and I asked in a whisper
what the hands were for.

'Many people come to this miraculous place,' she said in
broken English. 'Christians and Muslims alike come to pray for
their rheumatism to be cured. When these prayers are successful
they leave a silver imprint of their hand as a token of thanks. You
see, it has worked for many people.'

'And the icon by St Luke?' I asked. 'Is that still here.'

'Yes, yes,' she said. 'It is here, right here.' She pointed to a
thick panel of silver in the centre of the iconostasis. Though my
eyes had grown accustomed to the gloom I still couldn't see the
icon and asked her to point it out.

'You can't see it,' she said. 'It is kept hidden from view. No one
has set eyes on it for many hundreds of years.'

I remembered what Sir John had written: 'In this church,
behind the High Altar . . . is a wooden panel on which a portrait
of Our Lady was once painted . . . *but that picture is now seen but
little.*' Here it was still; still by the altar and seen by no one for
centuries.

This icon was once so famous that scores of legends sprung up
around it. The most persistent story is that it was the work of St
Luke; the first icon ever to be painted and the one which became
the theological justification for all others. Since St Luke lived at
the same time as the Virgin and must therefore have known what
she looked like, this icon – hidden away for centuries – is quite
probably the only accurate portrait of her. If only it could be
brought out for a moment; shown to the world for a few brief
seconds, we might finally know what Mary actually looked like.

The road from Saidenaya continues to wind uphill for seven or
eight miles towards the village of Maalula, famous for its
churches and clustered beneath an enormous rockface that

shelters it from the worst of the winter snows.

Nearly 90 per cent of Maalula's population is Christian and an enormous number of crucifixes and domes poke out from between the houses. At the top of the cliff, exposed and buffeted by gales, is St Serge which claims to be the oldest continuously working church in the world. It is a tiny building – a small dome propped up by four ancient pillars and built of stone the colour of old straw. As I entered the deserted courtyard a plumpish priest with a ruddy face and wispy beard came up to greet me.

'Father Michael,' he said with a friendly smile. 'How can I help?'

I explained how I'd become interested in a medieval pilgrim and was following his journey.

'Very fascinating,' he said. 'This is a subject I have been wanting to study for many years. It is sad that all the monks have left for I no longer have time to do much reading. But the eyes of the medieval pilgrims are the only way to understand this region.'

He asked me who else I had read and I told him about Ludolph von Suchem, Burchard and Felix Fabri. 'Now this is very fascinating indeed,' he said with great enthusiasm. 'You must write them down for me; the next time I go to Damascus I shall get them out of the library.'

He then led me inside the church, rapping his hand on the thick stone. 'This was here long before your knight,' he said. 'I am helping archaeologists to date the church for it seems to be one of the oldest in the world. Carbon dating from the wooden beams suggests it dates from the fourth century, but the altar is even older. Look . . . ' He led me to the altar which was carved from a single sheet of marble.

'Run your hand around the rim,' he said. 'Feel it carefully. Can you notice anything?'

The marble was smooth as glass and a rim ran right around the edge. 'Can you feel a hole?' he asked.

'No . . . nothing,' I said.

'Exactly . . . exactly. This is how we know it is a Christian and not a pagan altar. There is no drain for the blood yet the raised rim suggests it was modelled on the old pagan altars. Since the

Roman government banned pagan sacrifice when the empire converted to Christianity, it must date from the earliest days of the Byzantine empire. In fact, I've found documents showing that Maalula sent a bishop to the first ecumenical council in Nicea in AD325, so this church must have been serving a thriving community even then.'

When he had finished talking I asked if there were any people in the village who still spoke Aramaic.

'Oh, indeed there are,' he said. 'You know about Aramaic? It's an old Semitic dialect but it is only used by a few of the older people nowadays. It is a quite amazing survival – after all, several books of the Bible were written in Aramaic.'

With that he reached over and pressed the button on his ancient tape recorder, and a deep voice began reading the Lord's Prayer in Aramaic, a curious tongue which sounded like a blend of Arabic and Greek. This was the language Sir John would have heard, perhaps in this very church.

'And now,' said Father Michael with a devious smile, 'we must have a little wine. The wine here is excellent.'

I laughed and he asked me what was so amusing. Mandeville, I told him, had made exactly the same comment about the wine in these villages six centuries earlier.

'Well he knew what he was talking about,' said Father Michael as he poured the thick liquid into a tiny silver glass. We both drained the wine in a single gulp: it was sweet and heavy with the taste of over-ripe plums.

I would have liked more, but the cork was already back in the bottle.

7 A Medieval Chronicle

There are no Books which I more delight in than in Travels, especially those that describe remote Countries and give the Writer an Opportunity of showing his Parts without incurring any Danger of being examined or contradicted. Among the authors of this Kind, our renowned Countryman Sir John Mandeville has distinguished himself by the Copiousness of his Invention and Greatness of his Genius.

Tatler, No 254, **23 November, 1710**

Piecing together Mandeville's life became increasingly complicated, for the more fragments of evidence I unearthed, the more I found them to be either forgeries or fabrications. It was as if Mandeville's detractors had deliberately scattered my path with misleading clues in the hope that I would stumble, fall, or lose my way.

This was not the only problem; it was still extremely difficult to work out when Sir John himself was telling the truth and how much he had hammed up the role of knightly narrator. For all I knew, he could have invented not only his voyage but the story of his life as well. But if archaeologists can unravel the lifestyle of palaeolithic man from a couple of teeth and the odd jawbone I felt sure I could learn something about Sir John from the 61 leaves of vellum and the handful of documents that have survived the centuries.

Every once in a while I would stumble across a new chronicle or manuscript that would open up new avenues and different possibilities. Often I found such documents by chance – in the footnote or index of some esoteric tome – and although these snippets didn't in themselves tell me a great deal, I was able to slot them one by one into the framework of Sir John's life. A picture slowly began to emerge – a picture that bore a remarkable similarity to the one that he himself had presented.

One such piece of evidence was buried in a huge folio written by Samuel Purchas and published in 1625. Called *Purchas his Pilgrimes* it was an encyclopedic catalogue of all Britain's great explorers and included a lengthy entry about Mandeville. It told me many things I already knew about Sir John and several things I didn't. It repeated the mistake of his burial in Liège but this was hardly surprising for Jean d'Outremeuse's trick was widely believed to be true in the seventeenth century. It also claimed that Sir John was a physician but this, too, was a result of Outremeuse's fabrications.

Far more exciting was its claim to record a speech that Sir John had made in his lifetime. Purchas says that before he died, Mandeville had told people that, 'Vertue is gone, the Church is under foot, the Clergie is in error, the Devill raineth, and Simonie beareth the sway.'

Had Sir John made such a speech or was it another fiction? It was impossible to verify but it told me that by the seventeenth century people were beginning to recognize that the anti-papal sentiments scattered throughout *The Travels* had helped spread across Europe the mentality that paved the way for the Reformation. Long after Purchas's book was forgotten, writers and antiquarians were still quoting this speech in their accounts, and Mandeville's criticisms of the Pope came to be seen as more and more important.

Yet he was not as critical as many have suggested, perhaps because he was fearful of being excommunicated. Had Mandeville really wanted to launch an attack on the Pope he could have found plenty of ammunition for Clement VI was one of the most outrageous and extravagant popes ever to occupy the papal throne. On his election, he was said to have uttered the words, 'My predecessors did not know how to be popes'.

Within a few months his court had become the most magnificent social centre in Europe – a place to rub shoulders with kings and princes, warlords and aristocrats. Clement believed that Christendom should be a feudal pyramid with the Pope at its head. Kings were vassals of the Pope and the tribute they paid was the expression of their loyalty.

And so the courtly life began. A huge window was added to the chapel in Avignon through which Clement could bless the adoring crowd below, and church feasts – which under John XXII and Benedict XII had been subdued affairs – were now celebrated in the most extravagant manner possible. Merchants flocked to the court and the papal cellars were soon filled with fine Beaune wines, silks from Damascus, *objets d'art* from Paris, spices from India and gold from the Baltic. One visitor – a member of an Italian cardinal's entourage – rubbed his eyes in amazement:

> The meal consisted of nine courses, each having three dishes. We saw brought in, among other things, a sort of castle containing a huge stag, a boar, kids, hares and rabbits . . . after the fifth course they brought in a fountain surmounted by a tree and pillar flowing with five types of wine. The margins of the fountain were decked with peacocks, pheasants, partridges, cranes and other birds. In the interval between the seventh and eighth courses there was a tournament, which took place in the banqueting hall itself . . . The day was brought to an end with singing, tournaments, dancing and, as a climax, a farce which the pope and cardinals found highly diverting.

Such a lifestyle was not without its critics and stories abounded of dancing girls and tawdry affairs, at the centre of which was the figure of the Pope. Yet despite his love of the good things in life, Clement was a consummate diplomat who genuinely cared for his subjects. During the disastrous plague of 1347-8 he did everything in his power to alleviate the suffering and even took the remarkable step of condemning Jew-baiters. This, together with his political experience and natural charm mark him as one of the most talented men of his time.

Although Clement's luxurious living proved to be ruinously expensive, the highly organized system of taxation that he devised soon enabled him to recoup the money. But such taxes were deeply unpopular, especially in England where many people suspected the money to be going to support the French armies in their war against England. Such a charge was not without foundation: after all, Clement VI had been the French king's chancellor before he became Pope.

Some Victorian scholars, not content with taking Mandeville's sidewipes at the Pope at face value, developed the idea that *The Travels* was nothing short of anti-papacy propaganda and came up with ever more startling theories to support their claims. Some went so far as to suggest that the alphabets which Sir John scattered throughout his book were in fact a series of secret codes containing anti-papal messages. Their evidence was hinged on the dubious notion that the Greek alphabet doesn't look much like Greek:

The Arabic looks very little like Arabic:

While the Chaldean looks like little more than a set of meaningless squiggles:

This, they concluded, could only mean one thing: Mandeville was using his book to spread discord throughout the monasteries of Europe.

But there are strong objections to such a theory. If the alphabets really were a code then there would surely be other documents in existence written in this same code? If so, not a single one has survived. More troubling is the fact that the alphabets proved so popular with scribes that every time a manuscript was copied these scribes took it upon themselves to invent a whole range of new alphabets. Less than a century after Sir John's death there were copies of *The Travels* containing dozens of such inventions, including a bizarre language called Pentexiore as well as an entire alphabet said to be known only to the chief of the Ismailites.

Could these be new codes containing new anti-papal conspiracies? Most unlikely, for each time these different alphabets were copied they were further distorted so that any opponent of the papacy would have been left scratching his head and wondering what on earth they might mean.

Far more likely than any conspiracy theory is that Sir John included the alphabets to increase the sense of wonder and mystery that surrounds his voyage. He himself admits that he was fascinated by foreign languages and says he has recorded them so that, 'you may know the difference between these letters and the letters of other languages'. And while his book is indeed critical of the papacy and the corruption in the Church, there is not a scrap of evidence to show that he wished to see the Pope overthrown. Such a theory, in fact, suggested that the Victorian critics had misread the book and, in doing so, had failed to solve the riddle at its heart.

Samuel Purchas is Mandeville's last heavyweight champion: while he draws the line at believing the tales of monsters and giants, he defends the rest of Sir John's book and even argues that unscrupulous scribes had added all the more outrageous stories. Purchas also dismisses Mandeville's claim to have returned to England after his voyage, believing Jean d'Outremeuse's story that he had settled in Liège and almost certainly died there. But there were still a handful of writers in the seventeenth century who believed that Sir John really had died in St Albans – and some had evidence to prove it.

One such author – an antiquarian named John Weever – wrote a book in 1631 cataloguing every one of Britain's thousands of funeral monuments, and although exhaustively dull it held out the promise of accurate information about Mandeville's tomb in its page upon page of burial inscriptions.

After flicking through hundreds of pages I finally came to St Albans and, had John Weever been standing beside me, I would have shaken him by the hand for he provided me with the first concrete evidence to suggest that Sir John was telling the truth about his return to the town:

> This Towne vaunts her selfe very much of the birth and buriall of Sir *Iohn Mandevill* Knight, the famous Travailer, who writ in Latine, French, and in the English tongue, his Itinerary of three and thirty yeares. And that you may beleeve the report of the Inhabitants to bee true, they have lately pensild a rare piece of Poetry, or an Epitaph for him, upon a piller; neere to which, they suppose his body to have beene buried . . .

By the time Weever came here – some 250 years after Sir John's death – the good folk of St Albans were clearly no longer certain as to whether or not Mandeville had been buried in their abbey. But they were happy enough to accept the local tradition, and sufficiently sure his bones lay under its flagstone floor to inscribe an epitaph commemorating his life and his travels. This epitaph was an earlier version of the one I had seen in the abbey and it contained an additional (and significant) four lines:

> As the Knights in the Temple, crosse-legged in marble,
> In armour, with sword and with sheeld,
> So was this Knight grac't, which time hath defac't,
> That nothing but ruines doth yeeld.

These lines, then, make the claim that the abbey had once contained a marble effigy of Sir John: an effigy that had been destroyed by the passing of the centuries. I soon discovered that Weever was not the only person to have believed in such a story. Several other accounts supported his claim about an effigy of

Mandeville and one, dated 1598, even described it as standing directly over Sir John's tomb.

While such records were interesting they had one major flaw: all were written nearly three centuries after Sir John had gone on his supposed travels. If only I could find something – some tiny scrap of evidence – that had been written during Mandeville's lifetime.

And then, working late one evening in the British Library, I stumbled across an account of him that took me far back into the past. I had spent the entire day searching through journals, antiquaries and calendar rolls – anything, in fact, that contained a reference to Sir John – but all to no avail. I picked up the last volume on my desk, a monastic chronicle which was for the most part a daily record of local happenings in the 1390s. But it also commented on local men who had achieved things of note, and on one of the pages there was a fascinating entry, the significance of which even my schoolboy Latin could detect:

Eodem anno, Johannes de Mandavilla, miles Anglicus, in villa Sancti Albani oriundus, postquam in 36 annis per universum fere orbem pertransisset . . . scripsit de omnibus mirabilibus orbis, quae in ipsa peregrinatione 36 annorum cognoverat, volumen unum, et ipsum dicto Edwardo regi Angliae destinavit.

It spoke of Sir John Mandeville and more importantly it was written just a few years after his death. It recorded his travels, and although it didn't say he died in St Albans, it confirmed that he was born in the town. But there was something distinctly odd about this entry. For it was contained in a chronicle from Meaux Abbey – an account of local events in a few square miles of Yorkshire. Why on earth would a remote abbey, far from St Albans, have had any interest in Sir John Mandeville?

The answer lay in the identity of the author who was linked directly to Sir John through a chain of related people. The chronicler's name was Thomas de Burton who had been made abbot of Meaux on the orders of his overlord the Duke of Gloucester. Gloucester had married into the de Bohun family and inherited the family estates when the elderly Humphrey de

Bohun died. These estates were not the only thing that came into his possession: the old man's will clearly states that he was leaving his copy of Mandeville's *Travels* to Gloucester as well.

The link between all these people proved everything and nothing. The chronicler was a friend of the Duke of Gloucester. Gloucester had inherited *The Travels* from the de Bohuns. And the de Bohuns were the Mandeville's overlords. Since the chronicler was writing just a few years after Mandeville's death he – if anyone – would have been in a position to find out the truth about Sir John.

There was even more conclusive evidence to suggest that Mandeville had been telling the truth about himself. Bound together with a different set of archives I found a little document under the title *De Fundatione et Meritis Monasterii Sancti Albani*. It was written by the chronicler Thomas Walsingham and dated from the 1370s:

> Sir Iohannes de Mandevile, Knight, wanderer over almost the whole earth, and tested in many wars against the adversaries of our faith, but never once worn out, he composed a book in French about the things he had seen. He was brought forth from his mother's womb in the town of St Albans.

Since Sir John didn't return home until 1356 – perhaps less than 14 years before this was written – the case for believing his own version of events increases dramatically. For these were two independent witnesses – both of whom were alive during Sir John's lifetime and one of whom even lived in St Albans – concurring with everything Mandeville himself had written about the place of his birth.

8 Jerusalem

Mandeville wrote a book of his own Itinerary through Africa, the east and north part of Asia, containing a variety of wonders. Now though far travellers are suspected in their relations to wander from the truth, yet all things improbable are not impossible; and the reader's ignorance is sometimes all the writer's falsehood.

The History of the Worthies of England **vol 2,**
Dr Thomas Fuller, 1840

Cyril wasn't sure how many languages he spoke. Russian, of course, was his mother tongue so that didn't really count. French didn't count either, for he had learnt that from his parents. Obviously he spoke Hebrew, and was fluent in Arabic as well. That made four. Then there was English, German, Italian and Spanish. These he brushed aside as though they didn't even count as languages. Latin and Greek he used for his work. Oh yes, he could read Syriac and Aramaic, the languages I had heard in Syria. He paused and scratched his head for a moment – did he speak Amharic? No . . . that was one he would like to learn. By the time he had finished I had long run out of fingers.

'Well . . . how many have you got?'

'Twelve.'

'Twelve,' he repeated uncertainly, 'Hmm, I think there might be one more . . . '

I had telephoned Cyril the day I arrived in Jerusalem. He was the brother of a friend in Paris and as soon as I explained who I was he invited me to stay. He had a spare room; I was welcome for long as I wanted; it was important that I make myself feel at home.

Cyril had converted to Judaism when in his early teens although he explained that it was not so much a conversion as a return to his roots since one side of his family – centuries before – had been Jews living in the former Soviet Union. Soon after he had adopted the faith of his forefathers he left France and set up home in Israel. He had a job at the Hebrew University and had just been granted Israeli nationality. He hoped to stay for good.

His mastery of languages was a great help to me for he translated numerous passages of complicated medieval Latin and Greek that I had brought from England. As we watched American soaps on television, Cyril would calmly render esoteric inscriptions into perfect English, a scene which went something like this:

'*Cumque a mystagogo rogassem* . . . hmm.'

Screech of breaks, blast of the horn, and a loud smash.

' . . . *quid miraculi esset* . . . ahah.'

Three shots and a man falls to the ground.

' . . . *respondebar, obla* . . . '

'You bastard son-of-a-bitch. I'll get you for this.'

' . . . *latum illud olim* . . . '

A huge explosion and all three cars disappear in a fireball.

At this Cyril would look at the screen, clap his hands, then turn to me and ask how you would say *cantiorum* in English. Only when it came to closedown did he stop his translations for he was a great fan of national anthems. No sooner had the Israeli anthem been sung than he would switch over to Syrian television for their anthem – a martial number played by the sort of old-fashioned brass band you might find in Eastbourne. When that was over, he would switch channels again in order to catch the Jordanian closedown. And then it was back to Syria's Channel Two for an even more rousing second anthem sung by schoolgirls dressed in military uniform.

He lived on one of the hilltops that ring Jerusalem and from his flat there was a superb view across the roof of the Hyatt Regency hotel towards the lozenge-shaped old city. A noisy dual carriageway, the main road to Ramallah, swooped down from his flat towards the congested junction near Damascus Gate. But although the gleaming roof of the Dome of the Rock was clearly visible from up here, you had to look hard to see the great walls of the medieval city for – as with Damascus – they have been dwarfed by new buildings in recent years and the ancient hotchpotch of souks, churches and mosques are slowly being strangled by the settlements that ring old Jerusalem. Nowadays the obvious landmarks are all recent ones: in the west, the Sheraton Jerusalem Plaza Hotel rears its façade into the sky. In the east the Hebrew University is sprawled across a hilltop, while the Mormons have recently built a university on the northern hills – a vast building occupying the most enviable site in Jerusalem.

I tried to make out the Church of the Holy Sepulchre but it was lost among the rooftops of the old city; only in the newer parts of town do the churches still stand out from the more recent developments. The huge domes of the Russian Cathedral are visible for miles, as is the brick tower of the YMCA.

As we stood with Jerusalem spread out before us like an Oriental carpet, Cyril gave me a word of warning: 'All the tourists who come to Jerusalem visit the old city,' he said. 'What they don't realize is that the old city has little to do with modern life in Jerusalem. If you want to understand Jerusalem, you should spend some time in the new town for that's where you'll find the Christians who have influence these days.'

He handed me a map and suggested I pay a call on the Baptists at some point during my stay. 'It might be easier to solve your knight's riddle if you think laterally,' he said. 'Imagine who Mandeville would have wanted to meet if he was arriving in Jerusalem today . . . and imagine what he might have written about them.'

Father Baratto sat back in his creaking wooden chair and inhaled deeply on an unlit cigarette. 'So you've come to Jerusalem on the trail of Sir John Mandeville,' he mused.

'Have you heard of him?'

'Let me see now . . . John Mandeville . . . John Mandeville . . . John Mandeville . . . ' He blew out an imaginary stream of smoke, scratched his head, then rested his cigarette in the ash-tray. 'The funny thing is, I *have* heard of Sir John Mandeville. You see I used to work for the Franciscan printing press and spent many years publishing accounts of Jerusalem written by med-ieval pilgrims. So I have indeed come across your knight Mandeville.'

I had telephoned Father Baratto some days earlier and

arranged to meet him at his office in the Christian Information Centre – a voluntary organization which offers advice to visiting pilgrims. Several people I'd met suggested I pay him a visit, telling me that if anyone in the city would know about Sir John it would be Father Baratto.

With his bald pate, glasses and enigmatic smile he bore a striking resemblance to the Dalai Lama. But when he spoke it was the voice of a schoolmaster that addressed me, and our conversation settled into a question and answer routine until Baratto knew what he wanted.

'Remind me,' he said, 'where he was from.'

'St Albans.'

'Good. Good. Did he die in Jerusalem?'

'No, St Albans.'

'Does he say where he stayed when he came here?'

'No.'

'No? A pity. A *big* pity,' he said as he settled back in his arm-chair.

While he pondered over what I had told him, I examined the collection of executive toys on his desk. They included a metal horse perched on a balance and a brainteaser cube which had been fiddled with then left unresolved. They seemed singularly inappropriate for a monk and I wondered if they had been presents from some distant nephew in Italy.

'Am I right in thinking he left England in 1322?' asked Father Baratto suddenly, knocking the desk with his leg and sending the horse into a gallop.

'Exactly,' I said. 'At least that's what he claims.'

'Yes, yes, yes,' he continued, 'you see this is very interesting for I *think* . . . yes, I *think* the Franciscans were already living in the city by that time. And if Sir John really did come to Jerusalem then he would almost certainly have been looked after by Franciscans. One of their most important roles, after all, was to look after the welfare of western pilgrims.'

This much I knew, for I had read about the Franciscans in accounts written by chroniclers in the later Middle Ages. On landing at the port of Jaffa the dazed and exhausted pilgrims were greeted with the familiar sight of Franciscan monks who welcomed them to the Holy Land and accompanied them on the cross-country hike to Jerusalem. These Franciscans remained with them at all times, guiding them around the holy sites and giving them board and lodging. They handed out instructions on how to behave in front of Muslims and warned against carving their names into monuments or taking statues home as souvenirs.

The pilgrims were also protected by Mameluke guards, but such guards offered little protection against the bands of jeering Muslims who hurled stones at them and tried to push them off their donkeys. Some pilgrims record how locals even tried to snatch their clothes as their long train wound its way slowly inland to Jerusalem.

Father Baratto cleared his throat noisily and shuffled over to the bookshelves. 'Now . . . ' he said, 'let me have a look . . . '

While he sorted through his books I looked out of the small square window. His room overlooked Jaffa Gate, one of the eight surviving gateways that lead into the old city. Although it was chilly and dark inside his room, the outside world was passing by in a glare of warm spring sunlight. Taxis blared their horns as they careered through the gate; a group of pilgrims (all in orange tracksuits and matching baseball caps) chatted excitedly amongst themselves; and a young man dressed as Jesus rested his crucifix for a moment, wiped his brow and picked his nose. If Sir John had arrived in the Holy Land by sea, he would almost certainly have entered the city through Jaffa Gate.

Baratto took a book down from the shelf and brought it back to his desk. 'I can't promise to help but I think we should look into the Franciscans' presence here. You see the 1320s were not an easy time for a westerner to visit Jerusalem and Mandeville is much more likely to have stayed if they were already established in the city. What we need to find out is when, exactly, they set themselves up in the Holy Land.'

He lit his Gauloise cigarette for a third time but still it didn't catch. Without thinking he placed it in the ashtray and carried on looking through the book. Outside the pilgrims were ready to begin their tour. The group leader attached an orange flag to a stick, gathered them around him, and led them into the alleys of the old city where they were swallowed up by the stone. Jesus, too, was moving on. He adjusted his tunic, spat out his rollie, and picked up his cross once more.

'Ah,' said Father Baratto at long last. 'Here we go . . . this is what we need.' He cleared his throat and read a passage from the book: '"On August 9th 1328, a bull from Pope John XXII granted permission to the Provincial Minister, then resident in Cyprus, to send two of his friars to the holy places every year . . . in doing this, the Pope was formalising a phenomenon which, in reality, was far more widespread than would or could be declared in official documents."'

He skipped a few passages, murmured something to himself, then began reading again in a louder voice. 'Ah, this is it . . . ' he said. 'Listen to this. "There is historical evidence that proves the presence of Franciscans at the Holy Sepulchre during the period 1322 to 1327."'

He put down the book and smiled. 'Just as I thought. The Franciscans *were* here at that time. That's important evidence in Sir John's favour,' he said, 'and we might find more clues if we look at their history.'

In fact, the Franciscans had taken the decision to settle in the Holy Land more than a century before Sir John arrived, and Father Baratto had soon unearthed sheaths of information about how his spiritual forefathers had first come to Jerusalem.

'At their General Chapter meeting in 1217, the Franciscans took a momentous decision,' he told me. 'Instead of being centred in Assisi, they decided that from that point on they would attempt to extend the testimony of their way of life to the entire world. This was not some woolly notion or impossible ideal. St Francis himself pondered over how to achieve it. Sitting down with a map in front of him, he divided the world into Franciscan Provinces and directed his followers to travel to the four corners of the globe.'

One of these areas became the Province of the Holy Land and, as the land where Christ was born and died, was considered to be the most important of all. St Francis himself came here in 1220, settled some of his friars, and determined that they would remain against all the odds.

Father Baratto stopped for a second and looked up at me. 'Are you still following me?' he asked. I nodded, worried that he might put me in detention.

'Good, because now we must get down to the details and I suggest you take some notes. In 1291, Acre – the last town still in the hands of the Crusaders – fell to the Muslim forces and the Franciscans were kicked out of the country. But not for long. Remember, these were determined men who would give up their lives to return to Jerusalem. Within a few years they had settled here permanently and Robert of Anjou, ruler of Naples, bought from the Sultan the buildings on Mount Sion as well as securing the right to perpetual occupation in the Holy Sepulchre. From that point on the Franciscans really did have a foothold in the city and, well, they have been here ever since.'

Father Baratto, then, was a continuation of this tradition: he formed an unbroken link back to the monks who had made Jerusalem their home in Sir John's day and he, like his forefathers, still helped visiting pilgrims and still looked after the holy places. Apart from the spectacles, Baratto – his cassock tied around his waist with rope – was even wearing exactly the same garments as the monks that St Francis sent to settle here.

'So there you have it,' he said with a smile. 'It's certainly *possible* that Sir John could have visited the city at the time he says he did. And the fact that there were monks living here at that time greatly increases the likelihood that he really did come.'

But when I asked him the chances of finding any definite evidence in Mandeville's favour his smile turned to a frown.

'That won't be so easy,' he said. 'You could spend years in libraries sifting through old documents and never find a thing. Personally I would be extremely surprised if Sir John *didn't* come. Many pilgrims visited Jerusalem at that time and when I worked for the Franciscan printing press I was involved in publishing their accounts of their trips. If you want my advice I'd read what they had to say. In particular, look at a book by a man named Simon Fitzsimmons. He left England in the very same year as Sir John. They went to the same places at the same time – why, they might even have met each other.'

I scribbled down the name as he continued talking. 'And another piece of advice. Follow the Franciscan prayer tour along the Via Dolorosa. Sir John might have done that as well, for monks have been leading pilgrims around the holy places since the very beginning of their time here.'

In Sir John's day, Jerusalem was still contained within its huge fortified walls which had been constructed by the crusaders some two centuries earlier. The Pope himself had instigated the crusades, and when the massed expedition finally accomplished its goal and wrested Jerusalem from the infidel, the knights and foot soldiers from Europe brutally slaughtered all the occupants of the city.

By the time Mandeville came to write *The Travels*, the tables had turned. The western knights had themselves been evicted from Jerusalem by Muslim forces in 1244 and the city was now ruled by a new force – the Mamelukes of Egypt – who held Jerusalem until the sixteenth century. Although there was continued talk of another crusade in Mandeville's lifetime it was a forlorn dream for the Mamelukes had built their land into a powerful empire; when envoys of King Philip VI of France travelled to Cairo to demand the return of Jerusalem, the Egyptian Sultan contemptuously dismissed them from his court.

The Mamelukes had a passion for building and left their legacy in stone. They had already spent a fortune beautifying Damascus; now they turned their attentions to Jerusalem, constructing palaces, mosques, universities and public baths. For all their brutality on the battlefield, the surviving Mameluke buildings bear none of the hallmarks of ruthless oppressors. Instead of citadels and fortifications, they lavished money on the façades of their pleasure palaces, and the decorative interplay of pattern and texture suggests an instinctive appreciation of aesthetics and beauty. The Madrassa al-Tankiziyya is adorned with a striking pattern of black and white mosaics while the tomb of Turkan Khatun is built of pink and cream masonry. There used to be many more Mameluke buildings in the old city: sadly, many were bulldozed to make way for the huge precinct in front of the Wailing Wall.

Little is known of Jerusalem during this time for the city entered one of the few peaceful periods in its history. It seems to have been governed by officials banished from the hierachy in Cairo and these officials often found themselves arguing with European rulers about the city's churches and shrines: successive governors used their possession of these holy places as a bargaining chip when dealing with foreign powers.

There must have been a considerable native Christian population living in the city but few travellers mention it. Surviving records in Cairo, however, reveal that these Christians suffered from regular bouts of persecution – both from the local Muslims and from the Mameluke officials. They were forced to wear blue turbans, forbidden to ride horses or mules, and were not even allowed to raise their voices in public. When the pilgrim Ludoph von Suchem came to Jerusalem in the first half of the fourteenth century he watched a small force of local Greeks break their way into the Muslim shrine and trample on the religious texts. All were hacked to pieces by the soldiers guarding the building.

After leaving Father Baratto I wandered through the old town with a growing sense of detachment. These narrow alleys – now lined with souvenir shops selling religious tat – were the birthplace of Christianity, yet the more I became familiar with their stones and their walls, the stronger that detachment became. As I passed churches and patriarchates, met Coptic monks and Ethiopian priests, I found myself wondering where in the world I was. Only in the Arab quarter of Jerusalem is there any sense of being in the Middle East; the narrow street of Tariq Al-Shaykh Rihan is cluttered with stalls selling worry beads and headscarves; veiled women haggle in Arabic and the souks are packed with people, donkeys, mopeds and bands of children in tatty clothes. Turn into Harat al-Yahud, the beginning of the Jewish quarter, and the scene switches to the SoHo district in New York. The pavement cafés and bars are filled with Americans eating falafel and drinking Coke and the girls – all beautiful – are dressed in jeans and skin-tight tops. Even the streets are beautifully kept and many of the buildings bear signs recording that they were restored by wealthy American Jews. The Christian quarter is different again; packed with busloads of pilgrims – mostly from western Europe – its churches and priests seemed both familiar and utterly foreign.

The Franciscan prayer tour recommended by Father Baratto is held every Friday at three o'clock. Starting at the first station of the cross, where Jesus was tried, the tour visits each of the 14 stations and ends in the Church of the Holy Sepulchre, the traditional site of Christ's crucifixion, burial and resurrection.

We were a curious group gathered at the Chapel of the Flagellation and included among our number:

- a party of Slovakians accompanied by their own Franciscan
  monk
- a blue-rinse lady from Surbiton
- five elderly couples (Danish, German, Italian)
- four Australian backpackers
- two devout believers
- two devout atheists
- some curious
- one mad

By the time we had been joined in the shaded courtyard by the group of straggling Slovakian pilgrims there were several dozen people signed up for the tour.

I had expected us to be led by one monk who would give a short reading at each station. I couldn't have been more wrong. There were 27 Franciscans leading the procession, with four principal monks giving the readings in Latin, Italian, English and Slovakian. This was not all. The lead monk – the one reading in Latin – carried on his shoulder a portable microphone and amplifier so we could all hear clearly. He had no need to test it for loudness for the shrill screech of feedback had us all clapping our hands over our ears.

The readings began at the second station, the Church of the Condemnation where Christ was found guilty and carried away to be flogged. The monk began in Latin and Italian, and then there was a moment's pause as the microphone was handed along a line of cassocks before being given to a Filipino at the far end. He read in a thick southern American drawl: 'Here J*eeeeesus* was condemned . . . '

Just at that moment the *muezzin* from the mosque opposite began the evening call to prayer and the wail of 'Allllllllaaaaaaaah Akbaaaar – God is great' drowned out our prayers. For the second time, everyone clapped their hands over their ears and a few people allowed themselves an ironic chuckle. There was a moment's break in the Arabic and the Filipino began again. But no sooner had he started than he was once more interrupted by the Muslim *muezzin*. This time he struggled on bravely before passing the microphone back down the line.

The second station over, we moved on slowly up the Via Dolorosa with the lead monks chanting *Dominus, Filius et Spiritu Sancto*, as we went. The Via Dolorosa is the route walked by Christ on His way to the crucifixion and I had memories of it from pictures in my childhood Bible. On one page, smiling faces carpeted Jesus's path with palm branches. On the next, they jeered at Him as He fell.

Quite probably the street hasn't changed much in the last 2,000 years. It still weaves its way uphill through the old town and although the shops that line the street these days specialize in gaudy madonnas and flashing plastic crucifixes, the flagstones themselves date back to the time of Christ.

I felt a tap on my shoulder and looked round. There was the Filipino with a beaming smile on his face.

'Hi,' he said as he pressed his plump hand into mine. 'I'm Father Angelo. What brings *you* here.'

I looked at him. Did he know me? Some months earlier I'd been on holiday in Assisi – perhaps I had spoken to him there? But no, he was simply being friendly.

'And you must be Anglican,' he said. '*Woooow*. That's m*aaa*rvellous. You must have a chat with me after; will you have a chat?' Before I could answer he ran off to join the other monks at the head of the procession. We had reached the third station of the cross.

Although a Good Friday procession to the Church of the Holy Sepulchre has taken place since the fifth century, the stations of the cross are an invention of the west. It was the crusaders who established the Via Dolorosa and by Sir John's day it had become a fixed route followed by virtually all western pilgrims who visited the city. This had been made possible by a number of miraculous discoveries: diligent medieval researchers located Pontius Pilate's palace which gave a starting point to the Via Dolorosa, and it wasn't long before they had unearthed other stations of the cross as well: the fourth, for example, where Jesus faced His mother, and the seventh where He fell for a second time. The trend to visit such places was fuelled by Europe's spiralling spiritual crisis. Churches increasingly stressed the importance of reflecting on the sufferings of Christ, and there was no better way to do this than actually to pray at the place of His death.

As we followed this well-worn path the monks chanted and the devout prayed. We had begun our tour as any other tourist group: everyone was chatting, exchanging news, asking who had seen what. Shopkeepers stared at us as we passed. Some laughed. Some tried to sell us their wares. Small boys pushed past and women knocked us with their shopping. I, like most, had signed up for the tour with considerable scepticism but as we weaved our way through the narrow streets of Jerusalem I became aware that something had begun to change in our group. Despite the commotion and the noise around us, we moved quietly along our slow, inevitable path – a path worn smooth by centuries of pilgrims – and as we did so we became our own little community, cut off from the bustle just inches from our faces. Slowly, imperceptibly, a hushed silence had descended.

Others had also joined our tour and there were now several dozen of us, all following the robed Franciscans in silence. We reached the ninth station, the prayers were read, then we turned the last right-angle twist in the route. And there before us stood the huge Church of the Holy Sepulchre. We had arrived at the very centre of Christendom; the spiritual and geographical heart of the Christian faith.

Medieval pilgrims called it the centre of the world.

Wajeeh Yacob Nuseibeh was waiting for me at the entrance. He was wearing a well-cut suit and his neatly clipped moustache gave him the look of a retired RAF pilot. I held out my hand and he shook it firmly. 'You're four minutes late,' he reprimanded. I apologized and he acknowledged me with a nod.

'Now,' he said. 'You better sit down because I have a lot to tell you.'

Wajeeh is the custodian and doorkeeper of the Church of the Holy Sepulchre and it is his job to unlock the church doors every morning and lock them again at night. I'd heard about him from Father Baratto and had already tried to meet him unsuccessfully several times, for I'd been told that his father, grandfather, and great grandfather – and all his forefathers right back to the year AD1187, and possibly much earlier – had performed the same role as Wajeeh. A direct ancestor of his would have opened the door of the church for Sir John Mandeville.

This in itself was remarkable, but the strangest fact about Wajeeh's family is that they have always been Muslim. What I wanted to know, and what Wajeeh was only too keen to tell me, was how a Muslim had come to be in charge of the holiest church in the world.

'When Caliph Omar seized Jerusalem from the Byzantine army in AD638,' began Wajeeh, 'a member of my family entered the city with him. His name was Abdullah, and he came from what is now Saudi Arabia. Abdullah's family . . . my family . . . must have been a distinguished one even in those days for it was they who received the Prophet Mohammed when he fled from Mecca to Medina.'

He paused for a moment as two Orthodox monks passed. They bowed towards him and he respectfully acknowledged their deference.

'As soon as Omar and Abdullah had entered Jerusalem, the city's Patriarch – a man named Sophronius – offered to the Caliph the keys to the Holy Sepulchre, a symbolic gesture. The Caliph accepted them and is said to have handed them to Abdullah for safe-keeping.'

I already knew a little about the remarkable Caliph Omar. Unkempt and unwashed, his small band of highly disciplined followers laid siege to Jerusalem and had slowly strangled the city, cutting its supply lines in time-honoured fashion until its exhausted population were forced to capitulate. After entering the city the victorious Omar, riding a white camel, went straight to pray at the Temple of Solomon. Next, he asked to be taken to the Church of the Holy Sepulchre but as he toured the building the hour for Muslim prayer arrived. Sophronius invited him to pray in the church but Omar refused, predicting that if he prayed there his troops would insist the building was turned into a mosque. And if this happened, he would be forced to break the command of his prophet Mohammed – that conquered Christians should be allowed the right to retain their places of worship. And so the Christians kept their church and for the next four centuries Wajeeh's family lived in Jerusalem and, according to legend, remained in possession of the keys to the Holy Sepulchre.

'Our problems began in 1099 when the crusaders stormed the city,' said Wajeeh. 'Many of my family were slaughtered in the bloodshed that followed. But a few managed to escape to a village near Nablus and sit out the next 150 years while the crusaders held the city. We still have family tombs in Nablus – I've visited them myself.'

The crusader period almost spelled the end for Wajeeh's family as it did for many Muslims. But they somehow managed to survive and when the great Islamic warrior Saladin defeated the crusaders and entered the city in 1187, Wajeeh's ancestors were once again at his side.

Saladin smashed the bells of the church, took down the cross and expelled the Latins. For a short time the church was locked, but documents record that when the doors were re-opened, it was Wajeeh's ancestors who performed the honour.

For many pilgrims, entering the church during the Middle Ages was expensive: not only was there a special tax imposed on foreign Christians but many of the doorkeepers were unscrupulous characters who thought nothing of abusing their position by extorting vast sums of gold from the pilgrims. Some believed such a rip-off to be penance for past sins and, when the Franciscan monk Antonio de Reboldis came here in 1331, he recorded his satisfaction at spending the last of his money to enter the church: 'Blessed indeed, those seven florins that I gave. O how much sweetness from those florins.'

Once they had negotiated themselves passed the doorkeepers, pilgrims often spent several days inside the church while the courtyard outside – where I was now sitting – would be packed with merchants selling foodstuffs to be eaten within the Holy Sepulchre.

Wajeeh stopped talking and brushed his moustache. Two Franciscans came up and shook his hand. A Coptic priest bowed deeply. He appeared to enjoy the respect he was shown, yet despite a thousand years of deference he acknowledged their greetings with a gracious charm.

He unlocks the door at 4 am and closes it again in the evening unless there is a special festival. Once a year the key is re-offered to him by the Greek Orthodox, the Armenian Orthodox and the Catholics.

'This is a symbolic act to show that they wish the tradition to continue. To have a Muslim unlocking the doors is symbolic of the friendship between Christianity and Islam. It is also fulfilling Caliph Omar's pledge, even today. But most importantly it cuts down the wrangles between the different Christian groups. If the Greeks had the key it would be a Greek church. If the Armenians had it the church would be Armenian. But I am completely neutral and never take sides.'

He paused for a moment and placed his hand upon his heart. 'It is an honour and a privilege for me to hold the keys to the Holy Sepulchre and I am thankful to God that I have a son to continue the tradition.'

He finished speaking, fell silent, and reached backwards to unlock a cupboard behind the great church door: 'Here,' he said, handing me a bundle of faded sepia photographs. 'This is my father unlocking the church . . . and that is my grandfather.' They both had moustaches and both looked like Wajeeh. 'If you would like to take a picture of me,' he added, 'I will be only too happy to pose for you.'

He stood outside the door while I took a photograph. But he wasn't happy with the first picture and, once again brushing his moustache, asked me to take another. Then he shook me by the hand and I entered the church.

145

In the early years of Christianity the church stressed Christ's divinity rather than His human nature, and the fact that He had lived and died in the Holy Land was overshadowed by His teachings and prophecies. It was not until the time of the fourth-century Byzantine Emperor Constantine the Great that Jerusalem became every pilgrim's desire and goal, for during his reign there were a series of spectacular discoveries made in the Holy City.

Constantine's mother, the Empress Helena, travelled to Jerusalem at an extremely advanced age determined to find the true site of the crucifixion before she died. At first her search proceeded slowly and fruitlessly and chroniclers record that it was only when she threatened all the Jewish inhabitants of the city with torture or death that relics miraculously began to appear. Her own version of the story is somewhat different. On her return to the imperial capital she told Constantine how an elderly Jew named Judas was in the midst of a prayer when the earth began to tremble and emit a sweet perfume. Her Byzantine guards immediately began digging and had soon unearthed three crosses which instantly restored to life the corpse of a young man who was about to be buried. Sir John repeats this story about Helena's discovery, recording that, 'the Jews had hidden [the cross] in the earth under the rock of Mount Calvary; and it lay there two hundred years and more up to the time when Saint Helena found it.'

Whatever the truth, her mission was heralded as a triumph by the emperor who ordered a huge church to be built over the site. It wasn't long before thousands of pilgrims began to follow in Helena's footsteps, flocking to sacred sites all over the region. Venerating holy relics became widespread as church authorities taught that such relics could cure the sick, and richer pilgrims began buying up these healing souvenirs and carting them home with them. Bones, hair, limbs, even tiny fragments of the true cross reached western Europe and Sir John himself claims to have a fragment of the Crown of Thorns in his baggage.

The trickle soon became a flood and monasteries – with one eye on the finances generated by such relics – claimed to possess ever more ludicrous items. Walsingham boasted of having acquired the Virgin's milk. Next to arrive was Christ's breath in a bottle. Then the tip of the Devil's tail turned up, and in Venice one of Goliath's teeth was miraculously unearthed. Most famous of all was Hailes Abbey in Gloucestershire which became a huge centre of pilgrimage because of the phial of the Blood of Christ that was held there. Given by a wealthy magnate and personally authenticated by the Pope it drew tens of thousands of pilgrims to the abbey.

Today it is hard not to be cynical about such relics and I found it impossible to imagine the excitement felt by medieval pilgrims arriving at the Church of the Holy Sepulchre. For months they had travelled across dangerous and hostile territories, suffering great hardship and constant hunger, and now their goal was at last before their eyes. Crossing themselves, weeping, and chanting the *Te Deum*, they entered the holiest site in Christendom.

I, too, entered the enormous church and looked around for the prayer group. I had been speaking to Wajeeh for so long that I was sure the tour would have finished, but I soon heard the southern drawl of Father Angelo over the noise of the builders restoring the church. As I caught up with him a mechanical digger spun around the slab on which Christ's body was supposedly anointed, narrowly missing an elderly lady. A pneumatic drill joined the cacophony of noise as it bored into the stone floor. High above us, workmen called to each other across the scaffolding.

We moved slowly towards Calvary, scene of the Crucifixion, which is reached by climbing a series of steps. There was a great crowd of us following the monks and we jostled up a steep and narrow stone staircase before finding ourselves at the twelfth station of the cross, the site where the crucifix had once stood. There was a moment's pause in the drilling as we sang hymns, said prayers, and contemplated the site. Two chapels stand on this venerated spot – one Catholic and one Orthodox – and as the ever-jovial Father Angelo read from the Bible (Here J*eee*sus was cr*uuu*cified . . .) I looked across to the Orthodox altar where a bearded Greek monk stood motionless and in prayer.

After our prayers a few people stuck their hands in the hole in the rock where the crucifix was supposed to have stood. From here it is possible to look through a glass panel in the floor to the chapel directly beneath Calvary. The rock wall below is fractured by a massive split; the Bible records that this crack occurred during the earthquake that followed the crucifixion. More cynical guides will tell you it was caused by workmen quarrying the rock thousands of years before Christ.

We shuffled back downstairs, making way for a troupe of American Franciscans weighed down with cameras and camcorders. I watched them posing before the tomb and filming themselves with their friends while all the time the Orthodox monk looked on – a bemused expression on his face.

The Church of the Holy Sepulchre has a peculiarly unplanned appearance quite unlike the great European cathedrals. It looks as if a vast pile of stones have grown organically into the building that exists today. The interior is marked by the same disorder as the exterior, partly because the church is built over the last five stations of the cross with each station boasting its own chapel and altar. Nothing remains of the Byzantine church built by the Emperor Constantine: that was completely destroyed by an Egyptian warrior – the fanatically anti-Christian Caliph Hakim – whose hobby was torture and whose passion for darkness was such that he spent the night-time hours riding through the streets of Cairo in order to spy on his people. His eccentricities often bordered on the insane: at one point he banned honey from his territories.

In 1009 he instructed his army commander to raze the Holy Sepulchre to the ground, 'until all traces of it have disappeared, and to endeavour to uproot its foundations'. His workman did a good job. Within a few weeks nothing – not even the foundations – was left of the building. But 90 years later the crusaders arrived in Jerusalem and rebuilt the church that stands today.

The Holy Sepulchre is shared between five Christian churches who, for centuries, have argued over who owns what. The Greek Orthodox have come out best for they own the site of Golgotha. The rest is shared between the Armenian Orthodox, the Syrian Orthodox, the Roman Catholics, and the Copts. The Ethiopians, who have been in Jerusalem since the fourth century, lost their documents of possession in a fire in 1808 and, no longer able to prove their rights, were evicted as if they had been illegal squatters. They now live in mud huts on the roof.

The anointing slab of marble graphically illustrates the bitter in-fighting that dominates the life of the church. Though commonly owned by all the churches, each insists on having its own lamp burning over the rectangular block of stone. It is only after decades of bickering about who is responsible for which column and flagstone that the church is finally being restored.

Some pilgrims are overwhelmed when they come face to face with the site of the crucifixion and for a few the experience turns their minds. Every year, some 200 foreigners – usually American – fall prey to a psychiatric disorder known as Jerusalem Syndrome which frequently strikes at the Holy Sepulchre. Victims, overwhelmed by the religious experience, suddenly believe themselves to be either God, the Devil, Christ, or one of the disciples. Sometimes, less mainstream biblical figures surface in their minds: two years ago, a strong Canadian man was overcome with the certainty that he was Samson. All are carted off to Jerusalem's psychiatric clinic and make a full recovery on returning home.

Nothing so dramatic happened in our group although I did spot two men wandering around the church dressed as Jesus (one of whom I had seen from the window of Father Baratto's office). Both were American and both dressed in long cotton robes. They studiously ignored each other.

A final prayer brought us to the fourteenth and final station of the cross – the site of the tomb of Christ. 'The tabernacle,' explains Sir John, 'is eight feet long, five wide, and eleven high. Not long ago the Sepulchre was quite open, so that men could kiss it and touch it. But because some men who went there used to try to break bits of the stone off to take it away with them, the Sultan had a wall built around the Tomb so that nobody could touch it . . . The tabernacle has no windows, but inside there are many lamps burning.'

The tomb has changed greatly since Sir John's day. The great fire of 1808 – begun by an intoxicated monk who attempted to extinguish the flames with *eau-de-vie* – destroyed the eleventh-century tomb that Sir John would have seen. Even that wasn't the original: the earliest Byzantine sepulchre was smashed on the orders of Caliph Hakim.

The present tomb is a clumsy, box-like room that resembles a walk-in wardrobe. There is a long queue to enter, for it is so small inside that there is room for no more than three people at a time. As I awaited my turn I wondered what I should do at this holiest of holy sites. Should I cross myself or fall to my knees in veneration? Medieval pilgrims would have flung themselves to the ground in prostration, and many wept freely before the tomb.

Slowly the queue shuffled forward until at last I was at the front. A Greek Orthodox monk pointed at me then pointed into the tomb. Finally it was my turn.

It was tiny inside but quite bright, for there were dozens of candles burning and scores of silver oil lamps hanging from the ceiling. On the right-hand side lay a slab of greenish marble where Christ's body was laid out to rest. Suddenly the woman to my left sunk to the floor. I thought she had fainted – overcome with emotion or the heat of the room – and I went to pick her up. But I realized she was whispering prayers and quietly weeping to herself. As I stood there I found myself continually questioning whether this really could be the tomb of Christ and asking how anyone could be so sure after all these centuries. Who could trust the Empress Helena and her Byzantine 'archaeologists'? And if it wasn't the real tomb, then surely it was a little ridiculous to be standing in awe beside a simple slab of marble.

I was mulling such thoughts through my mind when the Greek monk pointed at me. Out. Now. I had used up my alloted time. I had stood before the tomb.

The woman got up from the floor as I left the room and slowly wiped the tears from her eyes.

The following day I walked along the ancient walls to get a view of the new city that surrounds them. But when I reached Damascus Gate I was stopped by a group of teenage Israeli soldiers who casually pointed their machine guns in my direction and refused to let me go any further, even when I showed them the ticket that gave me access to the walkway. Damascus Gate was as far as I could go, they said. It was too dangerous to walk any further.

This, in fact, was the point I was looking for. It was here, just a stone's throw from Damascus Gate, that General Gordon (of Khartoum fame) had stayed when he visited Jerusalem in the 1880s. He rented a room built into the old city wall near Damascus Gate, its windows facing outwards and, in the warm evenings, Gordon liked to sit on the roof and look at the rounded hill opposite.

He had come here as a pilgrim – to visit the sites of his faith and pursue his interest in biblical studies – for Gordon, like Mandeville, was a deeply religious man. And one day, while he sat on the rooftop relaxing as the sun went down, he was suddenly struck by how much the hilltop in front of him resembled the shape of a skull. And it was not just the shape: the more he looked at it, the more he became convinced he was looking at the skull of a long dead person. There were two deep sockets where the eyes would once have been and although the rock had crumbled over the years, the cheekbones were still clearly visible. The more Gordon studied the cliff-face, the more he felt sure he had stumbled upon something of great importance.

'You have the ordnance map of Jerusalem,' he wrote excitedly to a friend in 1883. 'Look at the shape of the contour Number 2459 – Jeremiah's Grotto, near Damascus Gate. It is the shape of a skull; near it are gardens and caves, and close to it are the shambles of Jerusalem . . . To me, this Jeremiah Grotto area was the site of the crucifixion.'

He was not the first to question the site of the Holy Sepulchre; for many years people had become increasingly sceptical about both the site of the church and the problem of the crucifixion and tomb being so close to one another. Even Mandeville felt it necessary to explain that the city walls had been rebuilt since the time of Christ and that the site would, at one time, have been outside the city as was the custom with Roman executions.

But one of Gordon's principal reasons for believing this new place – and not the Church of the Holy Sepulchre – to be the site of Christ's crucifixion was the fact that the word Golgotha means 'Place of the Skull' and this hill clearly looked like a skull. Closer investigation only increased his excitement for the cliff, concealed by undergrowth, was found to contain a rock-hewn tomb that appeared to date from the first century. Surely this was no coincidence? The skull-like face. The tomb. The garden. They all pointed towards one thing: that this was the *true* site of Christ's burial and resurrection and the Empress Helena had got it wrong after all. Millions of pilgrims throughout the centuries had prayed at the wrong place.

Excited archaeologists flocked to the site to examine it in greater detail. Many agreed with Gordon and it was decided to attempt to buy the site with money raised by public subscription: an advertisement was immediately placed in *The Times*. Yet even at the time people had their doubts and the new 'garden tomb' caused great controversy, sparking off a series of hostile letters from experts who had serious doubts about the veracity of the site. *The Times* itself concluded in an editorial that the garden tomb was nothing more than the figment of an overly religious imagination. Yet despite the adverse publicity the money was raised, the site was bought, and within a few months it had been established as a place of pilgrimage. The alternative garden tomb was born.

The officials at the tomb are certainly armed with impressive evidence to support their case. The garden borders the main Damascus to Jericho road which fits the biblical account of Golgotha. There is a huge and ancient cistern under the garden which suggests that this site was once cultivated land. Moreover, in 1924, they found an ancient grape press here: further evidence that this was a garden – and one that fitted the description of the garden that had belonged to Joseph of Arimathea.

Today, thousands of pilgrims are drawn to the garden tomb every year. Perhaps it has become so popular because it fulfils all the expectations of modern pilgrims who long ago lost the blind faith of their medieval forebears. In an age where seeing is believing, this lush plot of land, shaded by trees and sprinkled with flowers, looks exactly how a garden tomb ought to look.

'So many people come to Jerusalem expecting to find what they have heard in hymns,' explained John, my guide to the tomb. 'They hope to see a green hill far away, and all that. When they get to the Church of the Holy Sepulchre they are often bitterly disappointed for it has a strange and often unholy atmosphere and the monks can be incredibly rude. Our tomb comes as a pleasant surprise. This is more what they have been expecting.'

Wherever the real site of the crucifixion was, it certainly would not have been a green hill. Roman executions were noted for their brutality and cruelty and criminals were usually executed by the side of roads so that people could jeer at them and throw stones as they died. The fact that there is an ancient road running alongside the Anglican site was further proof – according to General Gordon – that this was the true site of Golgotha. But not everyone is so convinced.

'The Orthodox dismiss us as an irrelevance,' said the guide. 'To them we are upstarts who have been here for less than one hundred and fifty years. But Catholics tend to be less critical. They often say that if this isn't the real tomb then it ought to have been.'

The tomb comes complete with a grooved channel where the rolling stone would once have been. John slowly pushed open the door and we entered the tomb in silence. It was a small, box-like room with a low ceiling rough-hewn from the rock. The walls felt dry but smelt musty, as if damp had permeated the rock for the last 2,000 winters. On the right-hand side was the tomb itself – a raised stone platform chiselled from the rock. This was much more like it: there was even a Byzantine cross painted on the wall.

As I stood here in front of a tomb that fitted the biblical description almost exactly, I wondered who was right. Could it be possible that it was here, and not at the Holy Sepulchre, that the disciples once stood marvelling that the body of Christ had disappeared?

'I personally find it difficult to believe that the site of the crucifixion and sepulchre would have been so close together, as they are in the Holy Sepulchre,' said John. 'And don't forget, the Empress Helena found the site more than three centuries after the event. The Christians had been expelled from the city for much of that time. How on earth could the tradition have been kept alive after all those years?'

As we left the tomb and entered the garden again the rain began to fall. The sky had darkened to the colour of old pewter and the wet weather was settling in for the day. The garden looked more beautiful than ever, for the trees and shrubs had lost their thick coats of dust: as I wandered alone along the narrow, overgrown paths, the silence was in marked contrast to the noise of the Holy Sepulchre.

Possession of the garden tomb enabled the Anglican church to claim ownership of its own holy place. For centuries all the sites on the pilgrim trail had been contained within the old city walls and owned by the ancient churches, and even Sir John seems surprised at how many churches and shrines belonged to the Greek Orthodox. But Gordon of Khartoum's surprise discovery changed all that for one of the upstart newcomers at last had a convincing claim of its own.

St George's Anglican church is 200 yards up the road from the garden tomb and looks as if it has been plucked from a picturesque English village and planted in Jerusalem. There is a cloistered courtyard surrounded by Victorian Gothic arches, and behind this courtyard stands a squat, stone tower with the flag of St George fluttering in the light breeze. It's the sort of place where you expect to hear hymns ancient and modern, bump into Anthony Trollope, and drink tea with the vicar. But appearances can be deceptive, and the church of St George is not as English as it seems. True, the Dean, the Very Reverend John Tidy invited me for tea in his book-lined study. But that was the point where the English illusion came to an end.

'Our congregation is almost completely comprised of Palestinians,' he said. 'They are Christians who were converted during the flurry of missionary activity in the last century. But their families have lived in the city for centuries. In fact they are descendants of the Christians your knight would have met all those hundreds of years ago.'

The first Anglicans had come to Jerusalem in 1841 but they didn't make their presence felt until the end of the century when

Andaman Islands: ' . . . they have no mouth, but instead a little hole, and so when they must eat they suck their food through a reed.'

Andaman Islands: 'There are people who walk on their hands . . . they are hairy and climb up trees as readily as apes.'

Andaman Islands: 'There is another island where the people are hermaphrodite, having the parts of each sex.'

Indo-China: 'There grows a kind of fruit as big as gourds, and when it is ripe men open it and find inside an animal . . . like a little lamb.'

India: ' . . . in the wilderness are many wild men with horns on their heads; they dwell in woods and speak not.'

Valley of the Ganges: 'In the middle of the valley under a rock one can clearly see the head and face of a devil, very hideous and dreadful. . .'

India: 'Men had died in that land in deflowering maidens, for the latter had snakes inside them, which stung the husbands on their penises.'

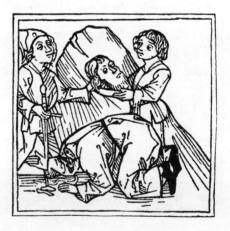

Tibet: ' When any man's father is dead . . . the priest strikes off the dead man's head and lays it on a great platter of silver.'

they built the church of St George and embarked on an ambitious missionary programme.

'The Victorians weren't simply content with living with the status quo,' said the Reverend Tidy, 'they wanted to change it. In those days the Church Missionary Society sent hundreds of missionaries to the Middle East and built churches, schools and hospitals all over the region in order to convert as many native people as possible.'

The church continued to serve the large expatriot community but the Palestinian congregation gradually swelled until it reached the size it is today – 9,000 communicants of whom a tiny minority are British. Most of the services are in Arabic and many of the priests, like the Bishop, are Palestinian. Small wonder that the sign welcoming visitors to St George's is in Arabic.

All this has caused considerable difficulties for the Anglican church for both its worshippers and leaders are generally supportive of the Palestinian cause, leading them into conflict with the authorities. And while the forms of discrimination against Christians have changed since Mandeville's day – they are no longed forced to wear blue turbans in public – the resentment against them is much the same: 'Being a Palestinian church means that you totally identify with the hopes of the Palestinian people,' explained the Reverend Tidy, 'and this has caused us many problems with the Israeli government. The Ministry of Religious Affairs closely monitors our churches and has occasionally made life extremely difficult for the Arab clergy . . . more tea? . . . for it stops them moving around the country and has the power to refuse requests for visas. We never know if there is a man from the ministry standing at the back of the church listening to everything that is being said.'

According to the Reverend Tidy, the government even monitors the church's day-to-day activities. 'We know, for instance, that our phones are tapped,' he said. 'They are so amateur it's unbelievable. You can actually hear them on the other end of the line. And our faxes are often monitored as well – you can tell because they take twice as long to go through the machine. We have to be careful. They obviously want to know where the bishop is going and what he is saying.'

'But we manage to survive the problems from the Israeli ministry,' he said. 'Their officials are not *too* bad. Things would have been a lot worse in Mandeville's day.'

When I returned to Cyril's house that evening he helped me translate a few more passages from difficult medieval Latin. Sir John's knowledge of Jerusalem impressed me greatly until I checked the writings of other pilgrims and discovered that many of his details were – as ever – lifted wholesale. He copies lengthy passages from William of Tripoli, Vincent of Beauvais, and Albert of Aix, as well as borrowing freely from the renegade German friar, William of Boldensele.

But while clearly indebted to Boldensele, he often differs from what the German wrote and at times disputes both his facts and his accuracy. He even takes the occasional sideswipe at the German, rubbishing his claim to have crossed the desert on horseback. And when Boldensele boasts about making the journey in record time, Mandeville comments on the unseemly haste of some travellers. Such witty asides endeared me to my medieval friend, for even if he had copied from other authors, he had at least infused their dry accounts with a sense of humour.

Father Baratto had suggested I look at the writings of Simon Fitzsimmons, a monk who left Britain the same year as Sir John and reached Jerusalem within twelve months. I managed to buy a copy of Fitzsimmons's account in the Franciscan bookshop but when I began to flick through its pages I found that it did little to clarify matters and often seemed to confuse them further. For while he visited many of the same places as Sir John, he all too often disagreed on details. Where Mandeville claims that the church on Mount Sion was still in use when he was in Jerusalem, Fitzsimmons assures his readers it was completely destroyed. Who was telling the truth? Since no other pilgrim mentions the church, it is impossible to know.

I tried a different approach, looking to see what Mandeville had *neglected* to mention in the hope that this might shed some light on his journey. But once again I was left scratching my head, for just as in Damascus he hadn't written about the tomb of St John the Baptist so, in Jerusalem, he doesn't mention Adam's skull which was kept in the Holy Sepulchre and venerated by thousands of pilgrims. This was strange, for scores of medieval writers described this gruesome object. It was said to have been found in a deep hole along with a pile of bones which were sprinkled with blood from Christ's feet. Digging it out of the ground caused it to deteriorate rapidly and by the time Felix Fabri saw it in the fifteenth century it had lost all its hair.

This was not the only object that Mandeville overlooked. While visiting the Mount of Olives, he recalls seeing the stone that was supposedly imprinted with Christ's left foot as He ascended to Heaven. But why did he not mention that an identical stone, bearing Christ's right footprint, was housed at Westminster Abbey throughout his lifetime? Did he forget? Or had he never been to Westminster Abbey?

Sir John, like today's pilgrims, did not just visit the Via Dolorosa and Church of the Holy Sepulchre; he lists a vast array of Christian sites that he was taken to while in Jerusalem. There was the Temple of Solomon, the tomb of Saint Simeon, the houses of Pilate and Herod, and the church of Saint Saviour. Here the pilgrims would stop to venerate the left arm of Saint John Chrysostom and fragments of Saint Stephen's skull. Then they would walk slowly up to Mount Sion where Saint Peter wept after forsaking Christ and were shown Caiaphas's house, the tree on which Judas hanged himself, and a chunk of marble which – they were told – was part of the table of the Last Supper.

Mandeville mentions all of these in passing but was especially keen on the church of St Anne, a finely domed crusader church built out of smooth blocks of stone. Today's tourists come here in their hundreds and as I sat admiring the simplicity of the architecture, no fewer than five pilgrim groups entered the church. Each sang hymns, read a communal prayer, then left. One group of evangelicals formed a ring outside and sang so loud that their voices pierced the thick stone walls of the church.

'Who is Jesus?'
'Jesus is the Lord.' (clap, clap)
'Who is Jesus?'

'Jesus is the Lord.' (clap, clap)
'Jesus, Jesus, Jesus, Jesus.'
Clap. Clap. Clap. Clap.
'The Saviour of the world.' (clap, clap)
'The Saviour of the world.'

I'd come to St Anne's in order to test Sir John, for he gives very precise details about the church – the burial site of Mary's father as well as of St Anne herself.

'As you descend *twenty-two steps* from that church,' he writes, 'Joachim, Our Lady's father, lies in a stone tomb. Once Saint Anne lay beside him, but Saint Helena had her translated to Constantinople.' Twenty-two steps. I walked over to the narrow stone stairwell that led down to the crypt and as I began to descend I also started to count. 'One, two, three, four . . . ' The stairs were roughly cut and very steep and they turned sharply at this point until they were almost descending back on themselves. 'Eight, nine, ten . . . ' There were a crowd of Catholic pilgrims in front of me who were blocking the stairs. They were singing a hymn, led by a priest who had vanished out of sight. The hymn came to an end and the group shuffled on while I continued counting. 'Eighteen, nineteen, twenty . . . ' I was at the bottom now, and had still only counted twenty steps. But the tomb itself was in a separate little room, and that was down a further step. 'Twenty-one . . . ' All I needed now was one more stair. But there weren't any more – Sir John was wrong by one step.

But then I looked down at the floor and saw that its shiny marble surface differed from the stone surrounding the tomb. I realized that this floor was a new addition, and that once there would almost certainly have been a further step – and that made twenty-two.

Although it is the Jewish settlers in the old city that always make the headlines, the ultra-Orthodox area of Mea She'ariim in the new city is far more interesting. Resembling a central European ghetto, its small houses are home to several thousand Orthodox Jews. On weekdays they wear long black cloaks and hats – the dress of sixteenth-century Poland – and on festivals they wear their *shtreimals*, or fur-trimmed hats.

Cyril and I took a short cut through these alleys which were festooned with washing from wall to wall and bore placards warning people to be properly dressed. When we reached the other side of the quarter we passed through a crowded vegetable market and were back in the modern part of the new town. It is this area of Jerusalem that is home to some of the biggest churches in the city. If you don't fancy the First Baptist Bible Church, then you could try the Jerusalem Baptist Church. If you prefer something more gutsy, why not pay a visit to the Church of God? Or the Church of God Prophecy? Or the Church of God Seventh Day (House of Prayer for all People)? There are dozens of such churches in Jerusalem but the one I decided to visit was the Narkis Street Baptist Congregation. This was a spanking new building just a stone's throw from the Sheraton and its doors, which led into a Baptist bookshop, had been flung wide open to embrace all comers. The face of a young man appeared from a bookcase when I entered and gave me a beaming smile. He had a mop of ginger hair, wore Joe Ninety spectacles, and was only too happy to help. 'What can I do for you?' he said. 'If I can't help, then I'm sure I can find someone who can.'

I explained that I was very keen to learn more about the Baptists and he gave me a knowing smile. 'Another one who's seen the light,' he said with a chuckle before excusing himself and disappearing behind a pile of books. He returned with the deacon, a man named Alan, who said he wished to have a little chat with me and give me a tour around the building – a sort of getting-to-know-you session.

The new chapel had only recently been completed and the smell of fresh paint still lingered. It was a pristine new building: unadorned with the usual clutter of churches. A drum set and guitars stood in the corner and bright sunlight filtered in through windows in the ceiling.

'For years there were only a handful of people coming here,' explained Alan, 'but in the 1970s there was a sudden outpouring of the Holy Spirit and a huge rise in the congregation. Perhaps that is why you have come?'

I shrugged my shoulders and asked if they had built the new

building to accommodate the ever-increasing numbers but Alan shook his head.

'No,' he said. 'The old chapel was burnt down by an arsonist. We had many difficulties trying to rebuild it but finally got permission from the Supreme Court.'

When I asked more questions about the fire he clammed up. 'If you want to know what happened,' he said, 'you must talk to Joseph. I am not able to speak about this.'

Joseph was the treasurer of the church but he, too, was unwilling to tell me about the fire. 'Of course I know the person who burnt down the building but I'm afraid I am unable to talk about it,' he said. 'I have received many death threats over this and the government did absolutely nothing.'

'Death threats?'

Joseph gave a cynical laugh. 'There are many people . . . Orthodox Jews . . . who wish we were not here,' he said. 'They'd like to see the back of us. Even the government wanted to move us out of the city. This is valuable land. They don't like us being here. We are Christians, and as Christians they try to block our every move.'

It is not just the Orthodox Jews who are antagonistic towards the Baptists. Many Israelis don't like them because of the way in which they are said to have a systematic plan to convert the Russian Jews to Christianity. These Russians are lonely when they first arrive in Israel. They are often in need of help and are unfamiliar with the ways of their adopted homeland. The Baptists – who have a Russian-speaking pastor as well as services in Russian – are only too eager to help.

'We only want to help them, not convert them,' explained Alan. 'We are not trying to substitute circumcision for baptism or anything like that. The Jews are welcome to remain as Jews and to accept the Lord Jesus as the Saviour. That fits the scriptures exactly.'

'So you're missionaries?' I said.

'You ask so many questions . . . missionary is not a word we like to use. We have outreach programmes. We do help these people. But we are not trying to convert.'

The two men began looking at their watches and Joseph told

me he had a meeting to go to. 'It's difficult to talk about such matters,' he said. 'But I am *extremely* glad that you are so interested in the Baptists and hope you might come on Sunday. Then you'll see all the good work we do.'

As I walked back up the Nablus Road, the sun was melting into the old city and the gilded roof of the Dome of the Rock had turned the colour of burnished copper. I wondered what Sir John would have made of the Baptists and the Anglicans. Most probably, they would have been his first port of call for he was fascinated with any faith that differed from his own. To him, they were like a strange and highly prized new wine: something to be examined, savoured and described to people back home.

9 The King's Pardon

> On investigating the sources of the book it will presently be
> obvious that part at least of the personal history of Mandeville is
> mere invention. Under these circumstances the truth of any part
> of that history, and even the genuineness of the compiler's name,
> become matter for serious doubt.
>
> *Encyclopedia Britannica*, **ninth edition, 1883**

In researching the history of the Mandevilles, I had ploughed
through church archives, monastic records and medieval
chronicles. What I hadn't so far looked at were wills, for I
assumed that few in the Middle Ages would have bothered to
record their possessions. On the whole this was the case, and there
was no trace of a will belonging to a John Mandeville in
Hertfordshire's County Records Office. To my great surprise,
however, I did find two short references to items that had appar-
ently once belonged to Sir John. The first was a sapphire ring
which he was said to have bequeathed to St Albans Abbey on his
death. It was recorded in a fifteenth-century inventory of the
possessions of the abbey and was described as, 'One gold ring
adorned with a good and precious sapphire of large size,
supported with tiny grips of gold. A gift of Sir John Mandeville.'

This was the only reference I could find and it was presumably
lost during the Reformation when St Albans' treasures were
carted off and dispersed.

The other object was altogether more curious, and the story of
its mystical properties was set down on paper in the sixteenth
century by an antiquary called John Leland, who compiled a
massive book called *The Laboryouse Journey and Serche of Johan
Leylande, for Englandes Antiquitiees*. Leland never completed his
work; he went mad and died long before it was published but he
left behind thousands of pages of notes. In these notes he claims
to have travelled to Canterbury Cathedral and seen a souvenir
that Mandeville himself had donated to the cathedral – a souvenir

that, just possibly, he had brought back from his travels. 'At Canterbury, the capital of Kent, I found an uncorrupted apple inside a hollow crystal globe, in the midst of the consecrated treasures of Thomas Becket. When I asked the clerk what kind of miracle this was, he anwered that in the past this little gift was given to the martyr by Sir John Mandeville.'

I checked the cathedral archives to see what happened to this gift but the relevant records had either been lost or destroyed. There was a tantalizing reference to an inventory of Thomas à Becket's shrine dated 1441 which might have shed more light on the gift, but the inventory itself had long ago been torn out and lost.

Could the stories about these items possibly be true? It was feasible that Mandeville had bought such items in Syria, the great marketplace for curiosities from the East, but unfortunately I had only Leland's word to go on, and since he was suffering from a debilitating mental disorder when he wrote his book, he was hardly the most reliable of sources.

This was not the only strange story about Mandeville to have been accepted as fact. Some scholars – keen to impose their medieval fantasies on *The Travels* – concluded that Sir John's jovial exterior was merely a disguise which concealed a sinister fascination with black magic. Such ideas were due, in part, to the fact that the manuscript at Chantilly is bound together with four others which deal with the magic arts and sciences; the sciences of 'augurie, sytrille, pyromanchie, ydromanchie, geomanchie, phyzonomie, cyromanchy'. Book Four includes a section on the magic properties of herbs while Book Five's tract on gemstones is compiled 'according to the opinion of the Indians from whom all the sciences of stones comes'.

It is most unlikely that Sir John had anything to do with these books. They appear with no other manuscript and bear all the hallmarks of Jean d'Outremeuse. But there is other evidence to suggest that Sir John had a dubious interest in magic; several manuscripts on alchemy survive in Oxford which purport to be written by a Johannes de Magna Villa.

But for all their medieval charm, none of these pseudoscientific tracts contains any proof to show they were written by Sir John Mandeville, the author of *The Travels*, as many have suggested. There were any number of Mandevilles alive in the medieval era – including several John Mandevilles – and any one of them could just as feasibly have been the author of such manuscripts.

Most of the medieval documents describing Sir John as a doctor can also be discounted. Antwerp used to possess a treatise *On Things Medical* by a Mandeville, while one medieval chronicler went so far as describing him as a man excelling in 'the art and genius of healing'. But such descriptions were all written in France where Outremeuse's deceits had long been accepted as fact. The chroniclers were merely multiplying these lies.

One particular John Mandeville interested me greatly. He was clearly forging a successful career in the diplomatic field for in 1320 he was sent by the king on an important mission to Robert Bruce, the king of Scotland who had annihilated King Edward II's army at the battle of Bannockburn six years earlier. This expedition was recorded in diplomatic archives and dated 7 January:

> Safe conduct for the undermentioned envoys of Robert de Brus, viz:

Sir William de Soules	
Sir Robert de Keth	
Sir Roger de Kirkpatrik	knights
Sir Alisaundre de Seton	
Sir William de Mountffichet	
Master William de Yetham	
Master John de Maundeville	clerks
Master Jakes Benne	
Wautier de Gauwaye	

This was not the first time that this particular John Mandeville had been sent to Scotland by the king; a previous visit, on 20 November 1312, had also earned him a mention of thanks in a roll of Scottish records.

Could this conceivably be Sir John Mandeville of *The Travels*? There is every possibility that it was, for if Sir John had indeed been a member of the Black Notley family of Mandevilles he would have been born and raised within a few miles of Robert Bruce's family home. Bruce, too, had lived in Essex and at least one of the Black Notley clan had married close associates of his family.

There were other links as well. When Sir Thomas Mandeville – John's possible father – was captured during the battle of Bannockburn, Bruce himself intervened to have Sir Thomas released. He even paid £94 – a vast sum of money in those days – to ensure that he was freed without suffering any harm.

Given the delicate circumstances surrounding the expedition to Scotland, a Mandeville from Black Notley would have made the perfect mediator.

The shelves nearest the main door of the British Library reading room are stacked with row upon row of identically sized volumes which are bound, for the most part, in red Morocco leather with chiselled gold lettering. Few people use this section of the library and for good reason. These shelves are home to Britain's state papers – a day-by-day record of interminably dull events. As you walk past row upon row of books you find yourself moving further back in time: two volumes cover the reign of George II; three deal with William III; there are dozens for Charles I, and a few plump books for Henry VIII. Two steps more and I was into the reigns of the Plantagenet kings, and at the bottom of one of the shelves found documents written during the reign of King Edward II. His affairs of state merited four volumes.

For some weeks I had been trying to verify an account which claimed that the de Bohuns – the overlords of the Mandevilles – had been involved in the murder of the king's favourite, Piers Gaveston. That Gaveston was brutally executed is not in doubt and the playwright Christopher Marlowe based his drama, *Edward the Second*, on sound historical facts. But it wasn't until I looked at the state papers for Edward II's reign that I realized that Mandeville was just as involved as the de Bohuns. For underneath the date, 16 October 1313, was the following notice written on behalf of the king: 'Westminster: Pardon to Thomas, earl of Lancaster, and his adherents, followers, and confederates, of all causes of anger, indignation, suits, accusations &c arisen in any manner on account of Peter de Gavaston, from the time of the king's marriage with his dear companion Isabelle . . . ' Surely a hint of irony here, for Edward hated his wife. ' . . . whether on account of the capture, detention, or death of Peter de Gavaston or in any other manner touching or concerning Peter de Gavaston, or that which befel him.'

The document went on to list all those pardoned for complicity in the murder of the King's favourite. This list began, naturally enough, with the most senior – Humphrey de Bohun, Earl of Hereford and Essex – but it also included all his retainers in order of rank. And whose name should appear halfway down the third column? None other than John Mandeville.

Was this my Sir John? He was certainly the right age. He was from the right family. He fitted the dates. And in every way he sounded like the author of *The Travels*. At last – I was sure – I'd found my man.

10 The Sinai Desert

Iohn Mandevile, Knight, borne in the Towne of Saint *Albons*, was
so well giuen to the studie of Learning from his childhood, that
he seemed to plant a good part of his felicitie in the same . . . hee
was rauished with a mightie desire to see the greater parts of the
World, as *Asia* and *Africa*. Hauing therefore prouided all things
necessarie for his iourney, hee departed from his Countrey in the
yeere of Christ 1332.

Illustrium Maioris Britanniae Scriptorum, **John Bale, 1548**

The journey from Jerusalem to Eilat began as drama and
ended as farce. The bus had scarcely left the outskirts of
the Holy City before the road swooped downwards and
continued to plummet for some 40 miles. By the time we reached
the Dead Sea we had dropped from 1,000 feet above sea level to
1,200 feet below.

Eilat is a further three hours' drive across the Negev Desert –
a bleak route with only the occasional army camp to break the
monotony of the landscape. The sparkling blue waters of the Red
Sea entice the eyes after the dust of the Negev, but any dreams of
an Oriental Côte d'Azur are shattered as soon as you enter the
half-finished concrete resort of Eilat. The Israeli Tourist Board
advertises the town as a year-round paradise but the snake in this
particular paradise is the airport which town-planners have
placed slap-bang in the centre of town.

Travellers heading onwards to Egypt must change on to a local
bus which runs to and from the military checkpoint at the border,
some 20 minutes from the town centre. Two hundred yards of
no-man's-land and several dozen well-equipped troops separate
the friendly states of Israel and Egypt.

A huge Hilton hotel stands right on the border, surrounded by
a cluster of tourist facilities. Built before the Camp David accords
handed the Sinai peninsula back to Egypt, this sliver of land was
disputed until 1989 when it, too, was signed over to Egypt. The

border was redrawn several hundred metres to the west, the hotel found itself no longer in Israel, and the tourists, put off by the sight of soldiers with guns slung from their shoulders, stayed away. Despite this, the hotel remains open to the few who choose to spend their holiday on a beach surrounded by barbed wire.

The scenery changes dramatically almost as soon as you enter Egypt. Where the Negev is bleak and uninviting, Sinai is barren but impressive. Dry scrub is replaced by waterless desert and dust-blown hills by brilliant pink mountains which centuries of desert sun have spliced into towering needles and tortuous chasms.

For thousands of years this wilderness was home to nomadic Bedouin who roamed the peninsula with their camels and wives in search of food and water. Sometimes they would journey to the sea where they could fish for their food but more often they wandered through the desolate heartland of the Sinai, living in black woollen tents and battling against drought and death.

There are still a few who continue this lifestyle, but most have abandoned hardship for the pleasures of a life by the sea. Tourist resorts have sprung up along the Red Sea coast and hotels are constantly under construction. In Mandeville's day the Bedouin murdered tourists. Now they serve them pizzas in air-conditioned hotels.

I had left Jerusalem later than I intended – it was after 10 am – and by the time I had crossed the border into Egypt it was past two o'clock. I was heading to the Greek Orthodox monastery of St Catherine's, which Sir John describes in great detail, but any chance of reaching this lonely desert outpost before nightfall was looking increasingly unlikely, especially when a couple of men at the border told me the last bus had already gone.

'No bus,' echoed a group of taxi drivers in unison. 'You come with me,' shouted one.

'Eh, monsieur, I take you to monastery,' said another.

'My car is a Mercedes,' boasted a third.

'How much?' I asked.

'Good price for you,' said the first. 'English we like. Gooood English . . . Gooood price.'

'How much?'

He looked me up and down and smiled: 'For you,' he said, bowing his head deeply in an attempt to stress his generosity, 'for you, the special price is 150 dollars.'

I laughed and the price plummeted. 'One hunded dollars.'

I smiled and it dropped again. 'Eighty dollars.'

There was a pause before he spoke again. 'Seventy?'

The price was still dropping when I was joined by Richard, an English tour rep who was spending his two months' leave in Sinai as he did every year.

'You're mad to take a taxi to St Catherine's,' he warned. 'Get the bus to Darhab instead. You'll be able to get a lift to the monastery tomorrow.' Twenty minutes later Richard and I, along with a couple of Germans and several Israelis, were en route to the Red Sea resort of Darhab.

It was dark when we arrived in the town but Richard said there would be no problem finding somewhere to stay. 'It's a great place,' he said. 'There are hotels, restaurants, bars . . . I spent a month here last year and loved it.'

He recommended the Moonlight Beach Hotel and was so enthusiastic in his praise that I decided to take him at his word. It sounded too good to be true: a friendly, family-run establishment situated right on the beach. But Darhab wasn't quite as he had described it; the town centre was little more than a collection of makeshift restaurants and bars strung out along a dirt track. The place was filled with young hippies slowly getting stoned as they sat on the rush matting of the restaurant floors.

Our hotel had enthusiastically embraced the easy-going lifestyle of Darhab. It didn't have any rooms, just thatched sheds where you could unroll a bedmat – if you had one. The owner, a thin man with nicotine brown teeth, seemed overcome with lethargy; he was slouched by an outdoor fire and made no effort to get up when we arrived and asked to stay. 'Sit down,' he said. 'Have some tea.' And he proceeded to pour over-stewed tea into glasses smeared with grease.

'You are welcome in Darhab,' he said as he handed me a bag of hashish. Richard intercepted it and exchanged the bag's contents for a bottle of duty-free vodka. I asked the price of the room and the owner said 60p a night.

'I said it would be cheap,' said Richard as he lay back in the dirt. 'Ah, Darhab . . . it's good to be back.'

As we sat around the fire and as the stars lit up the sky one by one, I asked Ahmad, the owner, if he was a Bedouin.

'Of course,' he said. 'I am from the Towarah tribe. My father came to Darhab for work and now I run this hotel. One day, I think, we will be rich.'

And the rest of his tribe? 'Pff,' he said as he swept his arm around his head. 'We are all over the place. I have relatives here in Darhab, in Nuweiba, in Sharm el Sheik, and even a few living in Cairo now.'

I was intrigued to know if he had ever heard of the Jebaliyeh tribe, for I'd been told that they were descendants of a strange Christian tribe from Europe. But Ahmad said I was talking nonsense. 'They are from Sinai,' he assured me. 'Jebel means mountain and they are Bedouin from the mountain.' There was a moment's pause: 'But why do you ask so many questions? Drink some vodka. Smoke some grass. This is Darhab.' And he sat back on the rug by the fire with a large grin on his face.

When I switched on my torch in the middle of the night I discovered that the room was seething with bedbugs and that the walls were splattered with blood stains. By the morning I was covered in bites. I got up early, paid my 60p and walked to the bus stop. I wouldn't come back to Darhab in a hurry.

Long before I set out from England I felt that Sir John's account of St Catherine's monastery would be a crucial test of his *Travels*. This was not simply because his descriptions of the buildings are more detailed than those of other places he visited: I had also been told that many medieval knights who travelled here as pilgrims had carved their names into the walls of the refectory. Could it be possible that Sir John, too, had left his name?

Staying inside the monastery, however, is no easy matter. The monks of St Catherine's have never been keen on outsiders disturbing their life of prayer and virtually all pilgrims who wish to spend a few nights here are told to sleep in the newly built hostel nearby. But I had one factor in my favour. A French friend of mine called Jean had spent several years as a monk at St

Catherine's, and had written a long and pleading letter to one of his former colleagues – a Frenchman named Father Justin – asking all at St Catherine's to help me with my research. I was pinning all my hopes on this letter as I set off from Darhab towards the monastery.

The bus slowly chugged across the Sinai peninsula – crossing numerous military checkpoints left behind after the 1967 Egypt–Israeli war – and finally came to a halt about half a mile from St Catherine's. Three of us got off and began walking up the narrow track towards the building, but we soon found ourselves joined by four air-conditioned tourist buses which pulled up and discharged a huge crowd of daytrippers from Israel. They were all clutching camcorders and bottles of Coke, shattering my expectations of a silent monastery under a silent sky.

Despite the crowds the first glimpse of St Catherine's is breathtaking. Built as a fortress and constructed from local materials, its huge mud walls appear to have pushed themselves out of the desert floor. Behind these walls, the massive bulk of Mount Sinai rears into the sky, while a second mountain looms over the far end of the valley.

As I walked up to the main entrance, elbowing my way through the crowds, I pulled the letter from my bag. With so many people arriving I felt sure that the monks would never let me stay.

'I've come to see Father Justin,' I said to the doorman. 'I've got a letter for him.'

'He is not here,' he replied. 'He's in the mountains.'

'When will he return?'

He shrugged his shoulders and held up his hands. 'Who knows,' he said. 'Maybe tomorrow. Perhaps not until next week.'

I explained that I wanted to stay in the monastery.

'Impossible. You can stay in the pilgrims' hostel down the road,' he said, 'but you can't stay in the monastery.'

'Is there anyone else I can ask?' He shrugged his shoulders for a second time and pointed into the courtyard. 'Ask one of the monks,' he said. 'They might know more.'

The narrow stone gateway opened into a cobbled alley that wound around the outside of the monastery's church. A monk stood gazing at the sky and although I coughed a couple of times to attract his attention, it was only when I began explaining my problem that he looked at me.

'You must speak with Father John,' he said. 'He is the only one who can give you permission to stay. You'll find him upstairs.'

Father John was sitting behind a large desk and he looked up when I entered the room. He had a clipped beard and white hair and he frowned when I handed him the letter for Father Justin. As he read it I explained that my wife was Orthodox and I'd been married in the Orthodox church.

'So you're looking for a knight,' he said with a perfect command of English. 'It goes without saying that you may stay in the monastery. How many days will you need . . . ?'

Holy men have been living in the Sinai peninsula from the earliest days of Christianity. Not only was this the place where Moses had heard the word of God, it was also far from the persecutions of pagan Rome.

But life here was not easy. Sinai is a desert with scant food and little water and many of the earliest settlers died of thirst or starvation. Even when they began to gather around the wells, life was little better for they were easy prey for the murderous Bedouin who had long ago adapted to the harsh environment.

The holy men continued with their struggle despite terrible difficulties and eventually built a small church on the site of the burning bush. An early pilgrim – a noblewomen called Etheria – visited this church in the fourth century and recorded her experiences of the place: 'There were many cells of holy men there, and a church in the place where the bush is . . . there is a very pleasant garden in front of the church, containing excellent and abundant water.'

The thick walls of the church did little to discourage the attacks by the Bedouin and eventually the monks decided that enough was enough: in the sixth century they wrote to the Byzantine Emperor Justinian begging for his protection. He granted their request and agreed to send assistance to help them build a monastic fortress on the site of the burning bush. This is the monastery that survives to this day; the monastery now known as St Catherine's.

It wasn't long before the monks faced a new threat, for in the seventh century the Sinai peninsula was conquered by Muslims. The building was frequently faced with destruction and it wasn't until the Prophet Mohammed himself intervened – or so the local legend goes – that the building and the monks were spared.

Even this didn't stop the occasional mad ruler from attempting to destroy the place. In AD1000 Caliph al-Hakim – the fanatical Egyptian Sultan who demolished the Holy Sepulchre – declared his intention of flattening the monastery and marched towards it with his troops. It was only when the monks met him in the desert and implored him to save it, claiming it was a sacred site for Muslims as well as Christians, that the fortress was spared. They even told Hakim that there was a mosque within the monastery walls and, as they slowly journeyed with him towards St Catherine's, they sent secret envoys back to the monastery to warn the monks to hastily construct a mosque.

It was about this time that a monk miraculously stumbled across a body on the summit of Mount Sinai. It was, he declared, the remains of St Catherine and it had been placed on the mountain by angels. The bones were immediately transferred to the church, and the monastery – which had originally been famed for its position beside the burning bush – now became known to all as St Catherine's. The fame of these relics soon spread far and wide and as the cult of St Catherine became popular in Europe, pilgrims began to make their way to Sinai to venerate her remains. By the time Sir John came here, thousands had visited the monastery, prayed beside her tomb, and taken home oil that oozed from the bones of the saint.

Sir John's description could almost have been written today. 'The monks who live there,' he writes, 'are Arabians and Greeks, and they are dressed like hermits; there is a large convent of them. They live on dates and roots and herbs . . . [and] are devout men and lead a pure life, and live in great abstinence and great penance.'

Though the number of monks has declined from some 400 in

the fourteenth century to today's 20, the way of life continues as it always has done: an endless cycle of prayer and fasting.

It was not the first time I had stayed in a monastery. Only a year before I had visited the monastic community of Mount Athos in northern Greece, staying in the great Byzantine monasteries that cling to the Aegean cliffs. But St Catherine's is a very different place. Surrounded by desert and troubled for centuries by Bedouin, its life is contained entirely within its massive walls. There is only one entrance – and even that didn't exist until recent times. Early visitors were hauled over the walls in a bucket.

Within these walls there are several churches, a mosque, a refectory, the library, the kitchens, and the living quarters of the monks. The collection of buildings has grown over the centuries so that there is no order to the place. Tiny alleys twist around the church and cobbled paths lead up steps, down steps and round corners before ending in blank walls. The only way to orientate yourself is to make a mental note of the few open spaces – splashed with sunlight and decorated with brightly coloured flower pots.

There is something intimidating about staying in a monastery and it took me several days to adjust to the peculiar way of life. Each day began long before dawn and the first few hours were spent in church listening to monotonous services in Greek. Even when the service came to an end, most of the monks – tired after a night in prayer – ignored me. Having no part to play in the community life of the monastery, and feeling totally irrelevant, I wondered how to fill the long, empty hours of the day.

But after a day or two the slower pace of life became more attractive. I woke up naturally at 4 am because I had gone to bed at 8 pm. The afternoons were spent reading. The absolute silence became appealing – intoxicating even – and soon every day rolled into one long, unchanging pattern of existence.

Only in the mornings was there any sign of life, for between 9 am and noon the monastery's doors were flung open to tourists and the silence would be shattered by a babble of voices. Day-trippers would flood into the courtyard, chattering, laughing and violating the sanctity of the place.

I grew to resent these three hours and the noise they brought. Yet the monks remained patient. Bleary-eyed and hungry, they would watch impassively while camera-clicking day-trippers posed next to them. These tourists saw little of the monastery and even less of its life. They were only allowed to poke their heads around the entrance of the church, while all the rest of the buildings were strictly off limits. I was lucky. Father John told me there were no restrictions on what I could and couldn't visit. The only problem, he said, was that he didn't think I should eat with the monks, explaining that the food was not so good. I was later told that the real reason was because I wasn't Orthodox.

At mealtimes I would leave the monastery and walk to the small pilgrims' hostel next door. On the first evening the cook served me my meal then handed me the bill, asking me with a puzzled expression if I was staying in the hostel. I explained that Father John had invited me to stay inside the monastery and an immediate change came over him.

'Father John . . . ' he said. 'In the monastery . . . well of course you don't have to pay. If you'd told me Father John . . . '

And he handed me back my money.

Father Nicholas was the first to speak to me. 'Morning,' he called out in fluent English. 'What brings you to St Catherine's?'

I explained about Sir John then asked where he learned such good English.

'Oh, I *am* English,' he said. 'I'm from Devon. But I've been living here for a few years now.' I began to wonder if every Orthodox monastery in the Middle East had a quota of English monks.

Father Nicholas had come to St Catherine's after a spiritual quest lasting several years. He had become interested in Orthodoxy while living in the West Country, had made a pilgrimage to Mount Athos, and was immediately taken by the monastic lifestyle.

'My mother was very worried when I went to Greece,' he told me. 'She said I'd become a monk and would never come back.'

But he did go back, to give Devon one more chance. Yet still he wasn't happy so when a friend suggested a holiday in

Jerusalem he jumped at the opportunity. The two of them visited the holy sites then popped to St Catherine's monastery for a couple of days. And as soon as he arrived, Father Nicholas knew he wanted to stay. He was rebaptized – this time into the Orthodox faith – became a novice, and has been there ever since*.

After vespers Father Nicholas offered to show me the library. St Catherine's library is said to be the second most important in the world after the Vatican. This is not because of the number of volumes it possesses – in fact it only boasts about 3,500 books – but because virtually every one is unique: ancient Bibles, codexes, writings of the desert fathers and prayer books. The very foundations of Christianity were built upon the works contained in this library.

I had vain hopes that there might be some record of Sir John's stay here: an early visitor's book, perhaps, or records left behind by western knights. But Father Nicholas said it was most unlikely. All the books, manuscripts and documents are religious works and even if Sir John had left anything behind, it would not have survived the centuries.

The library, built high into the back wall of the monastery, looks as old as the buildings that surround it yet it was built as recently as 1951. Father Nicholas unlocked the door and we stepped into the thick musty atmosphere. Shelves reached up to the high ceiling and were stacked with leather-bound volumes but when I took a closer look at these shelves I got quite a surprise. There was John Buchan's *The Thirty Nine Steps*, Nigel Balchin's *The Small Back Room*, and Jane Austin's *Sense and Sensibility*.

Father Nicholas laughed when I pointed them out. 'Most were left behind by visiting Anglican vicars,' he said. 'And when vicars write novels they often send a copy to us. But come over here . . . have a look at these.'

He pulled out an eleventh-century Bible, beautifully illustrated on every page. I turned the thick vellum with care: the swirling

---

*Only the monastery of St Catherine's and those on Mount Athos rebaptize Christians converting to Orthodoxy. It is regarded as controversial by many in the Orthodox church because, in the words of the Creed, 'I acknowledge *one* Baptism for the remission of sins . . .'

illuminations were in golds, cobalts and lapis blues – rich colours that hadn't faded in 900 years. When Sir John came to the monastery, this book had already been in the collection for three centuries.

'Now this item here is very interesting,' said Father Nicholas pointing to a document framed behind glass. It was a long sheet of parchment handwritten in Arabic and bearing the print of someone's hand.

'It's a letter from Mohammed,' he said. 'There's an old legend that relates how he visited the monastery and gave the place his own letter of protection guaranteeing that neither the buildings nor the monks would ever be harmed by Muslims.'

'And this is the original?' I asked.

'No, when Selim became Sultan of Constantinople in the sixteenth century he had 20 copies of the letter made for each of the monastery's dependent establishments. This is one of those copies. The original has sadly disappeared.'

Original or not, this document was of great importance for the survival of Christianity in the Middle East. Over the centuries it has been used to save churches from destruction and protect local Christian communities. Indeed it is said to have saved not only the Patriarch of Constantinople's job after the fall of the city to the Turks in 1453, but also to have protected many of the city's churches. More importantly it has helped to spare the monastery of St Catherine and its fabulous library.

There have, however, been dark periods in the library's history, the blackest moment of all being when a German scholar named Constantine Tischendorf visited the monastery in the 1840s. Tischendorf was one of the great nineteenth-century scholar travellers. Hugely erudite, wily and with a keen sense of humour, he found a basket of old parchment in the library which, he was told, were about to be used to light the bread oven.

On closer examination Tischendorf discovered – to his aston-ishment – that this parchment was a fourth-century manuscript of the Bible; one of the rarest books in the world. He managed to leave the monastery with a few scraps of the book and had them published in Germany. His sensational discovery set off a race among the scholars of Europe to acquire the rest of this Bible but

Tischendorf was not going to be outdone by Lord Curzon or Henry Tattam: with the support of the Russian government he returned to St Catherine's and began a desperate search for the rest of the manuscript. He couldn't find it in the library and the monks he questioned denied all knowledge of it. But just by chance Tischendorf spotted it in one of the monks' cells, surrounded by old tea cups and scraps of food. He later recalled:

> I unrolled the cover and discovered to my great surprise not only those fragments which fifteen years before I had taken out of the basket, but also other parts of the Old Testament, the New Testament complete, and, in addition, the Epistle of Barnabas and a part of the Pastor of Hermas . . . Full of joy, which this time I had the self command to conceal from the steward and the rest of the community, I asked, as if in a careless way, for permission to take the manuscript into my sleeping chamber to look over it more at leisure. There by myself I could give way to the transport of joy I felt. I knew that I held in my hand the most precious Biblical treasure in existence – a document whose age and importance exceeded all the manuscripts which I had ever examined during twenty years' study of the subject.

It was, it later transpired, one of 50 Bibles that the Byzantine Emperor Constantine had commissioned to celebrate the founding of the new Imperial capital of Constantinople. It was brought here when the monastery was founded and had survived the centuries, although even by Sir John's day, its significance had almost certainly been forgotten.

After lengthy negotiations with the monastery, Tischendorf was given permission to take the manuscript to Cairo to have it fully transcripted, but first he had to sign a pledge that he was borrowing 'under the form of a loan' as well as write a long letter guaranteeing that 'this manuscript I promise to return safely'.

He didn't. He had long since decided that the monks of St Catherine's had forfeited their right to possess such a priceless treasure and took considerable relish in recounting his deception: 'I set out from Egypt early in October and on the 19th of November I presented to their Imperial Majesties in the Winter Palace my rich collection of old Greek, Syrian, Coptic, Arabic and other manuscripts in the middle of which the Sinaitic Bible shone like a crown.'

The monks – only now aware of its value – were furious and tried to recover the book, but to this day they have never set eyes on it again. The Bible remained in Moscow until 1933 when the Soviets sold it to the British Museum for the massive sum of £100,000. The monastery could do nothing but protest. The monks had Tischendorf's promisory letter mounted and framed and hung it in a prominent place. Tischendorf is known to this day as 'the thief', and ever since his visit it has been extremely difficult to get access to the library of St Catherine's.

The British Museum's acquisition of the Bible seemed to mark the end of the Tischendorf story but one spring day in 1975 there was a small fire in one of the monastic churches. As the monks were clearing up the debris they unearthed an old cell filled with dust and rubble.

'One of the monks peered through the dust,' said Father Nicholas, 'and saw thousands of manuscripts just lying there, as they had lain for centuries.'

As these newly found treasures were lifted from the rubble, the full scale of the find became apparent. There were over 3,000 manuscripts, including another section of the Tischendorf Bible and scores of unique manuscripts from the seventh to ninth centuries – known as the 'period of silence' because of the lack of any biblical records. There were 60 further Bibles dating back to the fourth century, along with texts in Syriac, Arabic, Armenian, Coptic, Ethiopic, Georgian, Latin and Slavonic which provided a link between the first years of Christianity and the dawn of the Middle Ages.

No one knows why they had been hidden but the discovery caused a sensation, for never before had such an important haul of treasure come to life.

At the time Mandeville claims to have visited the monastic community of St Catherine's, the ruling dynasty in Egypt was in turmoil and the quest for the throne had degenerated into a bitter struggle between rival brothers, eunuchs, and slave girls.

The Mamelukes were slave soldiers who were brought back from military campaigns abroad, given a superb military training, then sold in the great slave auctions in Cairo. The best of these troops were employed by the sultan to enforce his authority but it was not long before they harboured dreams of wielding power themselves, and they eventually usurped the throne and established their own ruling line that controlled Egypt, Jerusalem and Damascus from 1250 to 1517.

By the fourteenth century the Mamelukes were entering their twilight years and Mandeville's description of their internecine warfare has been used by many to prove that he must have visited the country since no other western source recounts the period in such detail. Although he certainly copied some details from an Armenian book called *Fleur des Histoires d'Orient*, this account only deals with the history of Egypt up to the reign of Sultan al-Nasir. Mandeville is unique in naming the two rulers who followed, claiming that Sultan al-Nasir was followed by Sultan Mader and that he, in turn, was replaced by Sultan Madabron. But there is a problem. Scribal errors have distorted the names to such a great extent that it is difficult to know who – of the dozens of claimants to the throne – Sir John is refering to. 'Sultan Mader' probably refers to Mad-al-din who was crowned in 1342 while Madabron (the *on* is a suffix) could easily be a phonetic rendering of Mudhaffar, the ruler who succeeded in 1346. Unfortunately, neither of these men followed directly after al-Nasir. In the scramble for succession, they were the fourth and sixth sultans briefly to assume the throne before being deposed.

With characteristic bravuro Sir John never betrays the slightest doubts as to where he came by his information: 'I should know the organisation of his court pretty well,' he writes, 'for I lived a long time with the Sultan [and] he would have arranged a rich marriage for me with a great prince's daughter, and given me many great lordships if I had forsaken my faith and embraced theirs: but I did not want to.'

If Sir John arrived in Egypt in 1341 – as is suggested by his account of the reigning sultans – he would already have been travelling for some 19 years. This in itself would be enough to earn him a place in the history books yet at no point does Mandeville find the length of his journey in the slightest bit remarkable. Days, months and years drift through his narrative without comment and it is left to the reader to work out when he visited the towns and cities on his route.

Had he arrived in Egypt just a few years earlier he would have found himself in a golden age for the reigning sultan, al-Nasir, had been in power – on and off – since 1293 and had gradually eliminated all his enemies.

Al-Nasir was one of the most extravagant and outrageous characters of the whole dynasty. Fat, lame, and half-blind in one eye, he had a passion for beauty and never tired of lavishing money on ornaments and trinkets. As he toured his kingdom, he did so in ostentatious splendour, trailing vanities behind him.

On his return from one trip he laid out more than 4,000 rugs for his horse to inspect. No one recorded what his horse thought of them. While travelling across the Arabian desert on holy pilgrimage – a time when the devout abstained from all but the bare essentials – al-Nasir kept his table supplied with fresh fruit and vegetables grown in a travelling garden slung between forty camels. His son's wedding feast was an occasion for even greater excess. Lavishing gargantuan quantities of food upon his guests, he fed the wedding party with 20,000 animals and 18,000 sugar loaves, and lit the glittering affair with more than 3,000 candles.

Not content with adorning his own court, he next decided to adorn his country, beautifying his land with public buildings. When told about the difficulties of travelling from Alexandria to Cairo his solution was to build a vast canal. To ensure a constant supply of fresh water to Cairo's citadel he constructed a huge aquaduct. He founded mosques, baths and schools and built himself an exquisite new palace modelled on one he had taken a fancy to in Damascus. It cost five hundred million silver pieces.

Despite encouraging extravagance in his court Sultan al-Nasir himself lived a Jekyll and Hyde existence. He amassed thousands of jewels yet never wore any himself. He adored the pageantry of falconry yet never took part himself. He lavished gifts on his favourites yet preferred an ascetic lifestyle. He was an absolute despot – autocratic, iron-willed, arrogant and vengeful.

On gaining the throne he bow-strung one of his enemies who, years before, had refused to roast him a goose. Another enemy, the former viceroy, was condemned to death by starvation. As he lay in fetters and tortured with hunger pains Sultan al-Nasir relented and sent him three covered dishes. But it was a cruel deceit: when the viceroy opened them he discovered that they contained gold, silver and jewels.

Yet despite the barbarism, al-Nasir's reign was a period of unparalleled magnificence. His glittering court and outlandish public buildings mark him as one of the most brilliant rulers of the Middle Ages and ambassadors from all over the world flocked to salute him. Mongols, Persians, Byzantines, and Moroccans all sent envoys, soon to be followed by those of the Sultan of Hindustan, the King of Aragon, the Pope and King Philip VI of France.

He was equally popular with his own people. To pay for the luxury of his court he encouraged trade with the west. To reduce people's hardship he repealed taxes on slaves. He even repealed laws against Christians and Jews so that by the time he died, Egypt was in the midst of a renaissance. The last crusader states had been driven out of the Holy Land. The last Mongol invasion had been crushed in Syria, and al-Nasir himself had watched the defeated Mongols march through Cairo, every prisoner in chains and each one bearing a fellow Mongol's head dangling from his neck.

But he made one fatal mistake that was to plunge the country into disarray. He failed to nominate a successor, so that the next 41 years saw no less than eight sons, two grandsons, and two great-grandsons seize the throne.

It was just at this time that Sir John set foot in Egypt.

When he learned of all the terrible upheavals at the imperial court Sir John must have been terrified, especially since he found himself summoned to an audience with the newly enthroned sultan – the son of al-Nasir – who was far from secure in his position.

First, Sir John got himself acquainted with the intricate etiquette that surrounded the Mameluke court:

No stranger must come before the Sultan unless he be clad in cloth of gold or of Tartary or camlet – a fashion of clothing the Saracens follow. And whenever he sees the Sultan, at a window or elsewhere, he must kneel down and kiss the earth . . . and when any foreigners come to him, his men stand round with drawn swords in their hands, and their hands raised on high to strike him down if he say anything to displease the Sultan. No stranger shall come before him to ask anything without having his request granted, if it be reasonable and not contrary to their law . . . for they say that no man should have audience without leaving happier than he came thither.

As Sir John stood in silence, trembling at the knees and surrounded by soldiers waiting to stab him to death, he bowed deeply to the Sultan. He had heard that the Sultan never refused a request. Well, he himself had a small favour to ask. Could he possibly, er, would it be agreeable to His All Highness if he could have a permit to travel wherever he wanted? The Sultan agreed, the soldiers sheathed their daggers, and Sir John must have let out a long sigh of relief. But there was one caveat: the Sultan wanted a quiet word in Sir John's ear, in private, before he handed over the permit.

'He made everyone else leave his chamber, lords as well as others who were there, for he wanted to have a private talk between ourselves alone. And when they had all gone out, he asked me how Christians governed themselves in our countries. And I said, "Lord, well enough – thanks be to God." And he answered and said: "Truly, no. It is not so . . . ." '

What follows is the blistering and highly informed attack on the west, detailing everything that was wrong with the church, the state and people's greed. It is a fascinating speech – erudite, accurate, and all the more remarkable considering that the sultan of the time was just seven years old . . .

This young sultan had found himself thrust on to the throne as a result of political intrigue inside the imperial palace. His father's corpse had not even been cold when the struggle for succession began. At the forefront of the commotion were the imperial eunuchs who at last saw their chance of power after decades of holding positions without real authority. In the troubled years that followed al-Nasir's death they, in league with slave girls from the palace, assumed positions of unprecedented influence.

The seven-year-old Sultan al-Ashraf didn't last long. He was overthrown, his successors were murdered, and a whole new battle for succession began. Yet despite the political turmoil, court life was as luxurious as ever. Though the empire teetered on the brink of financial ruin and even the annual pilgrimage to Mecca had to be abandoned due to a lack of funds, there was an endless procession of singers and dancing girls streaming into the palace.

Such excess couldn't last for ever and life soon turned sour. Within a few years of Mandeville's visit, the Black Death hit Egypt, killing almost one million people. Cattle diseases accompanied the plague. The fish in the Nile were poisoned. The harvests failed and whole cities were abandoned by a terrified populace.

Though few western knights travelled to Cairo during these troubled years, a steady stream did reach St Catherine's, and Father Nicholas confirmed that many carved their names into the walls of the refectory and the doors of the church. 'Some of the walls are completely covered in the names and coats of arms of medieval knights,' he said. 'If you're really lucky, your Sir John might have done the same.'

First we went to examine the church doors, armed with a torch and magnifying glass. The sturdy outer doors dated from the eleventh century and were indeed covered from top to bottom with hundreds of scratches and carvings. But it was difficult to decipher these marks for the wood was often splintered where a name had been carved, and centuries of desert sand blasting the doors had erased all but the deepest incisions. Easier to trace were the numerous crosses carved in different shapes and sizes:

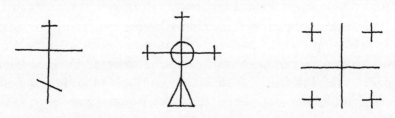

Many appeared to be Templar crosses and were carved, said Father Nicholas, by the Templar knights who came to St Catherine's while searching for the Holy Grail.

When we had finished examining the doors, we wandered over to the refectory where the western knights had slept. Although Father Nicholas had told me there were many coats of arms here, it was not until he switched on the light that I realized just how many knights must have stayed. The walls and barrel-vaulted ceiling were decorated with hundreds of coats of arms, along with scores of names scrawled in English, French, German and Dutch.

By the time of the crusades there were so many western pilgrims visiting St Catherine's that there was even a community of Latin monks permanently established within the monastery precincts. They built a Catholic chapel inside the monastery walls which was known as 'St Catherine of the Franks' and painted their own icons which are still housed here. And before they left on the long journey home, many carved their names and shields into the walls – medieval graffiti on a grand scale.

My biggest problem was that I didn't know exactly what Sir John's coat of arms looked like. English travellers who had visited Sir John's supposed tomb in Liège were shown a coat of arms displaying a silver lion with a crescent on its breast. This, I knew, could not have belonged to Sir John for no Mandeville ever had such a shield.

A second Mandeville shield was recorded in a fifteenth-century treatise on heraldry which had been compiled by a certain Sir Richard Strangways. This was very different – it was decorated with three vertical stripes of blue interlaced with three horizontal stripes of red, and underneath Strangways had written: 'Shield of Sir John Mandeville, Peregrinator'. Unfortunately, he fails to say where he came by this coat of arms. Was it genuine? As yet I didn't know.

To confuse matters further, I had with me a third coat of arms – that of Geoffrey de Mandeville – from whom all Mandevilles were ultimately descended. This was important evidence for heraldry works according to specific rules and can, in theory, be traced backwards in time. If I found a coat of arms similar to

Geoffrey's there was a chance that I'd be able to link it to the Mandeville line and perhaps even prove that it belonged to Sir John.

But there was another problem: although I knew that Geoffrey's shield was coloured in gold and red, it was almost completely unadorned, save for two lines which met in the middle.

In heraldic terms it is known as a 'simple quarterly shield; or and gules'.

Father Nicholas and I left the shields till last and began with the names. Some were easy to read while others had faded or been half-obscured with plaster. There was a 'Compeys', a 'Yawbhrey', and a 'Sallmy' while one on the end wall looked like 'Lebierorhimis', although its elaborate Gothic script was difficult to decipher. Many had only a few letters surviving – an 'S' here, a 'W' there, with the rest of the name obliterated by the passing of the centuries.

By the door we found dozens of inscriptions and some had dates to go with them. There was a Jaubert, an Amoirillon, (he must have been French) and a Borthen, whose name was dated 1458, more than a century after Sir John, while Jaubert had carved his in 1065, the year before the Battle of Hastings. If he hadn't come to St Catherine's, he might have fought in the battle alongside William the Conqueror.

'What's this,' called Father Nicholas from the other end of the room. I rushed over with the torch and examined the inscription more closely. It cerainly began with a 'Man' but, on closer inspection, tailed off into a completely different name.

When we had exhausted the names we began on the shields. But this proved equally fruitless. There were scores of them and many were beautifully preserved. Some were decorated with stars and some with lines, but all were far more decorative than Geoffrey's quarterly shield.

'Have you seen that one there,' said Father Nicholas, pointing towards the ceiling. 'That looks a little like the one you described.' I looked up. It was difficult to see clearly as it was so high up, and I asked if we could move the table nearer.

'Of course,' he said, and we both clambered on to the table for a closer look. And as I examined it I felt a thrill of excitement. The coat of arms was indeed a simple quarterly shield in gold and red and it contained just one small addition: there was a diagonal stripe on the shield which curved from one corner to the other.

'Well?' asked Father Nicholas.

'Well . . . ' I said. 'I don't know. It certainly *looks* a little like the Mandeville crest, but then again . . . '

It was a curious carving. It was carefully made and someone – at a much later date – had painted two elaborately carved helmets above it. I drew the shield and took a photograph of it. I wouldn't know the full story until I returned to London where, I hoped, the College of Arms would be able to give me an official identification.

One day, as I was busy transcribing crosses from the church door, the silence of the afternoon was rudely shattered by a shout from the courtyard.

'Coo-coo . . . is there anyone at home?'

I went to see who it was and found a ginger-haired American soldier dressed in army fatigues and a blue UN beret. Beside him stood another man, clearly not American, dressed in similar gear.

'Ron,' said the American, thrusting his hand into mine. 'Am I pleased to meet you.' His voice was overpowering in the absolute stillness of the monastery and everything he said bounced off the walls that surrounded the courtyard.

'Do you *live* here?' he asked, and the echo repeated his words. I explained that I was staying for a while.

'It looks kinda old,' he bawled. 'When was it put up?'

At that moment Father Nicholas appeared. He welcomed the American and asked, very apologetically, if he could possibly keep his voice down. 'Everyone sleeps at midday,' he explained.

'Understood . . . ' said Ron. 'Now who are you? Some kinda monk?'

'Yes, I live here.'

'Well that's just great,' said Ron as he turned to his colleague.

'Say, Scotch, this is a real monk. Bet you've never met one of these before.'

Scotch, who was Russian, began to speak in broken English. 'Er, yes I have. You see, my country is Orthodox too. We have monks in Russia.'

'Is that so?' said an increasingly amazed Ron. 'You know something? I never knew that until this very moment. Now Nick, tell me, how old is this building.'

'Well it dates from the fourth century . . . ' said Father Nicholas.

'The fourth century AD?' exclaimed Ron. 'No kidding? That's too bad.'

'But . . . ' continued Father Nicholas, 'the present church is more recent.'

Ron looked upset. 'How old is this then,' he asked, kicking the wall.

'This dates from about AD542.'

Ron smiled again. 'You were trying to kid me Nick, weren't you? Well, I still call five-forty something kinda old.'

'Now let's get straight to the point,' blared Ron, 'the thing is, we've taken some of your water for our jeep. We took it from the well.'

'That's Moses's well,' said Father Nicholas.

'Moses . . . right, Moses . . . the guy who spoke to God. Well, do you want some money?'

'No,' said Father Nicholas, 'no. I hope your jeep enjoys the water. It's the sweetest in the whole of Sinai.'

'She's a thirsty doll,' said Ron. 'By the way . . . ' he added, 'tell your boss you've got one hell of a place here. One *hell* of a place. This is what I call real history.' And with that he turned and, with a wave, he and his colleague left the monastery.

Mohammed, the monastery's cook, refused to speak to me at first. He was too busy, he said. He couldn't talk while he was working. Perhaps if I came to the kitchens later he would speak. But perhaps he would be too tired.

I returned at one o'clock, just as he had finished serving the meal. Big helpings of fish were being slopped into dishes, salad was being placed on the tables, and a few monks were hanging around in the doorway, hungry for their lunch.

'I'm sorry about Mohammed,' said Father George. 'He doesn't like to mix work with talk.'

Father George was a Greek monk who spoke fluent Arabic and he had agreed to translate some questions I wanted to ask Mohammed. In England I had read a curious story about the Bedouin who worked for the monastery: a story that claimed they were the descendants of a Christian tribe from Europe. Although the hotel owner in Darhab had ridiculed such a suggestion, I wanted to hear if the Bedouin themselves knew anything about their ancient ancestors.

While we waited for Mohammed to finish the salads I chatted with Father George. He spoke excellent English and I asked him where he learnt it.

'Oh, I used to live in London,' he said.

'Where?'

'West London, near Queensway.'

I explained that I lived near Queensway and he laughed. 'Do you know the pastry shop on Moscow Road?' he asked.

I nodded and he told me he used to go there every morning for his breakfast. 'Best pastries in London,' he added. We were interrupted by a sudden rap on the kitchen hatch. 'Quick,' said Father George. 'Mohammed is ready. Maybe you'll get to know more about the Bedouin.'

According to local legends, the Bedouin of Sinai are among the wildest people on earth. Even at the height of Sultan al-Nasir's power they had proved troublesome, frequently ravaging the countryside, slaughtering farmers and massacring the Sultan's troops. Sir John wrote of them:

They are people of evil condition, full of all kinds of wickedness and malice. Houses have they none, only tents, which they make of skins of camels and other wild beasts that they eat, and they drink water when they can get it . . . nevertheless they are strong men, good fighters; and there is a great multitude of them. They do nothing else but hunt wild beasts . . . and they do not care for their lives, and therefore they do not fear the Sultan nor any other prince of the world.

In order to reach St Catherine's, medieval pilgrims had to travel for 14 days through land controlled by these tribes – the same tribes who had tried to stop the building of the monastery some eight centuries previously. And this is where the peculiar story of the Christian Bedouin originates.

According to Byzantine chroniclers, the Emperor Justinian ordered 100 soldiers and their families to be sent to Sinai from Walachia in Romania in order to protect the monastery from the constant harassment. These soldiers were Christian and when they arrived they settled close to the monastery walls.

So far so good. But once they were established in Sinai the records grow hazy. Their descendants were definitely still serving the monastery when Islam spread through North Africa but, by the ninth century they had begun to resemble the lawless desert Bedouin, as a historian of the time recalls: 'After a long time they had many children and multiplied, [but when] Mohammedanism spread, which happened under Caliph Malek, they fell upon one another . . . some were killed and some fled and others embraced Mohammedanism, whose descendants at the monastery to this day profess.'

But not all the members of the tribe converted to Islam for travellers still record meeting Christian Bedouin hundreds of years after this, and one writer claims that the last Christian didn't die until the eighteenth century. And then there is silence. There are no more records of Justinian's soldiers.

The cook Mohammed was dark skinned and of indeterminate age. He could have been as young as 40 or as old as 60. His skin was wrinkled, but it was aged by the sun and not by his years. He reluctantly shook my hand, adjusted his headscarf, and asked why I wanted to speak to him. I told him – with Father George interpreting – the story of the Byzantine emperor and asked if any of the Bedouin were Christian.

'No,' he said, shaking his head. 'Not at all.'

'Had they ever been Christian?' He threw up his hands. Not to his knowledge. His father and grandfather were Bedouin. They were Bedouin of the desert and they were all Muslims. But here Mohammed inadvertently let slip a very interesting fact. I was asking about St Catherine and whether he believed in the legends, when he suddenly interrupted me. 'Of course we believe in them,' he said. 'We venerate St Catherine. We celebrate her feast day. And we venerate Elias and Moses too.'

This was fascinating. Two months earlier the Mufti of Cyprus had told me that there were no saints in Islam, yet here was a Bedouin, a member of a Muslim tribe, venerating a Christian saint. Could it be possible that Mohammed and his tribe were indeed the descendants of that small band of soldiers sent to guard the monastery in the sixth century on the orders of the Emperor Justinian? If so, Mohammed was serving the monastery in the twentieth century on the orders of a Byzantine emperor made some 1,400 years earlier.

I asked if his tribe worshipped St Catherine in church, but Father George stopped me. 'I am terribly sorry,' he said, 'but I cannot put these questions to Mohammed. Islam prohibits the worship of saints and what you are asking about is an extremely sensitive subject, especially with the growth of fundamentalism in Egypt. I will put any question you like to Mohammed, but please, I cannot ask such things as these.'

I had one last query. It was rumoured that the Jebeliyah accept the bishop of the monastery as the supreme head of their tribe. Was that the case?

'Indeed,' said Mohammed. 'We go to the bishop whenever we have a dispute over land or money. If two Bedouin are fighting one another we take our case to the bishop. He solves all our problems.'

One afternoon Father Nicholas said he would show me the church and the relics; the same that Sir John had seen all those centuries before.

And beside the High Altar are four steps leading up to the tomb of alabaster wherein the body of the holy virgin saint Katherine lies. And the prelate of the monks shows the relics of this virgin to pilgrims; with an instrument of silver he moves the bones of the virgin on an altar. Then there comes out a little oil, like sweat; but it is like neither oil nor balm for it is blacker. Of this liquid they give a little to pilgrims – for only a little comes out. After, they show you the head of St Katherine, and the cloth that it was wrapped in . . . and the cloth is still bloody and always will be.

The casket still stands in the same place although there are no longer as many bones as there were in medieval times for the monks, in their attempt to collect money for the monastery, travelled throughout Europe with the relics of St Catherine and on arriving in Rouen sold half of them to the cathedral. To this day, Rouen possesses more of St Catherine than the monastery itself.

Many European pilgrims were inspired to come to the monastery by the huge quantity of myrrh that flowed from the bones of the saint, and early visitors describe monks spooning liquid myrrh out of the coffin. By Sir John's time only a few drops could be scraped from the surface of the bones and now they have dried up completely, although there are still traces of their former miraculous properties.

'Put your nose to the casket,' said Father Nicholas. 'Can you smell anything?'

I inhaled deeply and smelt a thick, perfumed scent coming from the alabaster box. It was sweet like wood resin and did indeed seem to come from the bones. I asked Father Nicholas if we could open the casket but he shook his head. 'I'm afraid not,' he said. 'The relics are only brought out on feast days.'

But later that evening he had other bones to show me: the bones of long-deceased monks which are stored in the monastery's charnel house. In a small room as dry as old parchment are the bones of all the monks who have lived and died at St Catherine's.

Every time a monk dies his body is buried for a few years to help it decompose. The bones are then dug up, separated, the skull is inscribed, and all are placed on to their respective piles in the charnel house so that today there are vast mountains of tibia and fibia, skulls and vertabrae, stacked right up to the ceiling.

Strangest of all is the monk who guards these bones. Slumped in a chair and dressed in his black vestment is Father Stephanos – mummified. Ever since he died in the sixth century this monk, who used to guard the gateway leading to the top of the mountain, has sat in the charnel house presiding over the remains of the monks. From the bottom of his vestments, a mummified foot pokes out while above his head, a pile of tibias seem ready to come crashing down on top of him.

As I looked at this stockpile of bones it struck me that somewhere in this grisly room were the remains of the monks that Sir John would have met and chatted with. Perhaps he had spoken to the very skull I was now looking at: the one at the bottom of a pile whose few remaining teeth were curved into a fixed grin? Perhaps he had shaken the mummified hand that was hanging over a small rail, swaying slightly in the breeze that filtered through the door?

Had these men been saints like St Catherine? Had they sinned and confined themselves to a monastery as penance? It was impossible to know, for their stories were lost for ever among this pile of bones. Here was a place to marvel at the continuity of St Catherine's for this desert monastery is utterly unchanged since the day Sir John came here: a place where ancient, medieval and modern all roll into one endless continuum of history.

I had to leave the monastery the following day and went to thank Father John for his kindness after the morning liturgy. He nodded graciously and said he had something to give me. He opened his drawer and scratched around inside before looking at me with a smile.

'Here,' he said as he handed me a ring. 'This is for you to take back to England. We only give it to pilgrims who stay here in the monastery.'

I looked at it closely. It was a thick band of silver which had been inscribed in Greek with the words AI AIKATEPINA – St Catherine – with the beginning and end of the name decorated with tiny crosses. I thanked him again and was about to leave when Father Nicholas entered the room and said he also had something for me. It was a miniature glass phial filled with amber-coloured oil which was sealed with a tiny stopper.

'It's from the lamp that lights the relics of St Catherine,' he said. 'It's not the same as the myrrh that Sir John would have taken home with him, but take it and keep it. It's precious.'

'And did you discover whether your knight stayed here?' asked Father John.

I told him about the coat of arms and said I would have to wait until I got back to England to know for sure.

'Well there's one more thing to say,' he added. 'If you ever need to return to Sinai, you are welcome to stay in St Catherine's whenever you want.'

11 Onward to China

Sir John Mandeville, knight and doctor in physick . . . left a book
of his travels, which hath been honoured with the translation of
many languages, and now continued above three hundred years;
herein he often attesteth the fabulous relations of Ctesias, and
seems to confirm the refuted accounts of antiquity.

Vulgar Errors, **Sir Thomas Browne, 1646**

Many, if not most, of these Ctesian fables in Sir J. Mandevill were
monkish interpolations.

Notes on Sir Thomas Browne's Vulgar Errors,
Samuel Taylor Coleridge, 10 March 1804

ir John begins his book with the intention of visiting the
Holy Land. He sets out his reasons for going on a
pilgrimage and includes a few pious sentiments and a
selection of quotes from the Bible. It is only when he comes to list
the places he visited that he tells the reader he travelled a good
deal further afield than Jerusalem. Unexpectedly, almost casu-
ally, he says that his 34-year voyage actually took him halfway
around the world.

Before describing this second leg of the voyage, he once again
sets out his intentions and says that he hopes to visit the 'diverse
kingdoms, countries, and isles in the eastern part of the world,
where live different kinds of men and animals, and many other
marvellous things.'

All these marvellous things – monsters, pygmies, and savages
– found their way into *The Travels* and as Sir John reaches the
farthest flung corners of the globe, the pious platitudes are
replaced by lurid descriptions of an increasingly deformed
troupe of animals.

To modern ears, Sir John's fabulous tales about Java, Sumatra
and Borneo sound more like fables than the eye-witness
descriptions of a genuine traveller, but to his contemporaries

such monsters were very real creatures. His descriptions of the east were treated as hard practical information and cartographers filled the blank spaces on their maps with not only the abominable creatures that Mandeville claims to have seen, but also with pictures of the imperial palaces and eastern soldiers that he so vividly records. Two of the greatest sixteenth-century geographers, Ortelius and Mercator, both acknowledged their debt to Mandeville when they came to draw their world maps. Ortelius was so impressed he even visited Sir John's supposed grave in Liège.

Mandeville's reputation only began to suffer when the great age of exploration began, for the long sea voyages of the Renaissance geographers seemed to prove once and for all that Sir John's stories of monsters, giants and weird animals were nothing more than figments of his own imagination. It was concluded that his entire journey must have been a fiction and *The Travels* was soon mocked as a worthless piece of writing and consigned to the literary dustbin.

Yet even Mandeville's tallest of tall tales deserve closer examination. The practice of burning Indian women alive on their husband's funeral pyre sounds like one of his more colourful inventions, yet suttee was certainly practised in Mandeville's time and, though now outlawed, occurs in remote Indian villages to this day. His lavish description of the pepper forests of Malabar sounds equally suspect, yet such forests were also reported by the prosaic Marco Polo. The trees that grow flour may be an invention, but they sound remarkably similar to the sago-palm; while those that bear poison could well refer to the noxious upas-tree. Even Mandeville's story of the reed-beds of Borneo – where precious jewels are said to grow on the branches of the plants – has a rational explanation: bamboo emits a siliceous concretion which could easily be mistaken for gemstones.

It only requires a shift from a rational, to a lateral train of thought to find an explanation for many of Mandeville's more outlandish descriptions. Giant snails sound implausible – especially when Mandeville claims that 'three or four men can shelter in their shells' – until you realize he is referring to giant tortoises. Dog-faced men, too, sound monstrous unless they are descriptions of baboons which do indeed have snouts like dogs. And while there are certainly no pygmies on the Asian mainland, Sir John's race of midgets sound remarkably like the warrior pygmies who inhabit the highlands of New Guinea.

While none of these explanations proves that Sir John did travel, his claim to have visited the Far East cannot be dismissed out of hand. That the road to China was still open in the fourteenth century is demonstrated by a trickle of European travellers who did indeed reach the east and returned to tell the tale. Marco Polo had set out on his famous voyage in 1271, less than three decades before Mandeville was born, and the Nestorian monks Sawma and Markos had survived the journey in the other direction. Although the route was fraught with the perils of drought, starvation and murderous brigands, men did hazard the long journey and live to tell the tale.

If Sir John did make his journey east, he would have been one of the very last Europeans to travel overland to China until the nineteenth century, for within a few years of his death the Mongol Emperor Tamberlaine the Great swept out of China with his army and plunged Asia into anarchy for the next five centuries.

Mandeville does more than simply list monsters and pygmies in the second half of his *Travels*; he also presents concrete details about the places he visits. In India he gives precise descriptions of the emperor's army and how it does battle. In China he claims to have been welcomed by the Great Khan himself and recalls how he stayed in his palace for many months. In Tibet he recounts in great detail the burial rituals of the Tibetans. But, as with the first part of the book, Sir John pillaged from every available source for his supposedly truthful narrative. Two writers in particular provided him with many of his tales from the Far East: two exceptionally brave men whose accounts lie gathering dust in the British Library. The truth about Mandeville's voyage can only be judged in relation to theirs, not simply because he borrowed their stories, but because they really did make the journey and documented the perils and hardships of the road.

The first was a Franciscan monk called John of Plano Carpini who was dispatched by the Pope on the 3,000-mile journey to China in 1245. He was hopelessly ill-equipped for the task. Immensely fat, 65 years old and with no knowledge of Oriental languages, he had to bandage his body from head to foot in order to endure the pain of 15 hours' riding every day. His account of the voyage includes not only an eye-witness account of the Mongol court, but also gives a painfully graphic description of the hardships of the overland voyage: 'We were so weak we could hardly ride. During the whole of that Lent our food had been nothing but millet with water and salt, and it was the same on other fast days, and we had nothing to drink except snow melted in a kettle . . . We feared that we might be killed by the Tartars . . . [for] we came across many skulls and bones of dead men lying on the ground like dung.'

Despite the terrible hardship of the journey, this corpulent monk delivered the Pope's letter to the ungracious Emperor, returned to Europe and survived for just long enough to write up his travels before dropping dead from exhaustion.

The second traveller to whom Sir John was indebted was Friar Odoric, another Franciscan who travelled through Turkey, Iraq, Persia, India, Sumatra and Borneo, before landing in China where he baptized 20,000 people. He, too, survived to tell the tale in his *Itinerarius* and although his book has long been forgotten, Odoric was assured eternal remembrance when the Pope beatified him in 1755.

Mandeville lifted scores of stories from Friar Odoric's book yet he stops short of copying Odoric's more ludicrous tales. Whereas Sir John's monstrous snails fit the description of giant tortoises, Odoric describes the shells of such 'snails' bigger than the dome of St Anthony's church in Padua – more than 40 feet in diameter.

Mandeville's borrowings are always selective. Some of his stories are copied from Solinus, Isidore of Seville and Vincent of Beauvais. Several are lifted from Pliny, while his tale of the gold-digging ants of present-day Sri Lanka is taken straight from the pages of Herodotus. He must have chuckled to himself when he included the tale of the 30-foot-high giants he met in the east, for it is taken verbatim from Julius Caesar's account of the ancient Britons.

But not all Sir John's flights of the imagination have such obvious sources. Neither Friar Odoric not John of Plano Carpini describe the Indian court or the protocol that surrounded an appearance by the emperor, while many of his descriptions of China seem far more likely than the accounts of his peers.

By the time he reached India Sir John says he was weary from travelling. The overland journey had taken its toll and he had suffered great hardship. But as soon as he arrived at the emperor's court he found an unexpected delight for, after travelling halfway across Asia, he found himself in a land rich in food, well-populated, civilized and superbly governed by a wise ruler named Prester John.

Although Mandeville doesn't say how long he stayed with Prester John it must have been some considerable length of time for he gives a detailed description of his kingdom and its chief cities, as well as describing the richness and beauty of the Imperial palace in the city of Susa:

> That palace is so wealthy, so noble, so full of delights that it is a marvel to tell of. For on top of the main tower are two balls of gold, in each of which are two great fair carbuncles, which shine very brightly in the night. The chief gates of the palace are of precious stones, which men call sardonyx, and the bars are of ivory. The windows of the hall and the chambers are all of crystal. All the tables they eat off are of emeralds, amethysts and, some, of gold, set with precious stones . . . the steps up which the Emperor goes to his throne are bordered with fine gold, set full of pearls and other precious stones on the sides and edges.

This was not all: Prester John's power was as unlimited as his retinue was immense. He had seven kings serving under him; 72 dukes to oversee his every wish and whim; and 360 earls living at court in case he might need their support. But far more important than this – and the factor that mattered to Sir John – was that Prester John was Christian: a powerful emperor ruling over a vast area of land. He had a massive army, endless resources, and all his vassals and client kingdoms were Christian too.

Every time he went into battle he carried not banners, like western knights, but three huge crosses made of solid gold. Each one, says Sir John, was guarded by 10,000 men at arms and more than 100,000 foot soldiers. And although he had so far confined his battles to fighting the Persians, he had plans to wrest the Holy City of Jerusalem from the infidel.

What relief Sir John must have felt to arrive in India and find himself fêted by a generous Christian ruler. Except, of course, for one important point: it is most unlikely that Sir John ever went to India, and even more unlikely that he met the ruler of this Christian empire. For unbeknown to Mandeville, Prester John never existed.

He was not the only one to believe the stories he had heard about Prester John. Every monarch, nobleman, and priest across medieval Europe believed that the Indian continent was ruled by a powerful Christian emperor called Prester John, and all expected him – as Sir John himself writes – to march on Jerusalem with his huge army. Unfortunately it was not to be. For the letter that brought the news of this emperor to Europe some two centuries earlier was a hoax – perhaps the greatest hoax ever perpetrated in history.

It was the evening of 27 September 1177, and Pope Alexander III had just finished writing a most important letter. It was a reply to a long missive he had recently received from the king of India – a king he had only vaguely heard of – and it concerned a topic close to his heart: the recapture of Jerusalem. The Pope thanked this distant monarch for the letter, expressed his total support for the ideas it contained, and sent his papal blessing, addressing the ruler as, 'the illustrious and magnificent king of the Indies and beloved son of Christ'.

The letter from India had taken several years to reach the papal palace in Vitterbo and when it did arrive, no one could quite explain who had brought it or how it had been delivered. It was 12 pages long, written in good Latin, and contained the most startling information. For it related precise details of the strongest and most powerful Christian state on earth – an empire ruled by a priest king who now wished to perform his religious duty by recovering the Holy City from the infidel. This is how it began:

> Prester John, by the Grace of God, most powerful king over all Christian kings, greetings to the Emperor of Rome and the King of France, our friends:
>
> We wish you to learn about us, our position, the government of our land, and our people and our beasts . . . We let you know that we worship and believe in Father, Son, and Holy Ghost, three persons in one Deity and one true God only [and] that we have the highest crown on earth as well as gold, silver, precious stones and strong fortresses, cities, towns, castles and boroughs. We have under our sway forty-two kings who are all good and mighty Christians . . . know also we have promised and sworn in our good faith to conquer the Sepulchre of Our Lord and the whole Promised Land . . .

The letter goes on to recount the natural abundance of the land and the incredible animals that live there; it speaks of the palaces and monuments that adorn the country and records how the empire is ruled as a Utopian state, before finishing with the words: 'If Thou canst count the stars of the sky and the sands of the sea, judge the vastness of our realm and our power.'

This was not the first time that news of Prester John had been brought to the attentions of Europe. Some 30 years earlier a bishop from Asia Minor had visited the Pope in order to argue the case for a new crusade, and while staying at the papal palace this bishop had been introduced to a German historian called Otto of Freising to whom he recounted a similar story about a mighty Christian emperor of India.

Otto was fascinated by what he heard and when he wrote his famous history of the Middle Ages, he included all the details about Prester John. He described the emperor as a Nestorian Christian who was descended from one of the three kings and recorded how Prester John had defeated the huge Persian army but was forced to abandon his march on Jerusalem because the

River Tigris didn't freeze and couldn't be crossed by his thousands of troops.

Several decades before Prester John's famous letter even reached the papal court, this mysterious Indian emperor had already entered the history books and been accepted as a real person. It is hardly surprising, therefore, that when a letter from him did finally arrive Pope Alexander wasn't unduly surprised. It merely confirmed everything he had already been told.

But why had such a story, which was pure fiction, been so readily accepted by the west? And how did the person who hoaxed the letter manage to make it so believable that everyone – from the Pope and the monarchs of Europe to Mandeville and the world's great explorers – fell for it hook, line and sinker?

From the earliest times, the word 'India' had an important resonance for Christians. India was where the Apostle Thomas was believed to have preached and was said to have converted thousands of Hindus before being killed there, a martyr to his faith. Sir John would have known the story of St Thomas: how he refused to go to India because of his failing health: how Christ appeared before him and told him to pretend he was a carpenter: how he was eventually stabbed to death for daring to criticize the king.

With only sketchy knowledge of India, the Church and the crowned heads of medieval Europe all assumed that St Thomas had laid the foundations for the powerful Christian state now ruled by Prester John. Even before his famous letter turned up in Italy, there were many stories about this exemplary king circulating around Europe – stories which became more and more exaggerated as they were passed orally from country to country. One such tale was written down at about the time of the letter and was clearly known to Sir John for he includes snippets of it in his *Travels*. It is a far-fetched tale which describes how Prester John had one day travelled to Rome to tell the Pope about a strange mountain that stood outside his capital. This mountain had a church dedicated to St Thomas on its peak – a church which contained a huge silver vessel holding the uncorrupted body of the saint himself. At this point the story becomes very strange indeed; every feast day the patriarch would lift this body out of the vessel and place it in an armchair beside a large bowl of consecrated bread. The ghostly white apostle would slowly sit up, take a piece of bread in his own hand, and distribute it to the pilgrims. If any non-believer was there he would die on the spot.

Sir John reports this story and even claims to have seen the relics of St Thomas in the city of Mailapur, but he changes it slightly in order to make it more believable: 'His hand . . . lies in a reliquary and men of that country judge who is right by that hand. For if there be a quarrel between two parties and each affirms right is on his side, they cause the case of each party to be written in a scroll and put these scrolls in the hand of Saint Thomas; quickly the hand casts away the scroll that contains the false case, and keeps the other.'

Many similar stories about the relics of St Thomas circulated throughout medieval Europe and there is every possibility that there was indeed a church in Persia or India that contained some sort of miracle-working relic. If so, tales of its amazing properties would only have fuelled speculation about a Christian kingdom ruled by Prester John.

But there is also a remote possibility that Prester John really did exist: not a Christian king ruling a Christian empire but a powerful despot who commanded a considerable army. Historical records show that the Mongol ruler Yeh-lu Ta-shih defeated the Persian Sultan Sanjar in a pitched battle in 1141, and that the title of this Mongol king was Gur-khan. Change this phonetically into Hebrew and it becomes Yohanan, in Syriac it is Yuhanan, and in Latin Johannes – or John. And while Gur-khan – or John – was a Buddhist, many of his subjects and soldiers were Nestorian Christians. As the story of this battle was passed from merchant to merchant and as the language changed with the geography, it is not hard to see how Europe could eventually come to hear about, and believe in, the mighty ruler named Prester John. So that when an anonymous scholar decided to set down on paper a letter from Prester John to the Pope, it required no leap of the imagination for people to believe it.

Why the hoaxer wrote this letter remains a mystery. Perhaps he was intending to deceive? Perhaps he wanted to record everything he had heard about this king? Whatever the truth, one thing is certain: when a copy of this letter fell into the hands of Sir John Mandeville he, like the Pope, believed every word it contained. And once he set down the story of Prester John in his *Travels* – a book that was translated into every European language – it fooled a whole new generation of people. Many of the fifteenth- and sixteenth-century explorers who set out for India in search of the riches of Prester John, did so because they had read about him in Sir John's book.

Mandeville's description of China is also skilfully adapted from the information at his disposal. Once again he borrows heavily from Friar Odoric and John of Plano Carpini, but he also lifts from other books as well. He certainly consulted Haiton's *Fleur des Histoires d'Orient* – from which he had taken details about the Egyptian sultans – as well as copying from Vincent of Beauvais's encyclopedic *Speculum Mundi*, itself a compendium of dozens of books.

It is Sir John's skill as a writer that explains why his book was so much more popular than those of his contemporaries. Where Haiton merely records that he met a group of Chinese astrologers, Mandeville records his conversation with them and thereby gives the meeting an air of truth: 'I busied myself greatly to know and understand by what means these things I mentioned were done; but the chief craftsman told me that he was so bound by a vow to his god that he could show the method to no man except his eldest son.'

He does the same with stories borrowed from Friar Odoric. Odoric really did visit the imperial court and his descriptions of the pomp and ceremony surrounding an appearance of the emperor are based on his own experiences. But where Odoric's writing is clumsy and flat, Sir John's is vividly alive, especially when he describes the smells, the colours of fabrics, and the glimmer of candlelight on gold. At one point he even mocks Odoric, suggesting that the Franciscan teamed up with him for a particularly dangerous part of his voyage.

One of the finest passages, which Sir John adapted from Odoric's *Itinerarius*, is of an imperial banquet in China:

Beside the Emperor's table sit many philosophers and men learned in different branches of knowledge . . . At certain moments, when they see the right time, they say to men who stand near them, 'Let everyone be silent!' and one of those men says to all the hall, with a loud voice, 'Be silent!' Then says another of the philosophers, 'Let every man do obeisance and bow to the Emperor, who is God's son and Lord of the world, for this is the right moment.' Then every man bows his head to the earth . . . And at another instant another philosopher says, 'Every man put his little finger in his ear!' and they do so. Again, another philosopher says, 'Every man put his hand before his mouth!' and they do so . . .

Mandeville's book convinced his contemporaries because it is both witty and plausible – it is hard not to believe that he really has visited the places he describes. Yet a simple error proves that he didn't visit China: his claim that the emperor of the time was Guyak is impossible, for Guyak was khan when John of Plano Carpini visited China. He died in 1248, 74 years before Sir John claims to have left England.

For centuries, monks, critics, and curious readers have wondered what was in Sir John's mind when he came to describe the savages, cannibals and ghoulish creatures in the second half of his book. Had he simply included them for entertainment value or did such tales hold clues to a secret message that lay buried within the book's pages?

Even Mandeville's most ardent admirers were confused by the apparently uncomfortable way in which the two halves of *The Travels* sit together and found it difficult to reconcile the pilgrimage to Jerusalem – the first part of the book – with tales of savages and monsters in the second. The only obvious link was Sir John himself; the traveller and amateur philosopher with a keen eye for the marvellous.

Some dismissed the monsters as an irrelevance and claimed that Mandeville's aim, first and foremost, was to write a guidebook for pilgrims intending to visit the Holy Land. Others said he had written his book in order to preach the need for a new crusade. Many eighteenth-century readers disputed the worth of the *first* half of the book, saying that it was the monsters that gave *The Travels* its appeal. But whatever theories were put forward to explain Sir John's purpose in writing his book, no one managed to solve the riddle of why he had split *The Travels* into two separate parts.

Few clues can be found in the biblical stories and parables scattered throughout both halves for although Mandeville quotes tales from the Old Testament and parables from the New, no single theme links them all together. It is a similar story with the fables he recounts: in every case they appear to have been selected more for their entertainment value than for any obvious theme. Even the autobiographical passages about Sir John – one at the beginning and one at the end – shed no light on his possible motive for dividing his book in two.

I had spent months accompanying Sir John on his journey and knew he was a shrewd man – far too clever to present a random jumble of unconnected ideas. But it wasn't until I imagined myself as one of his medieval readers that it dawned on me that Mandeville had used his book's structure to play an elaborate game on the reader. *The Travels* was indeed a riddle – an allegorical attack on western Christendom – and the meaning of the whole lay in the relationship between its two halves.

For his riddle to work, it relies on the reader identifying himself totally with the pious pilgrim of the first half. He must travel hand in hand with Mandeville – praying at shrines, worshipping in churches, and slowly visiting the holiest sites in Christendom. Having undertaken the pilgrimage to Jerusalem – and armed with a new religiosity – the reader confronts the grotesque savages and pagans of the east with all the certitude of faith. And it is at exactly this point that Sir John reverses all the roles and throws the spotlight back on the reader. He describes these savages as far more pious than any Christian pilgrim could ever be, forcing the reader to see his own life as an ugly reflection of theirs.

The clearest example of Mandeville's method comes in his description of the burial rituals in Tibet. Firstly, he tells readers of the simple devotion of these Tibetans and then – in a horrific passage – describes their burial rites as a gruesome parody of Christian communion. The priest swipes off the dead man's head and places it on a silver platter. Then he chops the corpse into tiny cubes of meat and feeds the bits to the vultures and ravens that are wheeling around overhead: 'And then,' writes Sir John, 'just as the priests in our country sing for the souls of the dead *Subuenite, sancti Dei*, so those priests there sing with a loud voice in their language . . . the son boils his father's head, and the flesh from it he distributes among his special friends, giving each one a little bit, as a dainty. And from the cranium of the head he has a cup made, and he drinks from it all his lifetime in remembrance of his father.'

This last line would have set the alarm bells ringing in the mind of many a medieval reader, for every Sunday he would hear the priest repeating Christ's injunction to 'do this in remembrance of Me' before taking Holy Communion. Yet Mandeville doesn't once criticize the practice. Instead, he describes it as a touching and loving act and hints that although these Tibetans are most certainly not Christians, they perform their actions with a piety and tenderness that should shame even the most devout of Christian pilgrims.

He uses the same method when he describes his audience with the Sultan of Egypt. Having portrayed the Muslims as devout, humble and pious – sentiments that would have been shocking to Christian Europe – he records without criticism the Sultan's blistering attack on the lifestyles of these Christians. The reader finds his own life reflected in the Sultan's mirror – a Muslim mirror – and slowly becomes aware that his own behaviour is substantially *less* pious than that of his traditional enemy, the infidel. For a medieval reader, such a realization must have been frightening indeed.

Sir John uses this same device time and again throughout *The Travels*, challenging in the second half of the book everything that the reader has learnt in the first. The message of *The Travels* is a truly Christian one – one of tolerance and love – and what set it apart from all other travelogues of the Middle Ages is that Mandeville says this love should be extended not merely to fellow Christians but to Muslims and pagans as well.

So many centuries have passed since Sir John wrote his book that it is almost impossible to fathom his wilder claims. After two years of sifting through the surviving evidence I felt sure that his travels in India and China were a work of fiction, while his tales from Java and Sumatra came straight from the legends of the ancients. For although his contemporaries had believed his every word, there was little that was original in his account of the Far East except for the sparkling brilliance of his prose.

But even if the second part of the book was fiction, that still left the first half of *The Travels*. Was this true, or had Mandeville invented his journey to Jerusalem as well?

Before I slotted together all the facts I had unearthed while following his route through the Holy Land, I still had one last piece of evidence to check: the coat of arms I had found at St Catherine's monastery. There was just a chance that this would prove once and for all that Mandeville had travelled, at least as far as Egypt.

The College of Arms in London houses the largest collection of heraldic records in the country, and I hoped that somewhere among its geneaological charts and tables I would find a record of the carving from Sinai. But when I met the College's medieval expert, a man who liked to be known as Bluemantle Pursuivant, he warned me that identifying a random coat of arms could take years of research.

'I'm sorry to be so negative,' he said as he examined my drawing, 'but medieval heraldry is notoriously unreliable. It only takes one person to have altered their arms slightly for a search to become almost impossible.'

He suggested that we try a different approach and look through all the records of the Mandeville family instead. I already knew what Geoffrey de Mandeville's coat of arms looked like and had unearthed a considerable number of documents about Sir John's life. There was just a possibility we would be able to identify the St Catherine's carving from these pieces of evidence.

It didn't take long to discover several heraldic coats belonging to John Mandevilles but none of them looked remotely like the one I had found. One Mandeville seemed to fit the bill, and was even described as living in a village near St Albans where he, 'liked to hunt with his own dogs the hare, fox, badger and cat in Essex forest.' But when I checked the dates, I found he had died in 1275, more than 50 years before Sir John claims to have left England. Perhaps he was Sir John's grandfather?

It was a chance find in an eighteenth-century document that set us on to a more probable trail. This document recorded that a Halifax surgeon called William Alexander was granted a coat of arms in the mid-eighteenth century – an honour that inspired him to research his family history. As well as tracing his father's line he also investigated his mother's and grandmother's families, for his overriding concern was to link himself to noble blood. Any ancestor that sounded vaguely aristocratic came under his scrutiny and in such a way he eventually managed to link himself to the de Bohun family. The link was tenuous in the extreme but it contained one important piece of information. At some point during the Middle Ages a distant relative of Alexander's had married into the Mandevilles and I suddenly found myself with a whole new set of Mandeville coats of arms. But as soon as Bluemantle looked at these new coats of arms he frowned and shook his head. None of these could be genuine, he said, for the pointed star that adorned them – known to experts as an escarbuncle – was unknown in medieval heraldry. The Halifax surgeon had either invented the shield or copied it from a faulty manuscript.

Bluemantle had other bad news as well. He had been delving into numerous records of foreign heraldry and had become increasingly suspicious of the St Catherine's arms: 'I have to admit that I'm not convinced by these either,' he said as he slipped another book back on to a shelf. 'The shield you have drawn shows a curved line bending into one corner. We call that a bend sinister bowed towards the base of the first, but such a form appears to be extremely rare in English heraldry, particularly in the medieval period. The more I look at it, the more I have to conclude – I'm afraid – that this coat of arms was drawn by a knight of Continental origin.'

My last door had closed and my last avenue proved to be a cul-de-sac for the St Catherine's coat of arms did not belong to Sir

John Mandeville, the author of *The Travels*. But ten months of unearthing documents about his life had left me with a mountain of papers and a file of details. Although many riddles remained unresolved, I was at last in a position to construct a tentative portrait of him and his travels.

According to his own account he returned to England in 1356, 'a man worn out by age and travel and the feebleness of my body'. This statement was almost certainly true, for if Sir John had left England in 1322 as he says, he would have been a very old man by the time he returned home.

Although I had been unable to find any documents that recorded his birth, I had picked up a number of clues as to when he might have been born. If Sir John had indeed been one of the envoys sent by King Edward II to negotiate with Robert Bruce, he must have been at least 20 years old at the time. Since the expedition left London in 1312 this would put the year of his birth at no later than 1292.

But could a man born in 1292 still be alive in 1356? It is certainly possible, for even in the Middle Ages some people lived to a very great age. Sir John would have been 64 by the time he finished his book – a similar age to Chaucer when he died and several years younger than John of Marignolli who survived a long and arduous overland journey to China.

This early date also fitted neatly with the John Mandeville named in the document pardoning the conspirators who killed Piers Gaveston, as well as with the information I had unearthed about the Mandevilles of Black Notley. For Sir Thomas Mandeville, the head of this Black Notley household, appears to have spent at least part of his married life at his bride's family home near St Albans. If this was indeed the case, there is every likelihood that the young John Mandeville was educated at the abbey school in the town.

Having followed Mandeville on his pilgrimage to Jerusalem I felt sure that he really had travelled through the Holy Land, and the more I weighed up the evidence the more the balance swung in his favour. His book is littered with clues which I had checked and verified at every opportunity. In Constantinople he was correct in both his account of the jousting and his description of the statue of Justinian, and was even right in his claim that the globe was missing from the statue's hand. It had fallen out in 1317 and wasn't mended until 1325.

On arriving in Cyprus Sir John provided scant descriptions of the island's cities and towns but his details about people's leisure pursuits (the wine; the hunting; their eating habits) are all borne out by later travellers. His account of the Syrian monastery of Saidenaya was also accurate down to the last detail, and while it is possible that he had picked up information about Saidenaya from other travellers, this in no way proved that he had invented his visit.

Most convincing of all was his description of St Catherine's monastery which reads like an eye-witness account. Six hundred years after he wrote his *Travels*, I stood in front of the same buildings and relics that Mandeville himself had seen. Virtually nothing had changed.

There was one other factor in his favour: if he really had invented the first part of his voyage it is almost certain he would have made an accidental slip or error, for it is extremely difficult to sustain the deceit of having travelled. Yet despite putting his every phrase under the microscope I found scarcely a single mistake in his account of the route to Sinai.

It was not just these clues that convinced me that Sir John really had travelled: the very meaning of his book depends on the reader believing that Mandeville really had gone on a pilgrimage to the Holy Land. Without travelling with Mandeville in the first half of *The Travels*; without becoming a pilgrim like him, the second part of the book loses its meaning.

But even if Sir John did indeed spend a few years travelling through the Holy Land, it still leaves the question of how he filled the rest of the 34 years he claims to have been away. Unfortunately, this is a secret that he took with him to the grave. The most likely explanation – given the records of a Mandeville studying at the university in Paris – is that he spent at least part of this time living in France.

Mandeville dates his return to England as 1356 and all the surviving evidence suggests that he was telling the truth. For when Humphrey de Bohun – Earl of Essex and holder of the Mandeville honour – died at his home in 1361 he left a 12-page will detailing who he wished to inherit his possessions. Most went to his close relatives, but he didn't forget his retainers and kinsmen either. Halfway down the list is: 'Johan Maundeville, XX Marcs.'

Is this our man? Again, it is impossible to say. But if he really had been out of the country for years, the natural place for him to look for patronage when he finally returned would be at the home of his overlords the earls of Essex. Perhaps he lived out his declining years in their manor house at Pleshy, hastily compiling his *Travels* before arthritis robbed him of the ability to write? Such a hypothesis is well within the bounds of plausibility: the de Bohuns certainly possessed a copy of *The Travels* within a few years of Sir John's death, and perhaps during his lifetime, for a second family will records all the books in the de Bohun library, including a *rouge livre appellez Maundevylle*.

After Sir John's death there is a silence of some two hundred years before his name once again resurfaces. A handful of historians and antiqarians, intrigued by this knight from St Albans, tried to discover the truth about his life, but virtually all of them fell for the fabrications of Jean d'Outremeuse and Mandeville's reputation went into steep decline. Yet as soon as he had a brief surge of popularity in the eighteenth century, people began claiming descent from him once again – even though his branch of the family seems to have died out hundreds of years earlier. One copy of *The Travels* – sold in 1746 by a certain William Thompson of Queen's College, Oxford – has a note scrawled into the first blank page of the volume: 'NB: I had this book from a descendant by my mother's side, from Sir John Mandeville.' Can we believe this? Probably not for, by the eighteenth century, Sir John's family history was already shrouded in mystery.

Today there is just one Mandeville family listed in the St Albans telephone directory. I telephoned them just in case they had any knowledge of Sir John that I might have overlooked. But although Mrs Mandeville thought she might have heard of him, she seemed unaware of the illustrious pedigree that her name almost certainly entitles her to.

12 Epilogue

Copies of [Mandeville's] *Travels* were multiplied till they almost equalled in number those of the Scriptures; now we may smile at the 'mervayles' of the fourteenth century, and of Mandeville, but it was the spirit of these intrepid and credulous minds which has marched us through the universe. To these children of the imagination perhaps we owe the circumnavigation of the globe and the universal intercourse of nations.

Amenities of Literature, **Isaac D'Israeli, 1841**

hile Mandeville's tales of monsters and devils appealed to the ordinary man, and his message of tolerance and piety must have appealed to those churchmen who understood it, the book's importance in the first two centuries after it was written lay in its contribution to geography and exploration. This seems strange for, despite all his claims, Mandeville's *Travels* actually added very little to the world's storehouse of knowledge. Many men had travelled to the Holy Land – or at least heard tales from other travellers – and educated men could certainly have found books about Africa, Asia, India and China. Sir John, it is true, was claiming to have gone far further afield. But Marco Polo had also been to the uttermost ends of the earth and described the Far East in far greater detail.

The importance of Mandeville's book to medieval explorers, however, lay not so much in its description of India and China as in the 175 lines in which Sir John explains why he believes it is possible to circumnavigate the world.

These lines provided an answer to the great geographical debate of his age. By the time Sir John wrote his book the concept of a flat earth had long been disproved and most geographers accepted that the world was a globe hanging in the firmament. But three questions remained unanswered. Was there land in the southern hemisphere? If so, was it habitable? And most important of all, could it be visited?

The vast majority of people, supported by church teaching, believed that sailing around the world was impossible, and more than a century after Mandeville wrote his book Columbus's crew had a very real fear that their ship was going to topple over the edge when they crossed the Equator. Few people would countenance the idea of there being land in the southern hemisphere – arguing that because land was heavier than water it would obviously fall off the world – and even well-travelled and educated men did not believe in the possibility of circumnavigating the globe. The devout John of Marignolli had voyaged thousands of miles across Asia yet mocked the idea that it was possible to travel around the world, while the few who argued that there was habitable land on the underside of the earth were held up for public ridicule. Sceptics joked about men living upside down and rain falling upwards towards the earth.

Such ideas stemmed from the cloistered world of the Church which dismissed any theories that didn't conform with the biblical view of the world. As far as the Church was concerned, all mankind descended from Noah and if Noah had never been 'beneath' the earth then how and where did people in the southern hemisphere spring from? This was not the only objection: since the offer of salvation had been promised to the whole of mankind, how could an entire section of the world be cut off from this message. For if the apostles didn't go to the antipodes, that must surely mean that the antipodes could not exist. An inhabited southern hemisphere simply didn't fit in with Christian teaching and for this fact alone St Augustine considered belief in the existence of the antipodes to be not only wrong, but heretical as well.

Sir John's *Travels* dismiss centuries of the Church's teachings in a characteristically down-to-earth anecdote and 'proves' the world is circumnavigable by telling a strange story of a man who inadvertently sailed around it:

I have often thought of a story I have heard, when I was young of a worthy man of our country who went once upon a time to see the world. He passed India and many isles beyond India, where there are more than five thousand isles, and travelled so far by land and sea, girdling the globe, that he found an isle where he heard his own language being spoken . . . He marvelled greatly, for he did not understand how this could be. But I conjecture that he had travelled so far over land and sea, circumnavigating the earth, that he had come to his own borders; if he had gone a bit further, he would have come to his own district . . .

This story of a man who had accidentally traversed the globe seems to have struck a chord with Columbus for when he heard that two Oriental sailors had been washed up from a shipwreck on the coast of Ireland, he scribbled into the margin of one of his books: 'Men have come eastward from Cathay. We have seen many a remarkable thing, and particularly in Galway, in Ireland, two persons hanging on to two wreck planks, a man and a woman.'

Such a story is not Mandeville's only proof. He includes calculations based on readings from the stars to demonstrate that the world is a globe, and suggests that he himself would have continued around the world if he had found the necessary ships. But most important of all is the theological proof that he offers to support his theory. For while travelling in India he stumbles across a tribe of pagans who, like Job in the Old Testament, have absolutely no knowledge of Christianity yet worship God in a pure and simple way. For Mandeville, this is proof enough that God's law operates on every part of the globe. And if God is everywhere, it necessarily follows that man is able to travel everywhere and that the only difficulties are practical ones. 'So I say truly,' he concludes, 'that a man could go all round the world, above and below, and return to his own country, provided he had his health, good company, and a ship. And all the way he would find men, lands, islands, cities and towns.'

It is difficult to know where Mandeville might have formulated his theory of circumnavigation but there is every likelihood that the medieval records indicating a John of Sancto Albano studying at the University of Paris do indeed refer to him. If so, he would certainly have come into contact with John Buridan, who was central to these debates about the globe and had just put the finishing touches to his important treatise on whether the whole world was habitable.

Sir John was not the first to hold views about the possibilities of circumnavigation. But the writing by his contemporaries, in complex Latin, is technical, academic and extremely dull. John Buridan's treatise, too, is weighty stuff. The work of his fellow academics is so obscure as to be largely incomprehensible. What Sir John does is make it all sound plausible, arguing his point in a way that was accessible to the layman.

Sir John's assertion that it was possible to circumnavigate the globe, and the proof that he offered, had a particularly profound effect on the young Christopher Columbus. Columbus had long held the view that there was a quicker route to the riches of the East than the long and dangerous overland journey. A devoutly religious man who sincerely believed that 'the Lord would show him where gold is born', he delved into obscure and apocryphal biblical texts looking for support for his theory that it was possible to reach the riches of the east by sailing west.

Columbus wanted to put such theories to the test but had enormous difficulties getting anyone to support his project. The King of Portugal rejected his proposal out of hand and when he turned to the Spanish nobility it refused to back him as well. King Ferdinand and Queen Isabella of Spain were more interested and listened politely to his promise to return with gold, but they found Columbus's demands for a down payment ludicrously high. He insisted on being knighted and appointed grand admiral, he asked to be made viceroy of all the lands he discovered, and demanded that his family hold this title in perpetuity. Not only this, he wanted ten per cent of all the transactions within the admiralty. The King and Queen couldn't afford such proposals and Columbus was dismissed empty handed.

But when he returned to the court some months later he found the King and Queen in a more pliant frame of mind and by the time his audience was over they had agreed to back his voyage. It is impossible to know what finally persuaded them to change their minds but, in the official documents of the Spanish Admiralty recording Columbus's expedition, a new reason crops up. A book had come to light, perhaps brought to the court by Columbus himself, which was causing something of a sensation. It was taken far more seriously than the apocryphal biblical texts, it was far more recent than the classical geographer Ptolemy and, more importantly, it claimed to prove once and for all that the east coast of China could be reached by sailing westwards across the Atlantic.

It was a slim volume with no title but it was said to be by an Englishman and was generally known as *The Travels of Sir John Mandeville*.

The chronicler of the famous 1492 expedition, Andres Bernaldez, had no doubts about the debt Columbus owed to Mandeville. Of the mariner's great voyage he writes: 'Columbus navigated . . . towards that which he desired, which was to seek the province and city of Catayo [China], which is under the dominion of the Great Khan, saying that he could reach it by this route. Of it is read, as John Mandeville says, that it is the richest province in the world and the most abounding in gold and silver.' After explaining in detail how the riches of the east can be reached by sailing west, Bernaldez adds, 'Anyone who wishes to know the truth of this may read it in Mandeville's book.'

Columbus wanted honour and riches and his appetite had been whetted by Mandeville's *Travels*. The more he read the book the more he lapped up Sir John's tales of the fabulous wealth of India and the glittering prizes of China and by the time he set sail he was so convinced of success that he filled his ship with cheap trinkets with which he planned to relieve the eastern natives of their stocks of gold. He also took with him a learned man who spoke many languages in case he met the Great Khan of China.

Columbus never found the gold he so hungered for and nor did he reach China although when his ship finally touched land in 1492 he was convinced he had proved Mandeville to be right after all, recording that he was among 'the islands which are set down in the maps at the end of the Orient'.

He wasn't. What Columbus never realized, to his dying day, was that Mandeville's *Travels* had led him to discover America.

It was not just Columbus who turned to *The Travels*. Many other Renaissance geographers and explorers read Mandeville for practical information about remote areas of the world. Sir Walter Raleigh admits in his book *Discoverie of Guiana* that although initially sceptical about Mandeville, his own journey forced him to conclude that *The Travels* was true in every respect: '[Mandeville's] reports were holden for fables many yeeres, and yet since the East Indies were discovered, we find his relations true of such things as heretofore were held incredible.'

Sir Martin Frobisher also turned to Mandeville for advice when he set out on his voyage to discover the North-West Passage. Not only did his ship's library contain a copy of Mercator's world map, which itself relied on Mandeville for much of its information, but it also contained a copy of *The Travels*. The great explorers of the fifteenth and sixteenth centuries relied on Mandeville's book for information about the unknown, and few would have questioned Richard Hakluyt's decision to give *The Travels* pride of place when he came to compile his encyclopedic account of the country's greatest explorers, *The Principall Navigations, Voiages and Discoveries of the English Nation*.

What Sir John achieved in writing his *Travels* is far more important than the question of whether he himself went on his voyage. He gave a whole generation of explorers – men like Columbus who really did discover the world – a justification, both theological and practical, for setting out into the unknown. And when, in the decades following his death, men came to propose expeditions, it was to Sir John's book that they turned. He inspired them with his tales of the legendary east and fired their enthusiasm for discovery. And most important of all, he provided a motive for financial backers to plough huge sums of money into highly risky adventures. Within little more than a century after his death, men had taken Mandeville at his word and sailed to the other side of the globe, proving his theory of geography correct.

But in doing so, these early colonizers neglected the second point that Sir John was making. His message of tolerance, central to the book's meaning, was either misunderstood or ignored. Within years of discovering the new lands, settlers were colonizing them and the pagan natives that Sir John describes with such affection were being indiscriminately slaughtered.

Mandeville was once the most celebrated writer of his era and left a legacy that few can match. For not only did he inspire the world's greatest explorers, he also left his legacy in the great works of English literature. Shakespeare's plays are scattered with echoes of *The Travels*, from the Scythians who eat their parents in *King Lear* to the monstrous creatures in *The Tempest*. Spenser, too, borrowed Mandeville's men with waist-length ears for his *Fairie Queen*, while John Milton includes a troupe of Mandeville's monsters in his 1634 masque *Comus*. Ben Jonson, Jonathan Swift, Samuel Johnson and Daniel Defoe all turned to Mandeville's book for inspiration, while Samuel Coleridge was reading *Purchas his Pilgrimes* – which contained *The Travels* – shortly before writing his masterpiece *Kubla Khan*. Hardly surprising, therefore, that Coleridge's line, 'For he on honey-dew hath fed/ And drunk the milk of Paradise,' is lifted from Sir John's description of the land of Chaldea. Until the nineteenth century Mandeville's literary genius was freely acknowledged and it was he – not Chaucer – who was referred to as the 'father of English prose'.

But just as the discoveries of the sixteeenth-century explorers destroyed Mandeville's reputation as the world's greatest traveller, so the moralistic Victorians – disgusted by his fabrications – finally buried his literary reputation. Sir John entered the deepest trough in his career when the ninth edition of the *Encyclopedia Britannica* concluded that his book, his voyage and even his life were riddled with lies.

Today Sir John is still suffering from the batterings of the Victorian era. Although his book remains in print it is rarely taken down from the bookshelves, and in the three years I spent studying medieval literature at university, Mandeville was never even mentioned.

The peeling epitaph in St Albans Abbey is the last concrete reminder that Sir John Mandeville was an Englishman and once the most famous writer of the Middle Ages. But it will not be many years before the epitaph has disappeared completely. A few more damp winters and the last words of the inscription will flake, loosen themselves from the pillar, and be swept from the floor by a cleaner.

Only Sir John's book – the inspiration for the voyages that discovered the world – will remain as testimony to his genius.

Bibliography

There have been many editions of *The Travels*. The ones I have referred to are listed on page 225. The Penguin Edition, translated and edited by C.W.R.D. Moseley in 1983, is still available today.

Alexandris, Alexis, *The Greek Minority of Istanbul and Greek Turkish Relations, 1918-74*, Centre for Asia Minor Studies, Athens.

Atiya, A.S., *A History of Eastern Christianity*, 1968; *Crusade in the Later Middle Ages*, 1938.

Barcia, D. Andres Gonzalez, *Historiadores Primitivos de Las Indias Occidentales*, Madrid, 1749.

Bennett, Josephine, *The Rediscovery of Sir John Mandeville*, New York, 1954.

Bond, E.A. (ed), *Chronica Monasterii de Melsa*, 1866.

Budge, Sir E. A. Wallis (trs), *The Monks of Kublai Khan, Emperor of China*, 1928.

Burchard of Mount Sion, *A Description of the Holy Land*, Palestine Pilgrims' Text Society, vol XII, 1896;

Calendar of the Close Rolls, Edward II, 4 vols, 1892;

Calendar of the Patent Rolls, Edward II, 5 vols, 1894.

Charlesworth, J.H., *St Catherine's Monastery, myths and mysteries*, Biblical Archaeologist, 42, 1979; *The Manuscripts of St Catherine's Monastery*, Biblical Archaeologist, 43, 1980.

Clutterbuck, Robert, *History and Antiquities of Hertfordshire*, 1815.

Cobham, Claude Deval, *Excerpta Cypria*, Cambridge, 1908.

Dawson, Christopher, *The Mongol Mission; Narratives and Letters of the Franciscan Missionaries in Mongolia and China in the Thirteenth and Fourteenth centuries*, London and New York, 1955.

Edbury, Peter, *The Kingdom of Cyprus and the Crusades, 1191-1374*, Cambridge, 1991.

Forsyth, G.H., *The Monastery of St Catherine at Mount Sinai - the*

Church and Fortress of Justinian, Dumbarton Oaks Papers, 22, 1969.

Fortescue, Adrian, *The Lesser Eastern Churches*, 1913.

Fuller, Dr Thomas, *The History of the Worthies of England*, 1840.

Galbraith, V.A., *The St Albans' Chronicle*, Oxford, 1937.

Galey, John, *Sinai and the Monastery of St Catherine*, 1980.

Grant, Dr Asahel, *The Nestorians or The Lost Tribes*, 1841.

Gregoras, Nikephoros, *Corpus Scriptorum Historiae Byzantinae*, Bonn, 1829.

Gilles, Pierre, *The Antiquities of Constantinople*, 1729.

Hakluyt, Richard, *Principall Navigations*, 1589.

Hasluck, F.W., *Christianity and Islam under the Sultans*, 2 vols, 1929.

Hitti, Philip, *History of Syria*, 1951; *History of the Arabs*, 1958.

Hoarde, E., *Western Pilgrims, 1322-1392*, Jerusalem, 1952.

Howard, Donald, *The World of Mandeville's Travels*, Yearbook of English Studies, 1971.

Ibn Battuta, *Travels in Africa and Asia*, 1929.

Jackson, Professor Isaac, *Who was Sir John Mandeville? A Fresh Clue*, Modern Language Review, XXIII, 1928.

Jane, Cecil, (trs and ed), *Selected Documents Illustrating the Four Voyages of Columbus*, Hakluyt Society, 2 vols, 1930 and 1933.

Jeffery, G.H.F., *Description of the Historic Monuments of Cyprus*, Nicosia, 1918.

Kimble, G.H.T., *Geography in the Middle Ages*, 1938.

Kirk, R.E.G., *Feet of Fines for Essex*, 5 vols, Colchester, 1899.

Lane-Poole, Stanley, *A History of Egypt in the Middle Ages*, 1901.

Layard, A H., *Nineveh and its Remains*, 1849.

Leland, John, *Commentarii de Scriptoribus Britannicus*, Hall, A. (ed), Oxford, 1709.

Lethaby, W. R., and Swainson, H.S., *Church of Sancta Sophia, Constantinople, A Study*, 1894.

Letts, M., *Sir John Mandeville, The Man and his Book*, 1949.

Mandeville, Sir John, *Mandeville's Travels*, Seymour, M.C. (ed), 1967; *The Travels of Sir John Mandeville*, Moseley C.W.R.D. (trs and ed), 1983; *The Travels*, Hamelius, P. (ed), 2 vols, 1919 and 1923; *Mandeville's Travels*, Letts, M. (ed), 2 vols, 1953; *The Travels of Sir John Mandeville*, Pollard, A.W. (trs and ed), 1900; *The Travels and Voyages of Sir John Mandeville*, 1785.

McKisack, M., *The Fourteenth Century, 1307-1399*, Oxford, 1991.

Meyendorff, J., *The Byzantine Legacy in the Orthodox Church*, New York, 1982.

Moody, E.A., *John Buridan on the Habitability of the Earth*, Speculum, XVI, 1941.

Muir, Sir William, *The Mameluke or Slave Dynasty of Egypt*, 1896.

Nandris, John, *The Jebaliyeh of Mount Sinai, and the Land of Vlah*, Quaderni di Studi Arabi, 8, 1990.

Nichols, J., *A Collection of all the Wills of the Kings and Queens of England*, 1780.

Nicol, Donald, *The Last Centuries of Constantinople, 1261-1453*, 1972.

Norden, John, *Speculum Britanniae*, 1593.

Pantin, W.A., *The English Church in the Fourteenth Century*, Cambridge, 1955.

Polo, Marco, *The Travels*, 1958.

Prescott, H.F.M., *Jerusalem Journey*, 1954.

Purchas, Samuel, *Purchas his Pilgrimes*, 5 vols, 1625.

Rich, Claudius James, *Narrative of a Residence in Koordistan and on the Site of Ancient Nineveh*, 2 vols, 1836.

Riley, H.T. (ed), *Annales Monasterii S. Albani a Johannes Amundesham*, 1871; *Rotuli Scotiae in Turri Londinensi*, vol 1, 1814.

Round, J.H., *Geoffrey de Mandeville*, 1892.

Runciman, Steven, *A History of the Crusades*, 3 vols, Cambridge, 1951; *The Fall of Constantinople*, Cambridge, 1965; *The Great Church in Captivity*, 1968.

Rymer, Thomas, *Foedera*, 1818.

Slessarev, Vsevolod, *Prester John, The Letter and the Legend*, Minneapolis, 1959.

Southern, Richard, *Western Society and the Church in the Middle Ages*, 1970.

Stacey, John, *John Wyclif and Reform*, 1964.

Storme, Albert, *The Way of the Cross*, Jerusalem, 1984.

Suchem, Ludolph von, *Description of the Holy Land*, Palestine Pilgrims' Text Society, 1895.

Suriano, F., *Treatise on the Holy Land*, Jerusalem, 1983.

Toms, Elsie, *The Story of St Albans*, Luton, 1962.

Underwood, Paul A., *The Kariye Djami*, 4 vols, 1967.

Weever, John, *Ancient Funerall Monuments With In the United Monarchie of Great Britaine, Ireland, and the Ilands adiacent*, 1631.

Yule, Sir Henry, *Cathay and the Way Thither*, 4 vols, Hakluyt Society, 1913-16.

Ziadeh, N.A., *Urban Life in Syria under the Early Mameluks*, Beirut, 1953; *Damascus under the Mameluks*, Oklahoma, 1964.

Index